CW00688993

PRESENTATION FLY-FISHING

John,

for your great

efforts for the Eden

Jeremy Lucas.

PRESENTATION FLY-FISHING

Jeremy Lucas

ROBERT HALE • LONDON

© Jeremy Lucas 2014
First published in Great Britain 2014

ISBN 978-0-7198-0699-5

Robert Hale Limited
Clerkenwell House
Clerkenwell Green
London EC1R 0HT

www.halebooks.com

The right of Jeremy Lucas to be identified as
author of this work has been asserted by him
in accordance with the Copyright, Designs and
Patents Act 1988

A catalogue record for this book is available from the British Library

2 4 6 8 10 9 7 5 3 1

Designed by Eurodesign
Printed and bound in India by Imprint Digital Ltd.

Contents

Introduction

'This changes everything.'

The San tailwater was low and clear after two months without any rain whatsoever throughout Eastern Europe. The enormous Bieszczady forest catchment area in the border country between Poland and Ukraine was dry as tinder, and the lakes on the park's edge were low, exposing baked yellow mud along the shores. A group of us had been fishing for two weeks at the end of September and beginning of October. Each day we spread out along different sections of river, quietly and methodically searching, with nymph, spider and dry-fly techniques through the relentlessly sunny days. Usually there was little to show until the extraordinary pale watery and blue-winged olive spinner falls

San River, below the islands at Zaluz

of less than an hour's duration in the dying light of evening. Then, as the air thickened with the long-tailed spinners, like a billion sparks flickering against the reddening, sinking sun, it seemed as if every trout and grayling of this immense river was on the surface. To us it is a miracle of temperate zone nature: it will always be a marvel how, under the glare of daytime, when we think we can see every stone on the riverbed, the fish are nowhere to be seen and invertebrate activity is apparently non-existent, then there is this transformation in the dusk, and it is utterly magical. We who witness this spectacle are so very lucky. Then, the heavy heat of the day and the frustrations of fishing a sleeping river evaporate in a blitzkrieg of living urgency.

One day towards the end of our stay on the San, my friends asked me to give a demonstration of what I had termed the leader-to-hand technique. We chose the middle of the day when all was quiet, so no one would be over-anxious about missing fishing time. I set up a 9-foot #3 weight (which is a little short for ideal control) and the presentation leader as I had designed it at that time. I showed first single and double nymph set-ups and then the astonishing dry-fly delivery, and control, that is possible with this paradigm-shifting development in our sport. Even with the short rod, it was clear that we had taken a jump to a special place, where few had yet ventured. I was casting under the glare of the Eastern European sun and delivering the fly, at beyond 10-metre range, with no disturbance whatsoever, maintaining control of the drifting dry fly for up to 12 metres of drag-free drift with close contact throughout. Experienced river fly-fishers will understand that this is staggering and my friends were riveted, and in truth so was I, because it surprises me even now that we have finally found a better way. To see this level of presentation of a dry fly, without the disturbing clutter and crudeness of fly line, is remarkable. This book tells of such remarkable things within the esoteric sport of fly-fishing with a single-handed fly rod.

That afternoon we all fanned out to various parts of the river, mostly with hybridized fly line/presentation leader rigs, which were, in effect, very long leaders on #3 and #4 weight fly lines. I clearly remember wondering how my Belgian friend Elie Beerten, who had taken my own leader construction, would fare. Elie is an outstanding fly-fisher, typical of the adventurous-thinking modern Europeans, with considerable experience, and in the early days of the leader-to-hand approach, I very much wanted him to see the potential of what I was trying to broadcast. As we gathered before planning our positions for the evening rise, Elie climbed out of the river and on his face was an expression I had never seen before. He shook his head and smiled: 'Jeremy, this changes everything.'

It has done just that; in the first instance in the river sport, with nymph and, especially, dry fly. Even now, we are making headway into still-water applications and the potential here is enthralling. Who would have thought that, after almost fifty years with a fly rod in hand, one could discover something so radical that it would change the way we fish?

Presentation has preoccupied and fascinated me for much of my fly-fishing life. In recent years it has reached an obsession, because there is nothing – absolutely nothing – that affects one's performance as much as this one, immensely subtle and demanding factor. Of course, there are many other components of the whole – hundreds probably – but none so important to our success, or otherwise, as the way we make the fly behave in

and on the water. Through this incredible fly-fishing journey I have become increasingly focused on this central theme, the tenet of presentation, with its related factors of control and contact.

The ultimate among wild English trout; on the River Eden

There are many branches and disciplines of fly-fishing. My own has centred on trout and grayling, the former in both lakes and rivers. While I have fished for many other species, particularly freshwater non-salmonids, my passion is with rainbow and brown trout, and the enigmatic, beautiful European grayling; and thus my heart is in all those wonderful rivers of Scandinavia, Europe and Britain, and many still waters, where any of these species thrive. It might be any one of them, as in a Pennine lake, or all together, as in Slovenia. It matters not, so long as I can work out a way of catching them, being a little selective, particularly for the larger specimens, on a single-handed fly rod and an artificial fly. And this always brings me back to presentation.

A true fly-fisher recognizes skilful application no matter what the sector or technique within the sport. In terms of demand on skills and application my own view is summarized by the following series, with the most easily learned or mastered techniques at the beginning, with progressively increasing difficulty. Obviously, there is overlap and juxtaposition in certain circumstances.

STILL WATER: Dry fly from a drifting boat; nymph fishing with indicator from boat or bank; short-range traditional loch-style from drifting boat; long-range nymph (without indicator) or lure from boat or bank.

RIVER: Upstream dry fly in an upstream wind; fixed line (tenkara) with dry fly (upwind); fixed line with non-ballasted nymph, short range (6–10 m); indicator nymph fishing; duo style (nymph under dry); 360-degree dry fly incorporating casting across- and downwind to maximize presentation potential; Czech-nymphing (very short range); Euro-nymphing (longer range, approx. 14 m); streamer on floating line; streamer on sinking line; 360-degree micro dry fly; upstream (and across) nymph or spider without indicator (short to medium range); micro-nymph without indicator to sighted fish, with the difficulty increasing with depth and flow rate, particularly downstream.

At first consideration this might seem the wrong order to some readers, particularly those who, like me, have grown up from and through the classical English approach to single-handed fly rod fishing. After all, the upstream dry fly is a hallowed approach and almost defines the British river sport. This, however, has nothing to do with the level of skill required in its practice: it has to do with history and aesthetics, as well as with tired, bigoted doctrine. It is, after all, a never-ending delight to see a trout rise to our well-presented artificial, and this surely is reason enough for its endurance and status in the sport, and why it has become the favoured method for so many, including me.

In my book *Tactical Fly Fishing*, I concentrated on analysis, and those technical and tactical aspects that allow us to make the most of any particular fly-fishing situation, again focused very much on trout and grayling. Presentation is a function of all of the above and really, for the thinking fisherman, this is the grail we seek. Find how to achieve perfect presentation and therein is the ultimate achievement in our sport. It is a long journey, and in truth it is beguilingly never-ending, though I think we can get very close, for moments in our fishing lives. However, we have to go through all the processes that lead us in the right direction, making numerous mistakes along the way, as in anything that is worth-while in sport or cultural endeavour. Finally, for treasured, fleeting moments, we can find this special place and realize that we have reached it. There will be that drift, a perfect drift, as the dry fly touches down with supreme accuracy, high up the drift lane, 12 metres from your hands, and it will fall down the river on a 9-metre dead drift, poised among the naturals sailing there, moving as the river, completely unaffected by any interaction between currents and leader or tippet. And there will be contact all the way through the drift, so that when a trout kisses the fly away, you gently tap the hook home against the rod tip and the fish barely realizes that anything untoward has happened. What follows, as you tighten down, does not matter (though it is fun), so long as the fish is hooked cleanly and you can draw it to hand quickly enough for a few rapid photos, perhaps, before its safe release. What does matter is that drift, one which results from perfect presentation, with no distur-bance so that a wild trout, exhibiting absolutely natural feeding behaviour, accepts your fly as one of the naturals. I think fly-fishing cannot be better than this.

Wild English brown trout

It is a journey, ever refining itself towards the distant aesthetic of excellent presentation. It relies on both technical and instinctive factors, while experience is gathered as we travel further out from the fundamentals. It becomes a lonely pursuit too, because we find that eventually we have to depart from so much doctrine, diverging from so many historically trodden paths in the sport. Otherwise, we are doing no more than mimicking what others have done before us. That is fine, of course, for some, while to others it is a bit like the Apollo astronauts going to the moon, and then no one going back there again; just travelling a part of the way, which seems a pity to me. An extreme analogy, perhaps, but then I am looking at what completely captivates my imagination in our sport and I want something suitable with which to make the point by comparison. It is simply not enough for many of us to accept the presentation that can be achieved by relying on convention, or casting schools, or the mediocre and repetitive. This is just treading water, getting nowhere and, other than the enjoyment of being out fishing, it might be no more than this. There are those who are happy to exist in the mid-stream of ability and skills, and many who aspire to pass though this; and then there are the pioneers. Certainly, we are not fishing an artificial fly for the sake of catching our food. This is sport, which is about moving on towards that grail of excellence. Yes, it is also a lonely, aesthetic state.

*Storm breaking over
Helvellyn, Ullswater*

When I wrote *Fly Fisher*, back in the 1980s, young and first-time qualified for the England national fly-fishing team, I was very much a lake fisherman and while I had certainly put a lot of time into my pursuit, I know now that I was very close to the journey's beginning. I was not the fisherman I have become since – but the world was so very different then. We each had different perspectives and values. It all seemed simpler, but that is an older man talking; life gets more complicated, and everything moves on, including fly-fishing. Yet one aspect of all this I remember strongly, and that was the radical notion that real, unambiguous achievement in the sport was most strongly influenced by the behaviour of the fly we were casting at the fish; not just the fly itself, but the whole dynamic environment of a fly during a drift or retrieve. I think I was able to build a three-dimensional trajectory of the fly from the fish's viewpoint, or what I perceived this to be. For example, when I lost sight of the nymph after it hit the surface and sank, I tried to imagine its motion, and very early on I built in features to the nymphs I tied which would alter their behaviour in the water. I notice that most instinctively aware fly-fishers do this to varying extents. To be technically aware also helps, because not only the fly, but the entire tackle delivery and the skills of the angler, are called into play and have

an effect on the fly's behaviour, and indeed, the whole interaction process between fisherman, fly and fish, and the environment space they momentarily share.

All the disciplines within fly-fishing have their special requirements, and we each have our opinions about them, often bigoted at that. They have different demands, though common to them all is an essential understanding of the fly's behaviour on or under the water's surface – in the water column. Through the years this has given me the greatest respect for nymph fishing (which includes spiders), because in order to achieve good contact with, and control over, the nymph(s) in the water, particularly in running water, profound experience and skill are required. Even streamer fishing, which is so often derided by the ignorant, has considerable demands on the angler in this sense of being able to control the fly, often at long range, and sometimes at appreciable depth. Although my own treasured passion is for the dry fly it is (in spite of all the nonsense spoken about this 'pure' way of fly-fishing) the easiest method of all, either on lakes or on rivers – at least when fishing upstream in an upstream wind. It might often be the most appropriate way to fish and it is, arguably, the most aesthetically delightful way of catching trout and grayling on a fly, but this has nothing to do with comparative skill requirements. That said,

The ultimate prize for perfect presentation: wild Eden brown trout on the plume tip

I don't want anyone to run away with the idea that fishing the dry fly is all that easy! I mean, it has taken me the best part of fifty years to reach what I regard as a fairly consistently good dry-fly presentation in the full range of river and still-water situations.

Along the way one experiments in various disciplines with all manner of flies, and various approaches. I have seen a great many changes in my chosen or most favoured disciplines, of trout fishing on still waters and both trout and grayling on rivers. I have experienced methods come and go, and others which remain and develop to become significant elements of the sport. Most of these are small things that we gradually utilize and popularize, such as particular fly patterns. Some are fads that everyone thinks will change the sport forever, usually because the perception is that they will result in catching every fish in any river or lake. The ubiquitous gold-head hare's fur nymph on the river or the infamous fluorescent blobs of still water are examples of 'flies', while the Czech-nymph style on rivers or the indicator 'bung' on stocked still waters are examples of methods that were 'going to change everything'. It is salutary to note, however, that while most people considered all of the above to be detrimental to the development of the sport, as well as destructive, they contrarily all became rather popular; and so they remain to this day. Finally, by becoming more popular the only aspect they really changed was a slight, temporary reduction in anglers using other fly patterns or methods. None of the above, or countless other examples, really changed very much at all, with the possible exception of the Czech nymph: they are but small incremental developments and should be viewed as just that. As I have (almost) always said, if we don't like a particular method for any reason, we don't have to use it, and if we see others using it, well, it is best in my view if we just say nothing and allow them to enjoy their sport, which after all is very personal.

Huge changes are very rare. In the last fifty years I have experienced only three, with another happening right now. One, at the very beginning of the period, was precipitated by the enormous influence of a few river anglers such as Oliver Kite and most especially Frank Sawyer. The second was the proliferation of stocked still waters throughout the 1970s and 1980s and the adoption of entirely new techniques beyond the very British loch-style approach, including streamer or lure techniques borrowed from sea-trout and salmon fishing, and also the influence of the aggressive North American rainbow trout, including the migratory steelhead. We might include the simultaneous growth of competitive fly-fishing here. Thirdly came the giant influence of Arthur Cove who, as the most radical fly-fisher of an entire generation, really did change the way we approached still waters, particularly the bank discipline with his historically significant nymph approach. All of the above were paradigm-shifting episodes, the present-day side of which has left fly-fishing changed and considerably wealthier in a sporting, cultural sense.

In between the above are other events or changes of varying scale and impact, all of which have a developmental value. In the late 1980s I was one of the early promoters, on British still waters, of the 'strip and hang' technique. This involves using a team of flies on a fast-sinking line, usually from a drifting boat. Commonly, as I recommended, a brightly coloured 'disturbance' pattern (something like a hot orange hackled, fluorescent-tailed Dunkeld, of traditional wet-fly fame) was placed on the top dropper position,

and this was trailed usually by more imitative wet fly or nymph patterns. The idea was that the entire team would be cast to long range (in those days this was 30+ metres), and allowed to sink to the known or assumed feeding depth of the trout. It was then stripped back so that the bright top dropper would encourage an aggressive 'follow' reaction in the trout. Frequently, the fish would not take such an alarmingly bright fly, but when the strip was stopped such that the whole team hung in front of the boat – the 'hang' – any following fish, turning away, might discover one of the imitative flies and take it, as if not to waste their journey. Well, it worked and was a terrifically exciting and physical way to fish, which also made considerable demands on an angler's fitness in that many of us would do this for eight-hour sessions with breaks only between drifts! Definitely a young man's occupation; I do not care for this today for even a single drift. I can manage it, but enjoy other methods rather more.

Strip and hang and all the other approaches to lake and river trout fishing still work in spite of the advances of fashion and sophistication. This is the case for anything worthwhile in a particular fly pattern or technique – it becomes consistent and of long-term effect. I remember once in an England team debriefing session after a practice day, one

The thrill of it can only be enhanced by knowing that the capture resulted from good presentation: wild trout from the River Eden, with Streamflex two-weight

of my team-mates expressing his surprise when I told him that I had been catching on Cove-style pheasant tails. 'Surely, you don't still use those!' Well, as I reassured my friend, I did (and still do), and just because there are many other apparently more trendy patterns which will work in similar situations, this does not make the Cove PTN any less effective, and certainly not obsolete. Trout have not changed, even if we have, since the 1970s when Arthur introduced us to this outstanding generic nymph pattern.

We have come a long way since strip and hang. We have come a long way with both the tiny, compounded incremental steps, and with the pioneering exploits of Sawyer and Cove. Yet the childlike thrill of it all persists. Approaching 50,000 fly-caught fish later, I still yearn to discover, and to catch the next fish, and still enjoy almost every moment; but now there is more than just the catching. It has to be *in the way I want it*, or rather, in the way that all those trout and grayling have taught me is the most efficient and elegant way of going through this enthralling process. And it all comes down to presentation, which brings us to the fourth fly-fishing 'epiphany'; the extraordinary evolution of the contemporary state of the sport, which is the essence of this book.

Treasured moments hang there in the memory, like waypoints in the journey. After all those years with a fly rod they are many and varied. The first fish (a roach off a Wealden stream in Kent, 1960); the first trout off the river (a tiny fish from a tiny feeder stream running into the Clwyd in North Wales, the early 1960s); the first off the lake (a magnificent 2 lb brown trout on a teal and orange wet fly, Grafham, 1967); the first big sea-trout (black Pennell, top dropper on the drift; Loch Maree, September 1972). The first time double hauling through the 30-metre barrier (with a Hi Speed/Hi D fly line, from the bank of a small lake somewhere in southern England, 1973); the first time qualifying for the England team (a cool, breezy September day on Rutland Water, 1989). Hardly exhaustive, among the thousands of such moments in a fly-fishing life, but each one almost as intense as the day it happened – as was the big grayling that sipped the 21 yellow quill plume tip from the Eden's silken surface just the day before writing this. And I know also, being the age I am, that many of the moments are gone now, dispersed among the rich weave of five decades spent on the fresh, cold waters of the world, primarily in Britain and Europe.

Each time something happens, whether I catch or fail to catch a fish, there is discovery, even if it is but a consolation or strengthening of knowledge and experience. It is altogether a journey full of discoveries and wonders. It has brought me very close to nature, to the habitats where we practise our craft. It has brought me into contact, also, with the people, wildlife and landscapes of some of the most beautiful areas of the world, which for someone who does not particularly relish travelling, would not have been possible if not a fly-fisher. It has allowed me to experience true wilderness areas where I have discovered as much about myself as about fishing.

And then there was Team England, where I rubbed shoulders with the most competitive anglers in the world, and witnessed simply outstanding performances of the élite European masters (some of them my own countrymen). I could very easily fill a whole book with my experiences fishing for England. This covered two distinct periods, separated by almost a decade, in all the disciplines; lake bank, lake boat and river. It involved the hugely enjoyable river and loch-style home internationals (and my pride at winning both persists to this day) as well as the European and World Championships organized by the *Fédération Internationale de Pêche Sportive Mouche* (*FIPS-Mouche*). Very early in my fishing life, while in my early twenties, I was determined to qualify for England, and then to become an all-rounder within the team, and I was very proud, and genuinely lucky, to achieve these aims. Quite apart from the sheer joy and excitement of representing my country in my chosen sport, however, was the steep learning curve which finally resulted in travelling right out to the sport's frontier. Without my England team experience, I very much doubt that I would have made the leaps in river presentation that have occurred, at least in such a comparatively short time. There is something about the nature of competition that presses participants to the ragged edge as they seek the limit of what is possible within the rules – and sometimes, sadly, beyond them, because we competitive souls with our egos, particularly as young men, yearn for peer recognition at a cost that only the older, wiser man learns was not worth it.

Though there are remarkably few paradigm-shifting episodes in our sport, when they do occur they are grasped and broadcast and eased comfortably into the mind-set of us practitioners. Once the skills set has been achieved, they become commonplace and indeed we reach a point when we wonder how we managed before, and also why it took so long to reach these evolutionary benchmarks. I suppose this is just one of many humbling facets of the sport. And so it will continue. There are plateaux of skills and development but, with each one, we eventually reach the fringe, and look up to higher altitude. For sure we are on a high plateau now and I for one am rather surprised to be here, because it took me more than forty years with a fly rod before I even really glimpsed this place, and then the last few years to become comfortable here. I coach a young man, Tom, who has aspirations to repre-sent England, and it fills me with a sense of wonder that he is being injected immediately into this level of the sport. When he is my current age, and has gained all those river hours of experience, what fly-fishing place will he reach that none of us now can even imagine? In a way, though, this hardly matters, because right now, exactly where we are in the devel-opmental process is thrilling enough for us. It is tremendously fulfilling in a sporting sense to be opening doors to find a wealth of new territory reaching out beyond.

Although lonely at times, this sport is also like a family, and I think never more so than now because there is a delightful homogeneity about it, with shared experience that is disseminated more rapidly and further than ever before. It is perhaps one of the more pleasant aspects of the modern age. Neither has it spoiled anything of the mystery and magic of fly-fishing; rather it has really has opened it up for all of us, at whatever age and ability, to enjoy. Even if we cannot afford the historic, hallowed flows of the Itchen, say, or to hunt among the Alpine slopes of the upper Moselle, we can surely find fishing in stocked waters, at least, close to home – and perhaps even lakes and rivers where wild fish still exist in abundance in spite of the worst effects of modern, industrialized agri-culture. Fly-fishing is for all of us who have a love of clean, cold waters and the landscapes and habitats they flow through and occupy; where any species of fish will take the fly. It

Big Eden trout going back

is for the little boy on the Weald, thrilled at the sight of a plump roach sucking down a tuft of wool wound around a bait-fishing hook, as it is for the slower, middle-aged man quietly walking the manicured banks of a southern chalk stream, attentive to the vague hint out there of a rising brown trout in the seam of the water crowfoot. It is for the novices taking their first steps into the universe of adventures, or for the pioneers out on the rim of possibilities. It is for all of us who have this indomitable, instinctive passion to fish with fly in beautiful places. No matter how we evolve and move on, no matter by which water we prowl, we share the joy and excitement of it all.

✳ ✳ ✳ ✳ ✳

Before going through the process of development – my own and that of the sport more generally – I should give a definition of 'presentation fly-fishing'. It is an evolving boundary condition; the current limit of what can be achieved, with the tackle and the fly-fisher's skills, specifically in terms of having control over the presentation of the fly. This almost defines fly-fishing itself, and it should be noted that I am suggesting that all fly-fishing has nothing to do with how the rod or the line are constructed. The principle concern is the fly itself, being an artificial construction rather than a bait. How this fly is delivered is irrelevant to the definition of fly-fishing (although it is crucial to the excellence of presentation). Thus, the fly line, whether in the form of historically utilized woven horsehair or silk, or floss dapping lines, or the modern polymer composites, is simply not required within this definition. This liberates us from having to use such fundamentally crude fishing systems (although we acknowledge that the modern fly line does make the casting aspect of the process very easy). Instead, we are free to explore more radical means of delivering and then controlling the fly throughout the fishing process. It has been on rivers where departure from the limiting idea of employing comparatively heavy fly line has been most profound and we have discovered aspects of presentation which are revolutionizing at least this sector of the sport.

So, this book has to do with the core of fly-fishing, and is not limited to the oft-trodden territory of fly-casting, though the latter is a crucial aspect of the whole presentation-based approach.

CHAPTER ONE

Tackle and Approach

We have come a long way ...

The tackle we use dominates our sport; it stems from our history and suggests where we are going. We are rather lucky nowadays because the quality and availability of tackle is comparatively excellent. Older fly-fishers will remember the heavy rods and early PVC fly lines, for example, of the 1970s. It makes us shudder, now, because we endured it all, enjoyed it all, and caught a lot of fish in the process; but it was awful really. Yes, today we are fortunate in the choice for our requirements in all disciplines, with tackle eminently suitable throughout the range; for both the beginner on a stocked still water and the experienced angler wading the tumble of a wilderness river.

Beautifully marked San trout caught on state-of-the-art tackle in 2007: Hardy Marksman 9' four-weight

*State of the river art
as recently as 2009;
wild river trout on
Streamflex four-weight*

I am often dismayed by anglers who proudly show me some aged item of tackle that they have acquired or inherited, because more often than not I have to advise that it is mostly inappropriate for modern fishing, far surpassed in terms of performance by contemporary tackle. While it might have aesthetic, historic or financial value, it ends there because in almost every instance even the cheap versions of most tackle products nowadays are superior in terms of function, at the very least. I do still have one of the original Hardy Marquis reels from the 1970s. This reel has been loved. It was 'born' on Grafham Water where it was loaded with a double taper #6 floater and was identical to that used by Arthur Cove, which was why I had one. I can still hear the sound of the check pawl rasping away raucously as I stripped off line on those summer evenings among the smoke-like columns of buzzers. I think that sound would turn heads half a mile away. I used this same reel when fishing for sea-trout at night in the West Country, or on the lochs of northern Scotland, and I hated that sound, breaking the peace and silence of the summer nights; but I did love the reel, even putting up with the memory coiling that it put in my line because of the narrow arbor. I learned to disengage the pawl, so that it ran silently, though this also resulted in quite a few over-runs, many of them when big rainbows or sea-trout bolted, and not all of which ended happily. Finally, I filed a little of the hard steel from the tooth of the pawl, and the spool thereafter purred and seldom gave me the problem of over-runs. Some time in the 1980s the gun-metal anodizing begun

to peel and I laboriously stripped off the ugly remains of the rest to reveal the raw aluminium beneath. And so, I love it still, because I had many thousands of trout on that reel, quite a few salmon, and it travelled far and wide with me, even though the rods came and went. It was a faithful companion, even giving service during my first internationals. Yet nowadays, when I take it from its case, it is only to revel in the cascade of memories that the sight and feel of it ignites.

Hardy Marksman four-weight with AA rated silk fly line with furled tip, 2010

There is not a single item of the tackle we use, including the materials and structure of flies, that has not been developed, mostly to a considerable extent. Early carbon fibre, for example, was little better in function than the glass fibre it was soon to make obsolete. Indeed, in this period, many of us were still dabbling with split cane (and silk fly lines). Interestingly, though the performance of modern carbon fibre materials is unparalleled, there are those who still revert to cane, and even to glass fibre for certain uses; but we must all admit that contemporary high-modulus carbon fibre is simply outstanding for its purpose. As aesthetically delightful as a 7-foot Palakona cane rod was, and still can be, it will be outstripped in terms of performance by most carbon fibre tools in almost all circumstances. Similarly, the fly lines we have today are an utter delight compared with those memory-coiled, low-tech products which formed the foundation of the fly-fishing sport for many of us not so long ago.

Here, I am going to consider tackle development during recent decades only where it

Wild river brown trout with Streamflex two-weight and ultra-fine silk

has a significant bearing on our approach to the sport today. It is, however, an exploration at the frontier of development and in this context we will look at the state of the art in tackle design, and in some cases we will see how we have come full circle. You see, though we as anglers have changed, with new materials and developing experience and skills, our target species, the trout and grayling, have not. They still react to the fly as they always did.

Not so long ago, on the river, the de facto standard was a rod with an AFTMA #5 or #6 rating, loaded with a forward taper, or double taper, fly line; this was considered to be the 'balanced' outfit that could deal easily with wild trout and grayling, and even give service for sea-trout and steelhead. On still waters, there has been an obsession with distance casting, from bank or boat, and so rod ratings have been much higher. Here, a #6 would be considered fairly lightweight, and #7 or even #8 would be most anglers' choice. I know a few top 'loch-style' international competitors who prefer #9, even nowadays, claiming that the heavy line makes little detrimental difference, if any, to the presentation and thus to the trout. They prefer the feeling of control such heavy lines and powerful rods gives them, and even in calm weather continue with these lines, ignoring the noisy touchdown. Competitive fly-fishing has had a lot of influence on the modern approach, particularly on still waters, and while a considerable amount that is good in terms of development comes from the competitive sector, this particular issue might not be so. Finally, it is not possible to achieve very gentle touchdown with such heavy lines, compared with what is achievable with a sub-five weight, and this really does have an effect on fish close to the surface.

Oddly, this can sometimes be positive, in that stocked fish can be attracted to the noise of a fly line hitting the water (perhaps it sounds like trout pellets at feeding time). In fact the plop of a weighted nymph hitting the surface can sometimes have this effect even with wild fish. In most circumstances, however, our drive is towards the gentlest touchdown possible, no matter what the purpose and intention of some top international competitors targeting naïve fish.

From a very British-centred approach to trout fishing, which persisted into the 1980s, we observed the ascendancy of the American influence, and this was extended by (even originated from) the widespread introduction of rainbow trout in sport fisheries all over the world. This fast- growing, ferociously acrobatic salmonid, so ideal for the fly-fisher as a target species, thrives in still waters of all sizes and rivers of all types, so long as they are clean and cold. Rainbow trout are easier and cheaper to rear than brown trout and take well to a wide range of situations. Thus, fly-anglers demanded what were considered essential powerful rods. These were the typical (in this period) fast-action tools which had been, after all, designed primarily as streamer rods with perhaps due deference to nymph fishing. Of course, we used these rods for fishing the dry fly as well, typically with what were designated as #5 and #6 lines; but the heritage was definitely rainbow trout and streamer based and they were, therefore, only really suitable for the larger sizes of dry flies. It seems ludicrous, nowadays, that we used such rods in Britain for almost every-thing, including dry flies down to about size 20, with the only tippet material that was commonly available in those days (nylon monofilament) down to about 0.2 mm diameter and a breaking strain of about a kilogram, and thought we were sophisticated. Actually, we did rather a disservice to the trout population, because we left an awful lot of little flies in their mouths through the use of such over-powered rods with unsuitable terminal tackle. We did, however, also learn a great deal about still-water trout, particularly with streamer and nymph tactics, and significantly extended the traditional 'loch-style' approach. These were hugely exciting times. In Britain it was boom time for still-water fly-fishing.

The trend towards very powerful rods largely stemmed from the North American influence. Why else would Sage and others have produced those very fast-action rods unless they were in demand? In fact, these rods, designated for #5 and #6 weight lines, were not really properly line rated. The anachronistic (even then) AFTMA system was designed such that the rod would be optimally loaded with 30 feet of line out of the rod tip. We were all trying to cast way beyond this on still waters – the entire length of a fly line (90 feet), while loading the rod with up to 60 feet of line in the air, and these rods handled that amount of line mass remarkably easily. They might well have been designated #7 or even #8 weights.

Then came the European river masters and development in a different direction; immensely subtle and supremely elegant, and biased towards the river. The American fast-action rods seemed crude, or harsh; the longer, softer British style of rods somewhat better for this opening world of fly-fishing possibilities, at least in low line ratings. Yet the Europeans, many of them, from both east and west, were already on a higher plateau. In Britain

Perfection in the river approach: Streamflex two-weight with Rio triple zero

we merely glimpsed it at the time, only really coming into contact during World and European Championships where, after all, so much is always kept hidden and secretive within the nationalistic folds of teams. It was the European approach that really set the course for the presentation-based approach we have today, with the trend towards lighter lines, and rods to manage them, most especially on the river.

And here, I claim, is where we have the frontier of the single-handed fly rod sport; precipitated from the Sawyer and Cove schools (which changed so much), the proliferation of stocked fisheries, and the increased mobility of a generation of hunter anglers exploring new wild waters, particularly rivers. The tackle is now so beautifully tuned to our needs, though retaining some of the obsolescence and anachronism from more classical fly-fishing culture, while our mind-set is in that thrilling state of development that tells us all we are redefining, or rediscovering, the very core of the sport.

Purely in terms of tackle, the standards are currently focused on a #4 weight on rivers and #7 weight on lakes (and #8 for predator/salt-water). If you were to ask a hundred river anglers what line weight they most used, the majority would reply a #4, though you would find quite a number who more usually use a #3, or lower weight, and perhaps also some, fishing powerful torrent rivers, who would suggest heavier; but a #4 defines the benchmark, whereas just a decade ago it would have been a #5. There has been less change, and less development in many ways, on still waters. A decade ago the standard would have

been a #7, just as now. Only a comparative handful would lean towards a #6 or a #5, while lower weights might be considered somewhat radical. But why is this? It comes down to that long-range casting mentioned earlier, and of course to the comparatively large size of stocked fish (in fishery managers' attempts both to avoid over-predation and to supply what most customers want) and perhaps the larger wild lake trout and sea-trout. Big fish have always been equated with powerful rods, and only now, influenced by the river pioneers, are we understanding that this might be a somewhat misguided tenet, as we shall explore later. There is now a rapidly growing vanguard of contemporary fly-fishers who have a much more sophisticated or informed appreciation of presentation than formerly, and this is leading us evermore to question the established ideas of past doctrines. It is not so easy for most of us of conservative nature to change, yet inevitably, if we take steps towards this overwhelmingly exciting frontier, the most traditionally and classically minded among us must admit to there being a better way, and a new aesthetic in the sport. So, while the standard is for a #4 weight on the river, we are being led inexorably towards a #2 weight for optimum presentation.

While the journey has pushed the boat angler towards increasing complexity and a proliferation of tackle requirements, the roaming fisherman of lake shore or river has been both more adventurous and more minimalistic. Short casting range, mobility and shallow water – running or still – characterize the fishing habitat of the latter category

In 2012 this was close to the frontier, at the leader-only stage.

The ultimate in the Western-style? Wild river brown trout on leader-only, loaded on a Danielsson Midge and Streamflex 10' two-weight

of angler, and this has partly driven a simpler, more natural approach, which has in turn probably better developed instinctive ability and natural hunting skills. Not that technical development has passed the river angler by; rather it is an emergence of a level of ability with minimal tackle requirements on a very broad base of water types (which actually does not exclude fly-fishing from drifting boats on large lakes).

For general, all-round application in the Western-style the two-piece rod is obsolete, even the three-piece. We might have been stuck for years in the belief that increasing the number of sections, and joints, in a rod would spoil its performance, but the technology has moved us on from this. We now have multi-section 'travel' rods with the high-quality casting and fishing characteristics we require. Four sections represent the benchmark position today. The design of the single-handed fly rod is core to our sport; everything we do stems from this tool and it is now a very highly tuned compromise between light-weight material composites, length, flex distribution, ergonomics and the intangible qualities of aesthetics.

At this point I should make clear that the units described in this book are mixed! The reason is that in various countries we use different units, particularly in measuring lengths and weights (actually mass) and we also have the fly line loading conventions which are now dominated by the anachronistic AFTMA system, which in any case is arbitrary. The Americans are more imperial even than the British, using feet and pounds, while the British have our delightful mixture of these imperial units with SI (*Système*

International) units, stemming from our European connection, along with the conventional silk line weightings and AFTMA. Added to this mix is the new (to Western anglers) rod flex system incorporated in tenkara, which ranges from 5:5 to 7:3. It is a mess, but anglers everywhere tend to pick it up and do the necessary mental conversions into whatever they understand best. I tend to describe lengths of fish, depths and ranges, in centimetres and metres, and masses in kilograms, because this is a hangover from my time in international competition; but sometimes I revert to the old-school units of feet, inches and pounds. I grew up with the AFTMA system, so in spite of it being out of date to the extent that it is seriously flawed, I still describe line and rod weightings accordingly, even though I tend to make the necessary physical conversions in my mind in terms of the actual loading of a line on a rod – how it feels in the hand during casting – and I do the same with a fixed line rig, for which the ratio system ratings mean little.

It is perhaps clearest to see the whole gamut of tackle/approach possibilities when fly-fishing for trout (and grayling) in terms of the following spectrum.

On the small stream or upland lake where the fixed line approach is at its best, we also find that the Western-style with rods up to a maximum of #3 weight is perfect, and possibly preferable to fixed line if fish much larger than 35cm are commonly encountered. The Western-style rod length is less significant on this type of water than on any other, and the angler can more comfortably use a comparatively short rod. The only real problem with a long rod occurs on very overgrown streams where casting becomes a crucial, limiting issue. Even on such waters, however, a long rod can often be better utilized than a short one, with leader-only techniques, 'threading' the line through narrow gaps in the foliage and avoiding a back cast, or with fly line based rigs incorporating Spey and roll casts. As the size of river increases, the longer rod, from 9½ to 11 feet (Western-style) or 11–14 feet (fixed line), affords ideal control, with the Western-style approach offering greater range and also control in dealing with larger fish. Low AFTMA ratings (maximum #3) continue to have the advantage for ranges out to 15 metres (though ideally at 10 metres), allowing very gentle touchdown, cushioning of the take and setting the hook, and subsequent control over fish on fine tippets. Similarly, this is also the domain of the 5:5 and 6:4 rated tenkara rods.

As the size, or more particularly the flow rate and volume, of the river increase, the rod flex and line rating needs to increase, but *not as much as commonly accepted*: #3 and #4 weights can usually deal with most circumstances with nymph, spider and dry fly, as can tenkara 6:4 ratings. Neither should we think that leader-only rigs, including the fixed line, are disadvantaged on such waters, because it is invariably better to keep the range down to 6–10 metres (between hands and fly). Only as the flow rate becomes very high, or when large trout are encountered, do we really have a need for higher line ratings. On this sort of water, the tippet diameter will be high, upwards of 0.14 mm, and we need to have the ability to exert considerable pressure on a large, possibly bolting fish in fast water. This is also mostly beyond the scope of fixed line techniques, because it is simply irresponsible to attempt to hold a fish against fine tippets – which inevitably will break if the hook-hold does not fail.

Tenkara 12' 6:4 'Iwana',
plume tip and wild trout

The large rivers and still waters, at least where larger fish are encountered, are where Western-style now completely dominates and we are considering longer-range casting and control, also with the possibilities for streamer, necessitating more powerful rods and fly lines in the #4 to #6 category. However, it is certainly valid to be fishing lower line-rated rods on such waters, particularly with non-streamer methods at short range. Of course, on large still waters the #7 weight, and even heavier, will continue to have favour while anglers are focused on very long-range casting, from bank or boat, even when the size of fish does not warrant such stiff-actioned casting rods. It must be said, however, that all the above does not necessarily demand that, in order to deal best with the full range of water types, we need a similarly broad range of tackle. Other than a few extreme water types – mostly of very fast flow and volume – it is perfectly valid to manage comfortably with a single rod, something like the Greys Streamflex XF2+ #3, an outstanding all-rounder. In any case, we are now at the polar opposite of the spectrum from where the fixed line approach is supreme and find that the main issue is the ability to yield and gather line, and this is where the fly reel defines the Western style.

How a fly reel looks, sounds and feels in the hand is much more important to most of us than its function, which after all is pretty basic. In the river discipline – for trout and grayling – the reel is almost always merely a line store, seldom being required to perform beyond this function except on those occasions when a trout bolts over a considerable distance, stripping line from the reel. Of course, big still-water trout, sea-trout and steelhead, and numerous salt-water species, do often demand sophisticated brake systems and other subtle characteristics (such as vibration reduction) which come in at the higher end of the market, but for most fly-anglers the reel is actually over-designed. What most of us need is a lightweight reel with a large enough arbor to prevent too much coiling in line and backing, a fixed drag, or drag-less system, which avoids over-runs on a fast line strip, and an exposed rim on the spool which can be 'palmed' in the event of a big fish running. Also, with the trend towards very light lines and leader-only, a design which precludes these fine

One of the best 'river' reels ever made, the fixed drag Marksman; this one is loaded with Hardy Premium two-weight with horsehair furled tip

diameter lines becoming trapped between spool and rim is also essential. Aesthetics, however, are probably much more important to most of us and a reel which does not look and sound good to the user, even if it is perfectly functional, has the capacity for spoiling the experience. So, while my battle-worn Marquis saw me through into the 1990s, the Danielsson Midge, Hardy Marksman and Ultralite are now my companions of the day, and I consider these perhaps the pinnacle in terms of design and use of materials, with ideal functionality. I admit, however, that a reel costing a quarter the price of these beautiful tools might well serve perfectly in terms of function, if not matching the aesthetics.

While various contemporary approaches to the river discipline have involved limited use of fly line (if any), there has been a surge of interest in tenkara fishing, outside Japan where it originated. Although this fixed line technique does not employ the conventional fly reel, and nor does it involve fly line, tenkara is utterly enfolded within the sport as a completely valid fly-fishing technique, which also pushes the presentation boundaries. It is unquestionably both supremely elegant and delightfully minimalistic, lacking only in the range of presentation potential and the ability to deal with larger trout in open water situations, which is the territory of the fly reel based, Western-style approaches. Tenkara has caught on in a big way in the United States, and among river fly-fishers there it challenges the Western-style (conventional fly line and fly reel). In Britain, too, this trend is not far behind.

The perfection of the Streamflex two-weight, with one-weight line and wild trout

As pointed out previously, a reel can be a thing of great beauty, and highly personal, every bit as much as a fly rod. However, many fly-fishers put too much functional emphasis on the reel, believing perhaps that this item of tackle can and should allow control over the fish in play. In practice this can actually be a problem because, in most circumstances – in the river and still-water sport at least – there are much more important aspects of control, as we shall examine later. The most beautiful fly reels of all are those ultra-lightweight, understated, minimal function tools which just make us look at them, yearning to touch them and to hear them purring as line is pulled off. Strange, functionally contrary devices they might be, but to lose them from fly-fishing would be to lose some of the sport's character.

We should, however, be more pragmatic about fly lines, because these seriously affect presentation and are also every bit as central to the sport as the fly rod. In fact, the sport has been fly line orientated (rather than fish orientated) to a very large extent, with this factor determining the entire process of fly delivery. (In this context we must include the leader, though this is something for considerable exploration in later chapters.)

The fundamental design of the contemporary fly line has not changed very much since the introduction of polymer lines in the 1960s, though the materials and construction have improved hugely. Modern fly lines are outstanding casting implements, when married to suitable rods with the correct loading. Our convention for matching rod to line is the AFTMA system, in which the first 30 feet of fly line extended from the tip ring should load the rod perfectly and thus be ideal for casting; but there is a serious built-in flaw here. In practice, we almost never load the rod with exactly or even nearly 30 feet of fly line. On the river we usually have much less, while on the lake we have considerably more. We can go back to the 1970s and the Arthur Cove school to see this point exemplified. Then, we were aerializing perhaps two-thirds of a 90-foot fly line, thus loading the rod with more than double the mass suggested by the AFTMA rating, in order to achieve the very long distance presentation of nymphs from the banks of large still waters. This approach extended to similar long-range techniques in boat fishing

The outstanding Danielsson Midge, loaded with leader-only rig and horsehair furl

as 'loch-style' developed apace. Tournament casters similarly load the rod with much greater mass than the AFTMA rating would suggest. If we watch the modern lake fisherman loading a rod with the high-performance distance casting lines, such as the 40 plus from Airflo, we can understand that optimal loading, in relation to long casts (albeit involving considerable line-shoot) is way off the AFTMA scale for any particular fly-fishing rod (as differentiated from a tournament casting rod). The point is that modern materials such as high-modulus carbon fibre have a far greater range of performance tolerance than hitherto, and all we can really say about the old rating convention is that it offers only a very rough guide and we should not be overly swayed by its implications. There is considerably more to the marriage of rod and line than the loading convention. Indeed, modern 'high-performance' fly-fishing on the river is now focused on the rod being considerably under-loaded, as we shall see.

While many of us feel that the AFTMA system is antiquated, we do not suggest that conventional fly lines are obsolete. The various densities and sinking rates of today's sinking lines, for instance, have pushed the boundaries of possibilities for nymph and streamer presentation, particularly in still waters. The modern floating line is excellent for its function, even though this also limits its presentation potential – but here is the development occurring right now; here is the technical frontier of the sport, rather as skaggit lines are affecting the double-handed fly rod sport. This is sporting evolution and to deny it is to deny the reality of the situation.

*Wild brown trout and
Phoenix silk, AA rated*

In the sport's traditional development there is gradual change; countless little advances which add up to a homogeneity of progressions. And then there are the sudden jumps; the Sawyer and Cove moments that catch the imagination and sweep us all along in a storm of change. We are currently living through one of these and it is overwhelmingly exciting. Everywhere I look now, at home or beyond, there is evidence of the metamorphosis. It is far-reaching, encompassing the sophistication and attention to detail of the Americans, the adventurous eastern and northern Europeans, the enthralling tenkara emanating from Japan, and *pesca alla Valsesiana* from Italy; and it is all presentation-orientated. So, of course, we must question the validity of the tools and tackle with which we conduct our sport, every bit as much as the techniques we employ. This is the great driver that leads to development. Fly rods have swept ahead of the game and fly lines and leaders are following.

There is also the strangeness of the full circle. How extraordinary it is to observe the resurgence of horsehair and silk or thread furled leaders, and how the silk fly line has returned to the forefront of the sport. I began my fishing life with Kingfisher silk lines and now use them again (or the French equivalents of the day from, for example,

Phoenix). Today, as more of us question the AFTMA system and understand better the rod/line/leader relationship that improves our presentation, we rediscover the benefits of silk, and horsehair. These include the fine diameter-to-mass ratio, low stretch and low memory, among others; but in combination, and with appropriate leaders, these produce the best compromise possible today for a whole range of, particularly, river applications.

Perfection for tenkara: wild trout from a small north-country river

There is also a proliferation of other tackle out there. Some of it is essential to a successful approach in one or more of the fly-fishing disciplines, while other items have more limited application, but are useful from time to time. Others yet might be fashionable, though of lesser long-term value, and finally pass away; and then there are the contrary, the non-faddish and often disregarded items that are nonetheless utterly worthwhile and have a bearing on the very substance of what we are trying to achieve. Leader and tippet materials, including the structure of the various furls and braids, so central to the modern approach in both fixed and running line techniques, are considered in the relevant context in later chapters, as are the items of peripheral tackle.

I have often said that our success is the sum of many parts, which include the items

Ready to go at BWO time: Pat Stevens' kit, with apple harvest, by the San

of tackle and how we choose and assemble them, as well as their use in the whole gamut of circumstances we encounter. Each part of the whole, properly considered, might be worth the capture of a fish, or perhaps many more in a lifetime of fishing; but then there are hundreds, thousands, of these components. If we pay them due attention, the path of our fly-fishing adventure is a fulfilling one. The flip-side is, more often than not, a frustration. Through a lifetime there is a lot of trial and error – the trial is fun and, while the errors knock us back, they should also fuel further exploration taking us towards improvement. I deal with these parts of the whole both where they have a bearing in the text, and also in Chapter 7, Sum of the Parts.

To conclude this current chapter, there follows a description first of the tackle I most usually have with me on a typical day on the river, and then of that I have packed away for a more prolonged trip.

The Greys Streamflex XF2 10-foot #2 is my most usual companion, in conjunction with a presentation leader and/or a DT #2 floater, tipped with a furled horsehair leader, loaded on either a Hardy Marksman reel (which is a beautifully engineered, lightweight, fixed drag reel, with rim control), an Ultralite CC or a Danielsson Midge. I take a single,

small box of flies, a pair of line snips (which can incorporate a sharpening stone), and scissors/fine pliers combined (for the removal of flies taken deeply where fingers cannot reach). Usually I take a single spool, but never more than two spools, of copolymer between 0.09 mm and 0.14 mm diameter, according to prevalent conditions, to provide the tippet material needs. The most important item of peripheral tackle that I carry is red label Mucilin – it is utterly indispensable because, as detailed later, it is crucial to keeping the line or leader tip afloat.

Although obviously not essential, I nearly always carry a waterproof compact digital camera. I use no net (we are nearly always better off if we learn how to deal with fish without a net) or wading stick (because I no longer choose water where one might be tempted with a wading stick, which can often lead to a false sense of security in such situations). All of the peripheral tackle is placed in the pockets or top section of breathable waders, or on a leather lanyard around my neck. I still like felt soles on wading boots for their compromise between quiet footfalls and reasonable grip on slippery boulders, but the micro-studded, stealth soles of modern boots probably do have the edge in terms of grip. Clothing is as appropriate (I only use a waterproof jacket in persistent rain), but in this

Delightful simplicity, particularly when travelling: tenkara rig and tailwater grayling

context, a modern neck or head tube is strongly recommended. They are incredibly versatile – they keep the neck (and ears and head if necessary) warm, protect from biting insects and, in particularly hot weather, are great sun-shields. If dipped in the water and then wrung out, they also provide good cooling. High-factor lip salve is a must, even in northern regions – at a push this can be used (in combination with the head tube) to shield any exposed flesh, and even as an emergency replacement for uses on line, leader and fly which ordinarily involve Mucilin. I know, because I have used it, though the reverse does not apply; I don't think Mucilin is a good sun-screen!

Variations in the above will be a fixed line system, thus dispensing with the rod, reel and leader system as above, and my first rod of choice is the delightful 12-foot Iwana from TenkaraUSA which is designed as an all-rounder with a flex rating of 6:4. Also, for a still-water trip I usually replace the #2 weight with the Streamflex XF2+ #3, married with either a silk line (AA rated) or Hardy Premium DT floater. For a boat session, I use either the above, or a Streamflex 9½-foot #6, with usually a #5 double taper floater, or variety of sinking lines loaded on Hardy Demon or Ultralite cartridges.

For the longer trip, particularly if it involves air travel, I usually take both the 10-foot #2 and the XF2+, which is an extendable (9½–10 feet) #3, and have the back-up of a 9-footer in similar line designation, while also taking the 12-foot Iwana. Apart from the leader-to-hand rig (and the furled silk leader, or other, for tenkara), I include a Hardy premium DT #2 and the AA rated level silk line, on Marksman, Ultralite and Danielsson Midge reels. This is obviously river-based, and precludes streamer, though I am perfectly all right with the XF2+ #3 for all my own still-water needs.

All the other tackle is as for the simple day trip, though I also include a rudimentary fly-tying kit, and usually nowadays have with me a digital SLR (as well as the waterproof compact). Everything, other than the tying kit, is carried to the river (or lake shore) in a robust waterproof shoulder bag which, in the event of rain, can protect the SLR and anything else that needs to be kept dry or is simply not needed while out on the river.

The lake fisherman who needs to cast long distances, or the streamer fisherman, will naturally adjust the rod and line specifications accordingly. In my competition years, tackle would always include a 10-foot #6 or #7 weight rod and, apart from the floater, a range of lines with different densities, each loaded on a cassette for the outstanding Hardy Demon, which has today been superseded by the Ultralite cartridge reel. I hesitate to make any specific recommendations for rods in this area of the sport. There are many excellent, fit-for-purpose rods out there now. All I really want to mention is that there persists a tendency, particularly with the relatively inexperienced, to err towards tip action, powerful rods. These can be 'poker-like' and hugely unforgiving in terms of both casting and dealing with fish. They are very poor for short- to medium-range techniques with nymph, wet fly or dry fly. In the right hands they offer the ability to send appropriate lines to the 40-metre range, with teams of wet flies or streamers, and to deal with fish on heavy leaders, but in truth, when did I *need* to do this in my international career, on lakes? Actually, never. I always got away with rods of a maximum rating of #7, and was usually much happier with lower line ratings, right down to the #3, which is the preference nowadays.

It all has to do with presentation and control, and choosing the appropriate technique for the prevalent conditions, and invariably this involves gentler tackle than the faddy power tools with which we so often abuse our fishing. I am not, however, making a specific recommendation for ultra-light line rated rods for still-water use (though I certainly am for the river). A #5 or #6 represents an excellent all-round compromise between casting and presentation requirements, and will allow the safe use of fairly fine tippets and small flies, which are often so important.

All of the above amounts to a personal view, based on experience. If one were to seek the advice of, say, my former England team-mates John Horsey or Ian Barr, who are two of the most successful international competitors of all time, on still waters, their recommendations would probably be towards the #7/8 or even #9 weights, and they would convincingly argue the need for such. Then again, this might all be a part of that mysterious full circle. I remember back to times spent with similarly great still-water competitors, Chris Howitt and double World Champion Brian Leadbetter, who used to love the more through action #7 weights, while Chris Ogborne, like me, leaned towards lower line ratings.

The lake specialist generally will have slightly more tackle requirements than the river enthusiast, with boat fishermen in particular needing a net and probably a broad range of lines of different densities and sinking profiles, and arguably a greater range of flies. He will need a boat seat (or a float tube) and accompanying drift-controlling devices such as a drogue – though this can run out of control and lead to a conviction that the boat angler has requirements that are far greater than is practical and may finally amount to so much clutter and confusion. One of the great secrets of success in our sport is simplicity: removing variables and narrowing the choices (and resultant indecision). This almost always works to our benefit and, given the excellence of modern tackle and due consideration for our particular needs of the moment, leads to an altogether more satisfying experience. I think this is one of the greatest charms of latter-day river fishing, particularly with leader-only set-ups and the magical tenkara approach. These are also applicable to still-water fly-fishing, for all short-range techniques, whether from bank, boat or tube – although here the Western-style with fly line (and reel) and the more powerful rod remains the most versatile option.

CHAPTER TWO

Team England

The loneliness of the sessions ...

I spent many years of my fishing life utterly focused on Team England duties, and it was an extraordinary experience, unimagined at the outset. It changed the way I fished, and it changed my life – in both senses not always for the better. It set me on a crash course in competitiveness; of technical, pragmatic angling, in all manner of contrived situations. My competitive international career ranged from the loch-style and river home internationals, to the European open events and then the formal European and World Championships. In fact, I enjoyed two long periods, separated by almost ten years, and they were incredibly intense, filled with a spectrum of emotions from utter despair to overwhelming euphoria.

The England team at the European Championships in Poland, 2005; the author is third from left

I had dreamed of representing my country in my chosen sport for a very long time. I remember drifting over the expansive shallows of Loch Maree and Loch Hope in the north of Scotland, with dazzling catches of sea-trout; and the long drifts over Grafham ... I wandered the shores of numerous English reservoirs and lakes, and more than a hundred Highland lochs, in my pursuit of trout, and I did catch thousands. I travelled to Ireland, Europe and Scandinavia, and began my discovery of the enormous variety of rivers; and all this was before I was really ready to attempt my personal sporting summit. Having started fly-fishing very early meant that I was comparatively experienced, especially on lakes, while still in my twenties. I did not, however, possess the knowledge or the confidence – perhaps the courage – to go for it. Fortunately, I had my mentor figures to carry me over that hurdle – Arthur Cove, and particularly in the competitive sense, Tony Pawson, along with other members of the Confederation of English Fly Fishers (CEFF). I don't know if these great anglers saw in me merely youthful enthusiasm or some nascent skill in the sport, but I suspect (or like to think) it was a mixture of the two, the combination of which might or might not produce an international-class competitor. In any case, they did encourage me and I really was immensely lucky. In those days there was not the organization we have now in England, and many other countries, which encourages youth up to international standard, so without the kindness and attention of these gentlemen it would have taken me far longer to begin to realize my aspiration, and indeed I might never have done so.

Through my own progress I want to illustrate those aspects of which serious competitors need to be aware. Sometimes quite large, often tiny and subtle, they are all worthwhile if one is to be consistently competitive. There is not so much about technique in this chapter as there is in other chapters of this book, because here I am concentrating on the physical and mental aspects of preparation and participation in the top level of our competitive sport. In fact, I think that an awareness in this area is even more important than technical skill and I suppose at the outset I should express some caution, because there are many personality traits which do not take well to such competitiveness. I realized very late that my own personality, even lifestyle, had been altered, in most ways detrimentally: while becoming a much more effective technical and tactical fisherman, which I still relish, I did not become a better person, though I hope to have recovered the situation in later years! It can all become damaging to one's emotional state, and surely fishing should not be like that. On the credit side, the value of companionship of one's team-mates is immeasurable, and what one learns from those anglers is vast, far more than we can learn anywhere else. What we discover by being in close contact with team members of other nations is also huge, and in the World and European Championships we visit some of the most wonderful trout and grayling rivers that exist, which undoubtedly would be far more limited to us if we were not national team members. When it goes well, the feeling is utterly overwhelming, and sharing this with team-mates, friends and family lasts forever and makes the world an altogether better place. But I am getting ahead of myself.

Where it all started to gel for me was when I was mature enough to understand my own strengths and weaknesses. In the late 1980s, my strengths certainly lay mostly with

floating line techniques on still waters, a mixture of long-line nymph fishing from the bank, and traditional loch-style from a drifting boat, with a developing emphasis towards dry fly. This, after all, is how I had fished the northern lochs and the big English still waters, like Grafham. Although I was spending a lot of time with fast-sinking lines, streamer and deep nymph methods, I never particularly had a comfort with these or felt that I was doing anything exceptional, although I was one of those who developed the 'strip and hang' style mentioned in the introduction.

Having that broad experience, again mostly on lakes, compared with many competitors older than me, gave me an edge in terms of being able to analyse reasonably quickly the potential in a range of situations. I know that this is hugely important for a competitor, because the flip side, I'm afraid, is a feeling of not knowing what is going on and what to do, and that is hopeless. Related to this is preparation and, right from the outset, I always paid a lot of attention to this requirement. The confidence this gives is sometimes by itself virtually a match-winner. I remember once telling my team-mates that I had won a particular competition at the fly vice, meaning that all our pre-match preparation on the water and subsequently at the vice had allowed me to tie the right fly patterns which had infused all the confidence I needed. It does not always work like that, but attention to all forms of preparation is vital; one cannot survive without it.

The author fishing long-line nymph on the San tailwater in Poland, during the European Championships

The author's England team-mate Dave Parker into a big rainbow in dangerous heavy spate conditions during the European Championships of 2006

Beyond the obvious limitations in one's personal technical abilities, are those difficult emotional issues. These rapidly undermine confidence, and fatigue compounds them. In 1987 we had the inaugural European Open Championship, a precursor to the formal *FIPS-Mouche* European event, on Bewl Water in Kent. Tony Pawson, the main British organizer, had invited me to take part, alongside the England World Championship team, among whom was Brian Leadbetter, one of the all-time great England competitors and then current World Champion. I practised every day for the week leading up to the competition and on one of these days I was accompanied by Arthur Cove. The fishing conditions were poor; almost flat calm and cloudless, and we struggled through much of the day. We searched a lot of bank and in several hours fishing we managed only a fish apiece. Then I experienced one of those unforgettable 'purple patches' which resulted in four trout in fifteen minutes, and right at the end of the period that the championship would be fished.

I had been despondent through the day, because the weather was forecast to be similar on match day. As Arthur and I left the water, we talked about it. I probably said something banal about wondering what I should do in the competition in such conditions. Arthur replied, 'Well, you just have to rely on a patch like you had today. You might fish for hours without a take, but if you're doing it about right, and don't give up, you'll probably get your reward. *Never give up* until the very end.' Arthur did not allude to any of the fish he might have caught at the same time as me – it was a measure of the man that he simply

wanted to bolster my confidence. And this he did. While I was very tired on competition day – frankly over-practised – I was confident in what I was doing.

The competition day conditions did prove to be very similar to those we had experienced all week, with fish hard to come by. The morning, bank session went well for me, with a mixed bag of six rainbow and brown trout that gave me a section second place. The afternoon was relentlessly sunny and almost calm, testing stamina which can only be maintained by having confidence in one's ability. I 'scratched' a good rainbow and a small brown trout during the session and it was almost over when another good rainbow sipped down my dry fly off the edge of the ripple. It was this fish, netted within two minutes of the end, which tipped the balance, because it pushed me into fourth place in the afternoon session and the combination of my two session places gave me the individual European Open Championship. We worked out that, without that last rainbow, I would barely have made it into the top ten. I can still hear Arthur's voice – 'Never give up until the very end …'

I did have a very good start to my competitive career, and I was lucky; not because I was necessarily trusting too much to luck in the competitions themselves, but I always prepared very carefully, fished far and wide, and I had my mentor figures who helped me *immeasurably*. Also, the general standard on still waters was not as it was soon to become, while the river skills – in Britain – were frankly poor, and certainly uncompetitive in an

Alone in the sessions: the author on the San tailwater

*Incredibly effective
caddis imitation
by England team
guide Louis Perez*

international sense. This did not, however, give me a free ride into the England team. It took me to my third attempt, in my third year of trying, to reach this goal.

It was the 1989 National Final on Rutland Water on a cool, breezy September day. Again I had done my practice and was well prepared, so much so that I was committed to travelling up the limit of the South Arm to fish dry fly even though I knew that most finalists, and certainly most of the eventual team qualifiers, would be relying on sinking lines and 'pulling' techniques in the main body of the lake. With my boat partner, Ray Arkle, and boatman (England team-member Brian Thomas) in agreement, we headed off on the long haul down the Arm, wondering, of course, if we were passing over perfectly good water such as Yellowstone and Old Hall bays. However, based on what had happened the previous year, when I had weakened, I knew that to stop in such areas would be counter-productive. There was the bulk of the 100-strong field of finalists who could fish those areas at least as well as I could, and many of them better; I would in all probability be 'lost in the percentages' in such a situation, and one should learn early that this particular choice is rarely wise. Better to stick with what you know best, where your strengths lie, and right then mine were with dry fly in quiet, remote areas.

I fished a well-spaced team of three 'bits-style' dries and hoppers, and Ray was using similar. It proved a very difficult day; but this again was fortunate, because it was difficult all over Rutland Water, though we had no way of knowing that at the time. I caught four good trout, to Ray's three. There was one curious moment when I noticed one of my flies sitting on a large piece of floating weed. As I lifted off to re-cast into clear water, the weed turned into a big brown trout just about to take the fly I had removed! I wondered for the rest of the session whether that mistake would cost me my England team place. In the event it did not; on a day when most anglers were returning 'clean' or with a single trout, both Ray and I easily qualified for the England loch-style team.

It is not really possible for me to describe adequately this moment in my fishing life. Euphoria is the best single word, and I think this is what it was: an endorphin release that just went on and on. Here I was, at the gates of the place I had sought for so long and, as I thought at the time, the culmination, the peak. I had no vision, really, of anything beyond. I was in the England team, and if this was to be it, the end of it, then that was enough. My good friend John White also qualified that day, and this was justice, because we had embarked on our competitive journey at the same time, fishing Bewl and Grafham together for several years, honing our still-water skills. John is altogether more tempered and less emotional than me, but I know that he also felt the same sense of pride and was thrilled at his accomplishment.

Five years of fulfilling and broadening representation of my country followed, in lake and then river internationals, culminating in the World Championship which featured all disciplines from boat drifting to the banks of various-sized still waters, and rivers. It had not, after all, been enough for me to achieve an England team place. Very quickly I realized that I wanted to be an all-rounder, not merely a specialist in a single discipline. The learning curve was exponential, completely unimagined at the outset, and it is actually very difficult to convey this. Is not every fly-fishing trip a learning experience; the whole a journey of discovery? Of course it is, but there is absolutely nothing like inter-national competition to hone one's skills as a pragmatic fish-catcher, albeit within the somewhat strange and restrictive, and disparate, sets of rules that permeate the competitive sport.

Striving for all-round status makes the greatest demands of all, because it is not enough simply to practise and prepare on still waters, say, in order to achieve a suffi-ciently high standard on rivers. To do it all means that something else in life must suffer. I was lucky with my work (though even so, I stole rather too much time from this), but my family life was not so blessed. I spent the bulk of my time on waters, far and wide, focused on this one, tiny aspect of endeavour, and I was probably too selfish to appreciate the damage this was doing to other important aspects of life. To the immature inner man, at that time, international fly-fishing was life itself, and I would do just about anything needed to reach the top. Hardly any of my friends and family could possibly understand this. It was not, after all, a 'major' sport that might bring in enormous financial reward, which most would view as justification. In fly-fishing it is scarcely possible to make a decent living, and in the competitive arena alone, no one has achieved this. Those I know who have made fishing financially worthwhile have done so via some aspect of the tackle trade, or writing and media, or as an instructor or guide, and commonly a mixture of all. In 1990, none of this mattered a jot to me. Fly-fishing, particularly as an England team member, had become a lifestyle.

One of the all-time competitive greats, and inspirational for all those who aspire to international-level competition: Pascal Cognard (right), captain of another outstanding French team

Within the oddness of it all come numerous, wonderful facets beyond the skills one picks up along the way. The companionship of team-mates during an international is something indescribably enriching in life. My team-mate John Pawson, son of Tony, once said to me: 'Though you and I are probably so very different, there is an unbreakable bond between us. No one at home can understand it.' I think back to all those special relationships, bonds, that have been formed and realize that later, when we have all moved off in different directions (which is inevitable), the bond still exists, even if just locked away in memory space; but it is shared, and valuable beyond measure to those lucky enough to possess it.

In 1993 we were in British Columbia, Canada, a long way from the safe cushion of British still waters, where at that time the English were considered unbeatable (even though the Welsh and the Scots would argue this). We were, however, about to fish the World Championship entirely on still waters – the enormous lakes of the BC interior, centred at Kamloops. Even now, twenty years on, a blitz of memories crowd in on me: encounters with bears and snakes, and late-night chats in log cabins on the shores of lakes where the strange calls of loons would finally lull us into sleep; of stetsons and beer bottles flying in bars packed with locals and members of teams from as far away as Poland and Australia; and the fishing – such incredible fishing for wild rainbows …

It would have been easy to get carried away by the exotic flavour, the different perspectives, of fishing in such a place, and in the circumstances of the World Championship, but we were a better team than that, and led by one of England's strongest-ever team managers, Geoff Clarkson. I was one of the most competitively inexperienced, and youngest, members of the team. There were veterans Chris Ogborne and (my son's godfather) John Lindsey, as well as former World Champion John Pawson and still-water specialist Paul Miller, and as reserve we had the enormously steadying influence of John Braithwaite. Also with us was team coach Mike Childs and this, too, was enormously beneficial to the team. Practice sessions were nothing short of remarkable, fishing on those enormous lakes where ospreys would dive at cruising rainbows within 10 metres of our drifting boats, and great northern divers would appear from the depths in pursuit of fish we were playing, right up to the side of the boat; like killer whales, huge and menacing at that range.

It was the time of our sporting lives; for me one of its pinnacles. But as the actual championship drew closer I experienced an altogether new feeling, that of trepidation. It was not fun any more, and I even became somewhat blinkered from the awesome natural wonders that surrounded us. A deep and profound realization of what we were about to attempt replaced all the euphoria and pride with dread. I did not know it at the time, but I was always to experience this in major internationals, and it grew even worse over the years, feeding on me both mentally and physically. The day before the first championship session John Pawson, who recognized what I was going through, took me to one side: 'I know how you feel. You really don't want to go out there tomorrow. You hate the idea of it, what you and all of us have to do, putting ourselves right on the line. But, you know, you will never feel so *alive* as over the next few days, and when it's over you are going to miss it so very much. It will hurt.'

The next day, we all climbed on board our section coaches which were to take us to the championship venues. Each team member fishes a different sector of river or lake, along with members of all the other national teams taking part. We shook hands, hugged, caught each others' eyes and climbed the steps, leaving each other to our individual sessions. It is always thus; one is suddenly taken away in the very early morning hours to the championship sectors which are often far apart. Another team-mate of future years, Baz Reece, referred to this feeling as the 'loneliness of the sessions', and this does sum it up appropriately. In that moment you travel out without the physical presence of your team-mates with whom you have practised and lived for so long. You have, instead, only their best wishes as treasured company. There is also a heavy responsibility, because they are relying on your performance as much as you rely on theirs. This being my first-ever World Championship session, Mike came out with me, so I was not completely alone, at least until the start of the session.

It was a strange, two-hour journey out from Kamloops to Lake Tunkwa, high in the BC interior. It was very quiet on board, each competitor lost in their own private preparations and emotions. Mike spoke very quietly, distracting me with ideas about set-up, which we had rehearsed many times before in team briefings and practice sessions, and talking about matters such as fly selection and where I might aim to go on the lake. We had visited Tunkwa several times, though we were not allowed to fish it (like any other championship sector), so we had mapped it reasonably well and I certainly had my views on where I would like to go, if I could agree this with my boat partner for the day. When Geoff had taken me up to Tunkwa a few days earlier, we had stared out together over the expanse and he had confided: 'This is why you are in the England team.' Indeed, it had seemed that I was made for Tunkwa; to me it was like Grafham Water at almost 2,000 metres. That is how I viewed it, and surely it was bread-and-butter fishing for me; cruising rainbows on the nymph, long-cast from the boat.

I can still remember setting up, close to the boat mooring. Mike was so patient, because he just continued to talk softly and calmly, even though my hands were trembling and I could barely thread the line through the rod guides. I had already set up my leader, so it was merely a matter of attaching the fly (the rules in Canada were for a single fly, rather than teams of up to three flies as is more usual on lake venues). Mike went through the checklist of spare rods, lines and peripheral tackle, for the sixth time, and then took it on himself to find my boatman, and the competitor who would be with me that day. (I was to learn later that my boatman had been asked to look after me as best he could out there, with Mike explaining that this was my first-ever World Championship session.) Introductions over, I was ushered into the boat and thus onward to those excruciating moments leading up to the start of the session. I have known competitors be physically sick at this point, and I certainly came very close to it then and was probably saved this ignominy only because I had not eaten anything for almost twenty-four hours. This is when you are completely on your own; it is hostile territory right up to the boundary of the competitive sport, and nothing really prepares a competitor for it. It is incapacitating, demolishing the structure of reason in the mind. One's skills, and former experience, seem to evaporate and one feels like an absolute beginner. Competitors in most other sports also experience these horrible feelings. One usually gets through this phase, but not always. Sometimes this is the 'bridge too far' and we just cannot go beyond.

That day, away on the far shores of Tunkwa, I did go beyond, realizing that all the meticulous preparation, all the past experience of big lakes, all the support and teaching of my mentors and team-mates, was there with me. So, I was not really alone. I could hear Geoff's voice: 'This is why you're in the England team.' I fished a floating line on a 9½-foot Sage #6, alternating between a Cove-style pheasant tail, a Diawl Bach (little devil) and a black spider (remember that the rule was for a single fly), all of which had been effective for those wild rainbows during practice. I noticed that competitors on any boat we drew near during the session were using fast-sinking lines and pulling tactics, mostly with weighted streamer patterns. This was undoubtedly the percentage method and noticing this threw me back to Rutland Water and the National Finals. My first fish was a little under-size, and so would not count, but at least it gave me enough confidence to persist with the slowly retrieved nymph or spider on a long leader. Soon afterwards, I was utterly elated because I boated a fish that measured and so, in my first session, I had already avoided the dreaded blank. This completely settled me and at last I could really focus on putting myself in the places.

My chance came towards the end of that first session – 'never give up until the very end' – when a rainbow stabbed at my size 18 black spider, taken on the drop, and was hooked against the tight line. Knowing this was a big fish, my boatman told me to take it very easy: 'It'll go ballistic in a moment, and if you hold 'em too tight they often shed the hook.' Well, it did jump, twice, but the hook held and after perhaps five minutes I netted a magnificent fish of some 1.8 kilograms, at 50 centimetres, 'scissored' by the spider. The two fish gave me a section win, because although one competitor, from Poland, had caught three trout, their overall measurement was less than my two fish, by a single centimetre! Almost the entire field of twenty-two competitors (the number of nations taking part) had blanked.

It was a similar story in the second session, that afternoon, during particularly diffi-cult fishing conditions. I think there were three measurable trout caught, and I did not catch one of them, so suffered the blank. It was doubly infuriating for me because I did manage to hook a big rainbow that I had watched swimming, and rising, up a wind lane, intercepting it with the same black spider, only to lose it as it neared the net. It was with mixed emotions that I returned to the shore, where both Mike and Geoff were waiting for me. I could report the opposites of a session win and a blank. They passed on to me what they knew of my team-mates' placings, which were fairly good. Here we were, now in the midst of the championship sessions, two days left to run, with new sectors to come for each of us, but the start had been reasonable. In fact, as we were to learn back at the hotel, we even had an intermediate team first placing overall, narrowly ahead of the Poles, Czechs and Italians.

Strengths – *always rely on what one does best, never giving up to the end* – and over-coming the weaknesses – *just get through that feeling of not knowing what is going on* – were what carried our team through that championship. We could each overcome the loneliness of the sessions and could rely on each other to do the very best possible. Fishing each lake venue on a rota of sessions over the three days of the championship, we could feed back to our team-mates a lot of information about their upcoming venue. This proved invaluable. I remember John Lindsey, who had fished Paul Lake on the second day, telling me that he had noticed some rising fish in a particular area, where one of the top-placed competitors had fished. He felt there was enormous potential here and gave me incred-ibly accurate reference points so that I could find it in my sessions on the third day – this on a lake about ten times the size of Rutland Water! John told me: 'Look for a log cabin behind which is an almost hidden, old green Chevrolet and move down the bank about 300 metres until you find an extensive shallow area with large weed-beds and marl [a white chalky clay bed] patches.' It was better than having a GPS fix. I did find the place, along with my Polish boat partner, and managed several good rainbows, again on the deep, slow nymph, in each of the day's sessions, when, as on previous sectors and sessions, the general catches were poor.

England won the team gold comfortably, while I was top England rod with the individual bronze medal, at my first attempt. It was only possible because of my incredible team-mates, our pooled experience on a huge variety of still waters elsewhere, and our ability to share this. Furthermore, it would not have been possible without a shared history of a variety of mentor figures, including our manager and coach, who had lifted us, individually and collectively, to truly internationally competitive standing. (Tony, Geoff and Mike are all gone now, passed away to fishing heaven. They are probably there with Arthur and I bet they are on dry fly or nymph.)

There was also the enormously good luck we had, such as that big rainbow staying hooked on Tunkwa. We fishermen should never lack the intelligence to ignore the value of plain good luck – and bad – there is a lot of both in fishing.

The following year, 1994, luck was to deal a mixed hand. The England team, as World Champions, travelled to Norway to defend the title. Again we were in a magnificently beautiful environment, with outstanding trout and grayling fishing, and exploring a range of waters from high, remote mountain lakes to enormous rivers, including the Laagen. This was such very different fishing from the Canadian lakes, and that which we knew so well in Britain, though the lake fishing was comparable to that in the Highlands of Scotland where I had spent much of my fishing time in the 1980s. It was the rivers that really exposed our weakness, however, even if we only partially recognized this, or admitted to it, at the time. The Eastern Europeans were way ahead of the game on rivers, and no amount of our patriotic enthusiasm could disguise this. Typically, I fear, the English had been slow to develop river skills, relying on classically laid down ideas which were rooted in just so much dogma. It held us back for three decades! We were living through the still-water boom and, for most English fly-fishers, the sport was dominated by lakes and reservoirs. I believe it was indeed the World and European Championships of the 1990s that provided the springboard for development of the river discipline, and certainly the England team members of those years were exposed to some harsh lessons.

The Czechs and the Poles were great all-rounders, but their emphasis was on river skills. Coming into close contact with these anglers during the championships was invaluable. Some of my countrymen had already discovered that fishing teams of weighted nymphs, at short range, was consistently more effective than our classic, long-line upstream nymph and spider approach, but we were terribly crude in these 'Czech nymph' and 'Polish rolled nymph' approaches. We just did not get it. Our fly patterns relied on a lot of lead under the dressings, in order to achieve depth, and we gave scant regard to the sparseness of materials used in the nymphs, or their balance on a team, both of which are crucial to the behaviour of the nymphs in the water. Even our rods were wrong; essentially stiff action #6, following the American and British trends towards tippy distance-casting rods – utterly impractical for short-range fishing on rivers, with nymph or dry fly.

At the end of the first session we had all suffered blanks and therefore were in last position – twentieth. I remember, in the team debriefing, Geoff being utterly pragmatic and suggesting that now we really had the chance to show the world what we were made of; but it was up to us. In Canada, he recalled, we had led from the start. Now, in Norway, we were going to have to come from behind, very far behind. When it was time for the coaches to take us to the next sector, John Pawson stood up abruptly: 'I'm going to go and win my session, and you're going to do the same!'

That evening, we were alive again. We had all, indeed, won or come very close to the top in all our sectors, and we had climbed into the middle of the table, still with three sessions to go in the days to follow. I think we scented something special right then, and were bursting to fish the next sessions. Whatever little we had soaked up from the Eastern Europeans with nymph on the river, we put into practice, while I relied on my strength with dry fly in an utterly crucial session, and we each avoided further blanks on the very difficult mountain lakes. At the end of it all we actually reached the bronze medal position, narrowly missing out on the higher medals which were taken by Italy and Czechoslovakia; but to reach the podium, from a standing start after session one, was to us a finer achievement than the gold in Canada. I was certainly more proud of this, especially when the Czech captain presented me with a team tie, featuring a silver embroidered grayling, a mark of what he told me was admiration of my river skills. I don't think I really earned this accolade from a European river master, because I had just relied on what I knew with dry fly. In truth I still had a mountain of experience to gather with nymph on the river.

We were, however, slowly gaining experience with the competitive river discipline and I found an increasing amount of my fishing time was spent on rivers in my quest to become a true all-rounder. At that time, however, an England all-rounder was very much biased towards loch-style and other lake disciplines, with passable experience on rivers. It was, if anything, the complete opposite of the European teams and, in any case, was unsatisfactory to me: uncomfortably emphasized by the 1993 Home River International on the River Wharfe, in Yorkshire. Here, on home territory, we should have had the edge, but when I think back now to our performance it was simply woeful; our expectations and confidence were so high, amounting to arrogance, while our experience and general level of skill were poor.

The first two morning sessions went well enough for me, with a 42-centimetre grayling (which was to be the biggest fish caught in the international) in one session and two measurable trout in the next; but they were all rather lucky catches, possible only because of the water I had drawn, and I know now that were I to fish that water today my catch would, or should, be tripled. It was so different in the afternoon, when I managed to find a large shoal of grayling on my sector, with a few aggressively feeding trout among them. I hooked four fish in the afternoon sessions and lost every one. I had met similar conditions several times in the past, including on the Wharfe itself, with shoals of feeding grayling, and I cursed my inability to make the most of this. Summer grayling really are challenging fish, often feeding on particularly small food-forms, both dry and nymph, and completely preoccupied. They also spook very easily, but unlike trout do not inform the angler by dashing for cover. They usually continue to feed while their awareness of their environment, and the danger lurking there, is communicated throughout the shoal. Even so, they are catchable, though I was not able to do so that afternoon. Again, today, with a leader-only rig and flies designed for purpose, this situation is routine; but in 1993, in a home international, it was frustratingly elusive. My team-mates all had similar stories to tell, and we suffered the ignominy of losing to the Scots on our own river.

It was that international which really brought home the reality, whether my team-mates accepted it or not, that there were severe problems with the English competitive approach, and certainly with my own. I determined to change that and shifted my own emphasis far more towards rivers, taking every opportunity to fish the broadest variety wherever I travelled, which by happy accident related to my work, included the north-western United States. Also, in 1994, the rivers international was on the Tweed, in Scotland, and I went at this as aggressively as any competition in which I have been involved. Technique was better honed than it had been the previous year on the Wharfe, though honestly way off the mark with where we are today, while competitiveness was at its most intense. The morning sessions went well, though at the time I did not know how others were doing. It felt somewhat routine at the time, but my catches seemed good in the conditions. It was during the afternoon sessions that I realized I had crossed a threshold in competitiveness.

Remember that, in internationals, it is absolutely crucial to avoid the blank session. I was fishing an area where trout were rising well to a trickle hatch of blue-winged olives. During the first hour of the one and a half hour session I caught seven trout and felt that, without a doubt, this would win the session, but I had the distinct feeling that if continued I would exhaust the possibilities of this beat, and therefore make it very difficult for myself in the final session. There would indeed be the serious possibility that I would blank the final session and so ruin my own, and my team's chances. So, I stopped fishing, and just talked quietly with my controller, resisting the temptation to wade back into the river to pick off the last few rising fish. I think I was more proud of this single, tactical action than any other in my first period of representing England. I was able to go back out in the final session and catch three trout, which would not have been possible had I fished the last half-hour of the previous session. I had four first place sessions and we won the home international with ease, gaining a revenge of sorts, or a balancing of the books at least, by beating the Scots on a Scottish river. Tactical and competitive we might have been, but in the greater scheme of things, particularly in comparison with many of the European teams, our river skills were still poor. We were most of us in denial, and I think this really slowed down progress in England (while less so in Scotland and Wales) with the river discipline.

After the gift of a gold medal from the British Columbian lakes, the tremendous fight-back to the bronze medal position in the Norwegian World Championship and English domination in loch-style technique – but inconsistent river skills as exemplified by the mixed fortunes of the Wharfe and Tweed internationals – it was time to take stock. While I could bathe in a certain amount of success, I was very far from smug. I knew all too well that a lot of this had been down to sheer good luck; being in the right place at the right time, having the benefit of outstanding mentors, fishing companions and team-mates, while also having close proximity to some of the European river masters. Even then, the posturing surrounding the winning of a competition infuriated me. This is pathetic because, as in any sport, there is always a huge element of luck. All we can really say is that a competitive fly-fisher who can consistently make the frame, statistically smoothing out the bad results such that overall the situation looks good, is exceptional. I know without any doubt that when I have managed to win river, or lake bank sessions, it has been because I was on good, or at least mediocre, sections and while my skills were up to making the most of these, almost all other international-level anglers should have been able to do the same on such water. The real test comes when we draw poor sections – the so-called 'blank savers' – and have to do what we can to extract a single, measurable fish to avoid that destructive blank. Loch-style is somewhat different, because here a boat can drift anywhere on a lake and it is up to the occupants, the two competitors therein, to make the most of the session. Even back in the mid-1990s I recognized this mismatch in the competitive disciplines of river and loch-style, and it was a frustration, particularly since I considered that, except for a few individuals, England was resting on the comfort of loch-style success and putting river development very much on hold.

Retiring from the international selection process in the mid-1990s I began to miss the England team campaigns, and this feeling grew enormously over the years. Initially, it was manageable, as I spent more time on rivers, while still fishing the shores of large lakes; but I did very little boat drift fishing and this is what I missed, competitively, partly because loch-style was where I began my international-level experience and also because it was, as I perceived it, the fairest form of competition (and, under the current organization of international competitions, it still is). In any case, I finally missed it too much. Fortunately, circumstances arose such that I could afford the time to put into the demanding qualification processes, and so, urged on by my family and a few friends and ex-team-mates, I re-entered the fray.

Second time around was even more fulfilling and enjoyable than during the 1990s. I suppose I had outgrown the worst of the ego-drive of the younger man, though I do not think I was any more relaxed. I always fished intensely, whether in competition or not, and I still do to this day. I felt that I had less to prove to others than first time around, but rather more to prove to myself. I still felt that the bank still-water and river disciplines in particular were anything but level playing fields, but I also reasoned that there was no way I could affect change from the outside.

Again, I was very lucky in that I qualified for both river and loch-style teams at the first attempts and was immediately selected for the European Championship team, which I fished for four consecutive years. A lot, however, had changed. The general standard of loch-style practitioners had improved and become more consistent. It was much more difficult than in earlier years to see differences in either the competitiveness or skills among British team members (including Irish, Scottish and Welsh anglers). But it was on the river that most of the real advances had taken place. Now, anglers had discovered duo (nymph under dry), how better to present teams of nymphs (Czech-style nymph was now pretty standard), while rods had become significantly softer, and longer, than the comparatively crude #5 and even #6 weights of the 1990s. A few English river anglers had even

Paul Page, England team manager, at Cow Green wild brown trout fishery during a team practice session prior to our silver medals in Norway

discovered the French leader, and many more than hitherto were so much better with small dry flies than ever before. However, other than a few individuals, the Europeans were still way ahead of us. Actually, so were the top Americans, though very few of these were international competitors, so this disguised the volume of sheer excellence among river practitioners there. These changes should not be underestimated, because they are so developmental; tending towards where the single-handed sport is today. Without a doubt the presentation-based approach, from beginnings in Continental Europe, stemmed from this period and has cascaded into a standard in the sport that is barely recognizable compared to that of even a decade ago.

Competitively, the England team ranking had changed. We had been number one so far as loch-style was concerned, perhaps in the middle order for bank still-water discipline and probably about the same on the river. In the early years of this new century we were no more than comparable to all the other home nations, and several European teams and others (and Australia should be mentioned in this context) were at least as competitive as we were. Our bank still-water skills were comparable to earlier years. Indeed, with lake fishing generally, it was not that we had gone backwards; rather that there were many other nations who had improved hugely. As mentioned, it was on the river that the most exciting developments were taking place.

Stuart Crofts in action on the Sava Dolinka during the European Championships of 2006; Stuart was influential in Team England, putting greater emphasis on the river component of the sport

It was a new level of international experience, manifestly more competitive than hitherto, simply because of the ascendancy of many other teams. The instincts were the same; it was the technical aspects that had moved on, and this was very exciting. It was so obvious that most competitive river anglers were more pragmatic and less restricted by tradition or convention than in earlier years, indeed than ever before. The European influence, largely via the *FIPS-Mouche* Championships, had driven this. In order to remain competitive, we had to move along with what so many other nations were doing. Even so, we were terribly slow, in my view, with some of the fundamental changes, and I am sure that this was because there were comparatively few international-level anglers coming through the selection process. As in the 1990s, which were boom years, the competitive area of the sport in the 2000s was not widely broadcast through the sport at large, in Britain. There were still only a handful of main protagonists and I do not think we were terribly good at communicating and broadening the interest (a situation which continues to this day). Although there were positive initiatives at youth level, and these certainly bore fruit, one could not help but notice that there were the same old faces on the circuit.

It was good, obviously, to fall back into a crowd of familiar personalities, like going home after a long time away; but while these outstanding competitors of long acquaintance had developed their own skills, they were, in truth, only still at the top level

Stuart Crofts in a wild-flower meadow by the Sava, Slovenia, in 2006

because they had not been usurped by younger talent. (That said, we should never take anything away from their incredible accomplishments: what truly world-class competitors like Stuart Crofts and John Tyzack on the rivers, or Tony Curtis and Ian Barr on still waters, did for the standard of English fly-fishing should not be under-valued.) Even so, it struck me during the 2005 European Championship, in Poland, that the average age of the England team was in the mid-forties. Also, we could not really see where the new blood was going to come from: moreover, all of this seemed focused on the domestic loch-style scene, the disci-pline which is actually in the *lowest* demand in *FIPS-Mouche* events. I had no doubt that, were it not for this, I would have had little chance of being successful in re-qualifying for the selection process, though I was hugely grateful for my England team place, which I cherish as much today as even my first loch-style qualification all those years ago on Rutland Water.

We were blown out of the water in Poland, on the incredible San River. The Czechs, French and Poles fought it out for the podium positions, with a few close runners such as the Italians and Slovaks, but we languished in the midfield. Of course, we mostly blamed our poor luck in drawing bad sections of river, and to an extent this might have been justified, but honestly (and speaking entirely about my own sections) I know that I did not fish these at all well, or competitively, other than one section at the top of the legendary tailwater. I was fishing at that time much as any of the dedicated English river interna-tionals were fishing. We were so very focused on Czech nymph – having been destroyed by this frequently in the past – that we were, in fact, always playing catch-up. The top Europeans were well ahead of us, and even then moving off into a broader scope of pres-entation skills. Whenever I was pulled away from my comfort zone of dry fly, I felt that my nymph fishing was more or less like that of any competitor, and that in many cases it was inferior. There were a lot of fly-fishers on European rivers who were achieving something beyond the capability of the comparatively crude nymph set-up we were using. It was, however, this self-admission that became the driver to find out what was going on, so that we could more consistently emulate the European river masters.

In 2006 the European Championships were in Slovenia; my first of many visits to this incredibly beautiful country, from which so much development has occurred in the river sport. There is a national one-fly rule which is actually something of a leveller, negating any advantage to be obtained from, say, Czech nymph or other multiple fly set-ups. Also, these alpine rivers tend to be fast flowing, with significant depths, all of which makes dry fly more challenging, as well as finding the ideal depth when nymph fishing. This is hugely significant. On a typical British river, whether rain or spring fed, the range of holding areas and feed lanes are not as complex as on a long, swift alpine river. It is a matter of scale and of water type, and again we found ourselves out of our comfort zones, while awed by the wonderful fishing. The hatches were neither so strong nor diverse as on my home rivers such as the Eden, and dry-fly opportunities, at least on the championship waters, were limited (it is not always thus), and the nymph fishing was hugely more demanding. Back home, duo had been discovered and actually over-exploited.

The victorious Polish team at the European Championships, 2005

River anglers everywhere seemed to be using this 'percentage' approach and seldom changing. While a large number of anglers became proficient with the method, their other skills thus tended to stagnate. I found it significant that the French team captain forbade his team from practising with duo, claiming that there is always a better approach than this compromise method, even if the alternative was more difficult to master. I became bewitched by this idea and found myself eventually loathing duo. This was also timely, because there was absolutely no point prac-tising with two or three fly set-ups for the Slovenian championship, in which there was the one-fly limitation.

Consider the problem: fast flow, with fish preoccupied on sub-surface food-forms unless there is a strong hatch, and often at depths up to 3 metres. At least a partial solu-tion came from two members of the team: Paul Davison and Howard Croston. Both had been experimenting for some time with novel indicator sections in long leaders and an altogether more sensitive presentation, albeit for fairly shallow water, though they had practised quite a lot with winter grayling on the Tweed system, which meant depths up to about 2 metres. One day during our practice phase I spent quite a lot of time with Howard on the Baca, watching him use a surprisingly long fluorocarbon leader which incorporated one of Paul's indicators close to the fly line tip. Howard was casting only a few metres of fly line out of the rod tip. We fished very close together. At first, I caught well with dry fly during a reasonable hatch of midges, but when the fish stopped rising I noticed that they were still visible, but very deep. We estimated this to be typically around 2 metres. They would not be tempted to rise more than a few centimetres; still less to dry fly.

During our early days in Slovenia several of us had caught quite well on weighted size 12 pheasant tail variants (incorporating 2.8 mm copper tungsten beads), so I naturally gravitated to this, on what I felt was a reasonably long tippet beyond the indicator, at 4.25 metres. Giving the fish plenty of lead, so that the nymph would have a chance to sink to the target depth, I persisted with this, with poor return. For much of the time I lost sight of the nymph – even in the dazzlingly clear water – and relied either on signs of a take from the fish itself, or the indicator. I remember that I pricked two fish in almost an hour's fishing, and neither of these fish registered a take on the indicator, but were seen to move to take the nymph which I knew was nearby. I think that I reacted too quickly on both occasions and should have paused before setting the hook. Meanwhile, Howard was using a leader much longer than mine, at nearer 7.25 metres, and actually a smaller, slimmer and sparser nymph, but one that was more visible than mine, having a bright orange dot on the wing case. As Howard netted his third fish, in the time that I had pricked two, I stopped fishing and watched him more closely. It was a revelation.

The longer leader and slim nymph combination, along with a measured lead upstream of the visible trout, allowed Howard to achieve the holding depth, and maintain this for much longer in each drift than I had done. Nor did he need to be so accurate, and this was the real surprise. Whereas my PTN had needed to be very close to a fish in order to initiate a take (though rejection was the norm), Howard's nymph, which was an 18, enticed a reaction over much longer range. Twice I saw fish break station and move at least 2 metres, across and downstream, in order to intercept the clearly visible orange dot.

We felt at the time that there were three important triggers at play here, and we discussed these with our team-mates: the establishment of deep presentation for an appreciable period of each drift, the small fly and the highly visible dot. These seemed perfectly reasonable. Depth is always a prime consideration for any river or lake fly-fisher. During the rise, when I had caught well with dry fly, this was obvious – the fly had to be on the surface. The fish dropped away, still feeding, but my comparatively clumsy presentation, of a large nymph, was way off the mark. Howard's longer (and finer) tippet allowed a much smaller nymph to be in the killing zone for much longer. The size of the fly is also utterly crucial, exemplified by this occasion. Focusing on close-copy imitation, while a delight at the fly vice, is pointless. The general impression of size and shape (GISS), is what is important, and I would go further and suggest that the shape and overall structure are what really matter. I have fished so many times in hatches of large Ephemeridae, such as March browns and olive uprights of *danica* mayflies, to find that an artificial of similar size to the naturals is rejected, and have needed to downsize, often considerably. Indeed, nowadays, during hatches of these large olives, my starting size is a 19, and if I need to change this, it will be down to a 21. Exactly the same principle applies to nymph fishing, in my view, although as in almost everything in comparison between nymph and dry fly, the former

is usually more complicated. In any case, the discovery of the supreme efficacy of small, sparsely dressed flies is one of the most important among the many in a trout and grayling fisher's journey.

Then, there is the fly's visibility. We all felt that this was of importance both in terms of the fish being able to see the nymph at range and of us being able to see the fly, falling down towards its target. Now, I think that the latter is much more significant. I am convinced that fish can detect their prey food-forms very easily in a clear water river, and even in healthily stained flows. It is highly apparent, however, that even a big nymph is usually invisible to the angler unless it is brightly coloured, or has a hotspot of colour in its makeup. In a clear water river, as in Slovenia, a highly coloured fly spooks more fish than it catches, and a hotspot is what is required, and this for the angler's visibility rather than that of the fish. This whole idea troubled me in 2006, but nowadays I am convinced: there are circumstances, usually involving early spring rainbows, or stocked trout at any time of year, when bright colours are attractive. Sometimes, too, flashy, 'disturbance' patterns can knock fish off preoccupied feeding behaviour and precipitate a sudden attack instinct. Daphnia feeders in lakes give the classic example. But wild fish, and big brown trout and grayling in particular – I don't think so. I have spent too many years taking flash and colour out of my flies in my pursuit of the larger specimens to want to go the other way. A touch of colour, to help us pick out the fly – maybe – but not to attract the

Stalking with an ultra-fine line approach on a Catalunyan mountain river in the European Championships, 2008

Big grayling for the controller at the European Championships, 2006

fish, because I am absolutely certain that this is a mistake with big brown trout and spec-imen grayling. For the latter, go small, sparse and take out the bright colour. We did not know it at the time, but some of the European teams, notably the French, were already working on their small ceramic nymphs for circumstances as described, and this put them at the forefront of presentation possibilities.

Aided somewhat by the experience with Howard, we performed a little better in Slovenia than on the San, with two of us in the top twenty, seriously competitive, and this entirely on river venues. I fell in love with the country – a sprawl of pristine rivers ranging from snow- and rain-fed torrents running off Triglav to spring-fed chalk streams meandering through wild hay meadows ablaze with summer flowers. The fishing was nothing short of startling. I often think we are very lucky in Britain, to have such varied rivers, lakes and reservoirs, and even our wild fishing in the north and west continues to be envied in spite of the environmental vandalism of modern agriculture. In Slovenia, however, we were all to discover how rivers and riverside habitat really can be when indus-trialized agriculture is taken out of the equation. It was a rapid ascent of discovery for all of us and the fishing was magical. We had encounters with marbled trout and huge grayling. During practice I caught a 53-centimetre grayling from the Idricja only for team manager Paul Page to catch one the same day at 56 centimetres! The rainbow trout fishing was spectacular, though we were under no illusions: the stocking with these is intense in most Slovenian rivers – which are heavily fished – though truly wild-bred rainbows are always in the mix. The one and only concern, really, is that popularity with fly-fishers, because it necessitates the massive stocking programme. This has led to an issue with wild brown trout, which, it is said, might already be extinct in several of this country's rivers. In spite of this, though, here is a place of intoxication for the fly-fisher.

Team England moved on, surging ahead with Paul Page's plan to see us back on the podium within five years. In our third year the championship was held in the Sunnfjord area of Norway, certainly one of the most spectacularly beautiful regions of all Europe and Scandinavia, and another trout-fisher's paradise, both river and lake. We were a very well bonded team by this stage, and well practised on British waters that had at least some of the characteristics of the Norwegian waters. The fundamental difference between northern European rivers and lakes and those of Southern and Eastern Europe is the substrate. In the latter it is nearly always pale, making the water appear crystal clear. In Norway the water is often almost as clear, though with the darker substrate background this is not immediately apparent. In Slovenia we could frequently see the fish we were targeting; in Norway this was rare and necessitated fishing 'blind' and a heightened sense of watercraft. Whereas in Slovenia, as in Poland the previous year, the championship venues had been dominated by rivers, in Norway there was a complete mix of disciplines, ranging from river to lake from both bank and boat. We practised painstakingly, therefore, across the range of waters beneath the awesome Jostedal Glacier. Much of what we had learned in earlier years, however, was redundant here, because we could revert to methods that were much more generic for rivers and lakes like these; essentially more British. As a consequence, our practice buoyed us considerably and by the time of the championship we felt ready for the challenge.

It was then that I discovered something in my own competitive make-up that had hitherto been only glimpsed. Any young competitor should be aware of this. By this time, in my early fifties, I kept myself fit by long-distance running almost daily. I was always blessed with reasonable stamina, which had served me well for the marathon, loch-style domestic internationals and rapid movement and wading over treacherous river terrains. Mentally, however, in spite of the experience of numerous internationals, in all the competitive disciplines, I suppose I had reached a point beyond which is the unknown, where few can successfully venture. This is consistent with all competitive sport. At the BBC Sports Personality of the Year Award in 1993, I had a discussion with Damon Hill (who in 1996 was to become Formula 1 World Champion) about this and, I think, we both echoed each other's thoughts about this single-most intangible competitive component. Without it, no matter what skills one might possess, one can get nowhere, but with that competitive ferocity within … I think this is independent of the actual sport.

On the San and in Slovenia I had suffered a stress-induced migraine during the championship and this had undoubtedly affected my performance, even though the help of my team-mates, particularly Stuart Crofts and manager Paul Page, saw me through the

Stuart Crofts, during one of our European Championship campaigns

ordeal. In Norway, I had a nightmare first session, when my controller did not turn up on time, and then disappeared for a period, and I lost a lot of competition time as a result. I managed to salvage five trout to leave me in the mid-order of the section, but I felt that several places had been lost. This affected me badly for the afternoon session and again I found myself in the mid-order, with four trout off a lake where I knew I should have been in double figures. That evening I was right up at the emotional boundary and I think it was only because I was rooming with Stuart that I was in any state to carry on the next day.

We fished from the shore of a massive lake and it felt as if the circumstances were just made for me. Looking out over my section I was mindful of Geoff Clarkson's words all those years earlier in British Columbia on the shores of Lake Tunkwa: 'This is why you are in the England team.' The wind was gentle, mostly from left to right. A gradually sloping gravel bed met with a rocky drop-off about 20 metres from the shoreline and the whole section was etched by weed-beds. At the downwind limit was a boulder field off a small promontory. The bank behind me was mostly birch woodland and, with some branches overlapping the water, I had to take care with the back cast throughout the session. There were few areas where I could really let fly a 30-metre cast, but then this was not necessary: at that range the water was deep (more than 3.5 metres) and I reasoned that the fish would mostly be patrolling the rocky ledge and hunting up into the weed-beds and over the gravel. The sight of it, along with my team-mates' support before going out into the 'loneliness of the sessions', as well as the memories of Geoff Clarkson, blew away the doubts and the emotional ravages of the previous day.

I used a Greys Streamflex 9-foot #5 and Rio Selective Trout line throughout, with a long leader and three flies, all of which had been honed in practice sessions: a pink Wickham spider on the top dropper, the inevitable PTN on the middle with a Billy (a black and red nymph-like pattern with a small copper tungsten bead) on point. It was a tremendous session for me, with trout coming slowly, but steadily, throughout. A quiet cast was essential, pitching the team of flies out beyond the drop-off, allowing them to sink and then timing a slow figure-of-eight retrieve so that the point fly would sink deep enough, but avoid catching on the rocks along the ledge. Most of the takes came at this point and it was here that I learned to pause slightly and then draw the flies up from fairly deep in order to induce the patrolling trout. Several fish took the flies right up on the gravel, within 6 metres of where I was wading. It became methodical as I explored everywhere along the sector, catching on all three flies and never having to change them. I lost the first hooked fish, and missed several takes, but this is in the nature of fishing for cruising, actively feeding trout, and enough came to the net to give to my controller for measuring. I also had a clear view of the French competitor on the neighbouring sector and could see that his catch rate was not so consistent, further bolstering my confidence. With a session second place, I had repaired the damage of the previous day, though at the end of it I found myself completely exhausted. I had thrived for so long on adrenalin, which seemed to have been surging through me since the morning before, and even through the almost sleepless night.

That evening we learned that the team had nudged into second place, with great performances from the ever-consistent Stuart Crofts and Ian Barr. The points situation was, however, very tight between the top seven teams. As so often before, it would all hang on the last day. This is where the mind can destroy a competitor, and in consequence a whole team. You can know you have the skills, are very well practised and can rely completely on your team-mates and yet, compounded with fatigue, all of this can disintegrate, as a house of cards, leaving you hardly able to know what you are doing. Since the age of five I have had a fly rod in my hands for much of the time and yet, coming into that last day of the 2007 European Championship, with it all to lose, I felt like a tyro. Stuart's voice seemed distant and I thought that I noticed doubt in Paul's eyes. The morning session was not good and I heard during the mid-day break that we had slipped out of the podium positions, though we were not too many points away. Of course, it was down to the last session and here I was on another lake, this time from the boat.

I felt numb, one small step away from cracking completely. I had drawn ace Czech competitor Dan Svrcek as my boat partner and this at least proved very good, because I would not have to make all the decisions.

Dan was, at that time, one of the very best river competitors in Europe and he was also perfectly proficient on the lake; a pragmatic hunter. Based on the knowledge of where fish had been caught in earlier sessions on this lake, including by my team-mate Simon Kidd (hence the name of his outstanding fly, the Billy) that morning, Dan and I immediately headed that way, but fished a fruitless drift there before very quickly agreeing to abandon the area and heading out where our instincts drew us, to the remote, least-fished far shore. Our boat lady, Becka, a student from Oslo, was incredible as she put her considerable energy into the long row (competitors are not allowed to row until the end of the session). This was a mental agony for me, as I'm sure it was for Dan. We were already half an hour into the session, fish-less, and with a lot of travelling time yet to do. We had not seen any other fish caught in the 'hot' area, but this did not help much.

At last we set a drift along the shore. The Billy, PTN and Wickham team was cast towards the stones and I automatically set into the routine of long cast and fast retrieve

Dan Svrcek, Czech river master, demonstrating here at Corwen on the Welsh Dee

which we had honed in practice. Luckily, I did not really have to think beyond this, having found an area which my boat partner and I were sure would hold trout. Very quickly I had a take, played the fish and lost it at the net. This could have been crushing, were it not for an automatic re-cast without pondering the loss and hooking another on the second pull. This one was netted and meant that I had saved the blank. The very next cast, just as our controller was returning the first fish to the lake, I hooked and netted another, slightly larger than the first. I could see that poor Dan was shocked. Those fish, over a drift length of only 30 metres, could so easily have come to his flies, yet all three takes, for two fish netted, had come to mine. My own relief felt as overwhelming as the breath of life itself. Whatever happened now, having more than saved the blank, I would be on the score sheet; this in the last session, when there were bound to be a lot of blanks.

The wind lifted through the remaining two hours of the session and the fishing became increasingly challenging. Dan's afternoon went from bad to worse as he hooked and lost four trout, breaking on the last one. I managed eight more takes, for four trout netted, giving me a total of six fish. I wondered, as we rowed back to the moorings, whether or not this catch would be enough to put our team back into the medals, and also at the extraordinary change in emotions. In the morning, still stunned really by what had happened two days earlier, and lacking sleep, full of self-doubt, I had been in a place which I can only describe as despair, but now it was utter relief. I knew that my six trout would be very high on the score sheet and whether or not we, as a team, had done enough, I could hold my head up and know that I had done my bit. I also wondered, however, at how Dan's and my fortunes could so easily have been reversed. Not for the first time I realized all too well that luck had played a significant part in the outcome – and fly-fishing is like that, even if we do not have the intelligence to accept it. I felt very much for Dan, imagining him going back to his team-mates to report his blank, facing the repercussions of what this would mean to the Czech team's results. Deep in his own mind, the loneliness of the sessions would continue.

We were seated in the championship hotel restaurant, picking at our suppers. Paul had been gone for half an hour. The day's competition had been mixed for the team and we simply had no idea where we were in the final rankings. Paul returned looking sombre and I remember feeling rather sick. 'Well Barny [Ian Barr]', he said finally, you managed to hold on to the silver.' He paused for what seemed an age, time enough for me to really believe he was going to tell us that the team had lost the podium: and then, 'and so did we!' We all leapt from our seats and what followed was a pandemonium of cheering and hugging. I don't think a silver medal in our sport has ever been so welcome and celebrated. It meant more to me than even the World Championship gold and bronze medals, and was on quite a different plane from the domestic international wins I have experienced. I don't know who was more delighted – Barny for his double silver, Paul for having achieved his goal of an England team podium within his personal five-year schedule, or me for having gone from the terrible fortunes of the competition's beginning to the euphoria of the last session and what it all meant to our final placing. In any case, I think we all considered this somewhere very close to the pinnacle of what it is possible to experience in our competitive sport.

And then I probably should have walked away, because had it not been for those friends and turns of event that saw me through the championship, the final circumstances could have been dire. I had also noticed that I was beginning to dread the big internationals. I never liked travelling far from home, even though I have always adored finding new fishing; but I was very happy at home on the Eden system, which now gave me just about everything I wanted in the sport. I was still qualifying for the home international teams, however, and thus was eligible for selection for the *FIPS-Mouche* Championships. It is very difficult to walk away, and it was especially so after the result in Norway.

In 2008, Paul Page and the CEFF committee reselected me for the European Championship which was held in the mountains of northern Spain. That strange mixture of delight and dread was more intense than ever before. Even though I worked very hard at maintaining fitness – which is a key to remaining competitive – I felt tired when we arrived in Spain, and I think that this was largely because the constant stress of dreading what was to come just wore me down.

Practice was terribly lean. The rivers of the Catalunya Highlands contain wild brown trout, in low population density. This was a shock after coming from the relatively teeming trout waters of northern England – and remembering the incredibly prolific fishing in western Norway the year before. In hindsight this was very good for us as individuals and

The author with grayling during a European Championship practice session

as a team, simply because much of the wild fishing throughout Europe is like this and competitive international anglers should learn how to adjust to prevalent stock density every bit as much as to any other specific local conditions. Paul had also arranged to have Louis Otano Perez as the England team guide and this proved to be a fortuitous turn of fate. Louis was in the first division of Spanish competitors and was superbly tuned to the local rivers. His coaching was to be an invaluable waypoint for me in future years, if not in the championship, as I explored subtleties of presentation.

The practice sessions forced us to explore 'out of the conventional box' but often also undermined our confidence. We had sessions when five anglers caught a single trout between us, though there were others when we averaged two or even three each, but this was the maximum. We never found a river where we could rack up the numbers (as we had done in most sessions in Norway, Slovenia and Poland, quite apart from practice sessions back in Britain). Here, under Louis's guidance, we had to redefine the aim, and the whole approach. This was inspiring for me, though at the time I could focus only on the championship.

Hot day followed hot day as we hunted for the elusive Catalunyan trout. On many thin, mountain rivers duo was out of the question, being far too crude, and we explored with dry fly or single micro nymphs. Louis demonstrated the Spanish adaptation of the French leader system, using very fine indicator coils, and we discovered a whole new level of subtlety with nymph presentation that I am sure few, in England, had experienced at that time. I remember one session on an upper mountain stream when Louis, having been watching me for some time, took my rod and demonstrated his own approach to a fish we had both seen moving close to the far bank, under the cover of overhanging foliage and the protection of very fast water in mid stream. I had been unable to achieve reasonable presentation with the leader system and had managed only to spook the trout.

What I now observed was an entirely different casting regime. Louis managed to do this with my 10-foot #4 weight, even though it would have been much more comfortably

Louis Otano Perez, England team guide in the Spanish European Championships in 2008; seen here in hunting mode on the Miera

achieved with the #2 or #3 that the top Europeans were using, even then. This significant developmental step had been completely missed by most English anglers at that time. We had been struggling, frankly, with the French leaders as we comprehended them, missing the point that these were not designed to be cast in their own right, but required the mass of a nymph. We were also stuck on #4 and 5 weights which are too stiff for a low-mass casting system, such as the French leader. What Louis managed to demonstrate, even with my rod (but beautifully with his own 11-foot #2), was conventional overhead (or side) casting, using a long pause after the back stop point and directing the power stroke so as to incorporate the wind, and delivering a consistent turn-over which was, finally, both accurate and gentle. Enough of this soaked in at the time for me to realize that the key lay in the long, soft rod and a more appropriate structure of leader than the much-vaunted French constructions that were being blindly copied by all and sundry. We did not catch that trout, but after Louis's demonstration I took my rod back and headed off into the increasingly thin water upstream where I managed three lovely mountain trout which I am absolutely certain I would not have caught without such a delicate leader-only system.

What can happen in the loneliness of the sessions is astonishing, and without warning. I went into the first day of the championship tired and lacking confidence, and facing the inevitable challenging sections of river. They were mostly fast torrents with just the occasional pocket or 'held up' water close to the banks, under cover, where trout might be reasonably expected to hold. We had all remarked during every practice session that on a typical English trout river, almost every such location would hold at least one fish, but in

Incredibly valuable wild trout on orange-collared PTN during the Spanish Euros

Spain we had come to expect most of these same, attractive lies to be empty. In my morning session I had one particularly good-looking pocket and three, possibly four, others which were marginal. In the best lie I managed to catch a measurable fish fairly early, but soon afterwards lost another larger fish, and this killed that area for the rest of the session, which forced me to search everywhere else, including the least-likely places, from which I managed only a few undersized trout. Yet I had avoided the blank, which automatically placed me in the mid-order on such a difficult venue.

The afternoon session yielded a section that was lower down the same river and generally much faster, deeper water. Heavy nymphing proved useless, and I was unable to achieve any reasonable control, even with the long leader which avoided the worst of the drag from the fast flow. I concentrated on the few slacker sections, but these were all deep, and mostly protected by torrent. There was one little side stream on the far bank which caught my eye. If I were a trout, that is where I would be; out of the maelstrom. The problem was that between the bank where my controller was (and had to remain under *FIPS* rulings), and the beach of stones I needed to reach in order to fish the stream on the far side, was the fastest water in the whole section, among a frothing boulder field. On any normal fishing occasion I would simply have passed it by, but in the European Championship there was no other option. Here was the only possibility, as I reasoned, of saving the blank.

Just crossing the torrent once was pulverizing, though I was to do this several times that afternoon. The air temperature was well into the thirties, though the water was cold. Climbing up onto the beach rewarded me with a close look at the tiny stream that had attracted me, and I immediately knew that the danger of the pounding waters on the boulder field was worthwhile, because I noticed a trout rise, just downstream of an over-hanging bush, halfway along this rivulet. I was immediately down on my knees and in both analytical and tactical mode. At the outset I reasoned that this was utterly the most important fish on my section, being the most exposed, and actually feeding, in water that could actually be covered properly, with dry fly. But I also knew that if I made a mistake, and failed to catch this fish, there was unlikely to be another chance.

During what felt like a very long time, but in reality was probably less than ten minutes, I inched over the stones until I felt I was in the ideal casting position. I took off the nymph I had been using earlier and retied a reasonably long leader and tippet (4 metres – remember this was in the days before we developed leaders which could be cast without the aid of a weighted nymph or fly line) and tied on a single size 19 plume tip. I hesitated, noticing the fish rising again to something unseen, possibly a midge or some tiny terrestrial dropping from the bush upstream. The plume tip was too big and rather than risk spooking the trout by attempting a presentation with the big fly, I replaced it with a size 21 heron herl shuttlecock plume tip which was at least closer to the size of the naturals this fish was taking. At last, I put in a short cast, keeping the rod tip and fly line low. Another short cast followed, easing my way towards the target, and then a final delivery, almost hitting the water-dibbling leaves of the bush, which placed the fly exactly on the feed path. On the first cover the fish snatched the plume tip away and it felt miraculous to set the hook and ease a perfect Catalunyan trout into the waiting net, which meant having avoided the blank on an almost impossible torrent section.

Then recollection gradually becomes more blurred. I remember crossing the boulder field and the roar of spray, kicking off my waders and up into my face, and passing the fish to my controller for measuring (and I think he was almost as happy as I was at that moment). And I know that I re-crossed several times, almost losing my footing, and also searched elsewhere for any possibility of another trout, but these moments and episodes seem distorted. Finally the session was over. I was wading almost in mid river and my controller called out that it was time. I looked at him and froze. The trees and mountains beyond were floating, swimming in a sea that seemed an extension of the torrent in which I stood. I felt as if I were diving into this cold, welcoming place. Incredibly, I managed to wade to the shore and remember my controller's outstretched hand, pulling me from the river; but then I plunged away into the abyss. There was nothing more, until three hours later I awoke in Santander emergency unit.

Clinically, it was no more than dehydration and depleted blood sugar, though mentally I knew, as did our manager, Paul Page, that a serious problem had been exposed. 2008 at the level of the *FIPS-Mouche* Championship, while in my fifties, in high air temperatures and pounding waters far from home, yielded the final competitive lesson. I could no longer

Close to where I collapsed at the end of my championship second session – air temperature 32 degrees/water temperature 8 degrees – Rio Pas, northern Spain

live at this dizzying altitude. I had avoided the blank, and that was certainly good enough, and something of which I remain enormously proud to this day; and yet there was even more to come.

The following day I was incapable of competing and both *FIPS* and Paul forced me to stay in the championship hotel, while team reserve Vince Brooks fished in my place. On the final day I just had to be back on the water, because (under the *FIPS* rulings) we had no more reserve sessions in hand. The exhaustion had turned into a migraine-like headache, including nausea and sensitivity to bright light. The final session was a lake sector, high in the mountains and fished from the boats. The target fish were wild rainbows and previous sessions had yielded few of them, with one fish being a respectable catch and between three and five producing a section win. Dosed with aspirin and paracetamol, I could hardly walk to the boat, but Paul and Vince helped me in. Paul's parting words were: 'It's almost over, J; just see this one through – one fish and you can curl up in the bottom of the boat if you want to. Then you can go home to Jennie.'

So, out there among a place of distant islands, wind and waves, I did see it through; and see my international career out with not one, but two gorgeous wild rainbows, as welcome as the journey home. They came on the strip and hang, hammering into a spider on the dropper, and I felt this was just, in that my competitive life had really come full circle, on another still water, on the drift. But it was over, even though the following year, as if I yet had something to prove to myself, I entered the loch-style qualifying system, on

Stocks and Bewl, and managed to get through to the 2009 England team. My heart was no longer in it, however, and frankly I knew that I was no longer up to it; not, at least, to the top flight of the *FIPS* Championships.

Perhaps we should all know our limits, and certainly when it is time to walk away. Is it not always a mistake to carry on when one has had the best of it? I had done it once before, in the 1990s, when my team was truly competitive at world level, and I had finally discovered that, in spite of the wonderful experiences in my 'second time around' leading up to Norway in 2007 and here in Spain in 2008, I had reached my own limit. My great friend and team-mate Stuart Crofts had also reached the same conclusion and together we retired from the international selection process. Remembering how I had felt in the 1990s, however, I did this with reluctance, because I thought I would miss it desperately, as John Pawson had told me I would all those years ago on the eve of my first World Championship: 'You will never feel so alive, and when it's over …' Norway had been a warning, and I had nearly gone under there; but Spain affirmed the real situation, and there was no other sensible option. I needed to be home, on the Eden.

There has, however, been an extraordinary wealth of fishing experience after my international career, and curiously it has been both technically and practically a revelation; but this is for other chapters – the other side of the waters. Right now, I am thrown back in memory to all those cherished moments on rivers and lakes all over the world where I have been a part of the peculiar arena of international competitive fly-fishing. Apart from a few unpleasant experiences, such as my collapse in northern Spain, I would not swap a single moment. The first qualification for the loch-style team; the European open title, in 1987; the huge rainbow on Tunkwa, BC; the incredible fight back to the podium in Norway in 1994; winning the rivers international in Scotland and the loch-style international in Wales – ten years apart – and the fantastic support and friendships of so many team-mates; and the strength of great managers like Geoff Clarkson and Paul Page who were able to put us on the podium on waters far away, where it counts most. These are memories more than enough to fill a whole book; I could not be doing without any of them.

For a while, I had overcome the loneliness of the sessions, and was able to survive at the highest altitude of international fly-fishing, often far from home. It was a gift in a sporting life that had accelerated my technical and competitive abilities. It was tremendously fulfilling to be a part of this flow of fly-fishing development. It would not have been possible had I not managed to reach the England team while fairly young. Most of the anglers of outstanding ability that I know are, or have been, international competitors, though there are a handful who are not. Arthur Cove was one, and an outstanding example of another in the modern era is Paul Procter. The point is that there are those with great skills and there are great competitors: the two are not necessarily the same, and in fact rarely are. What one does observe, however, is that to survive for any length of time at international competitive level, one needs the skills, the broad range of experience, the cutting-edge competitiveness, and a deal of good luck. I have been graced with two long periods in the England team, fuelled by various measures of these.

CHAPTER THREE

The Other Side of the Water

Living without fly line ...

Because of the personal intensity I put into the England team I worried a lot about missing it all when I retired. Knowing that it made sense did not really help when I felt that the skills were still there, made keener by experience. Luck was again on my side, however, because with the extra time I was able to spend on the water away from the constraints of competition, an extraordinary period of development cascaded. This never occurred to the same extent while I was in the team, and I think the reason was that, to a large degree, one just has to be a team player, and to forge ahead in some individual, maverick direction is unsettling for a team. Now I was able to explore, unfettered, with only the success or failure of my own fishing at stake. That being the case, I must admit that, had it not been for that experience in international competition, with my team-mates, I would probably never have reached the stage from which I could venture into this territory, which I perceive as the frontier of the single-handed (freshwater) sport.

Time to explore alone, amid the island water of the San at blue-winged olive time

I have long been obsessed with the necessity for a good approach on a target fish, particularly in the river. While I acknowledge that the fly and numerous other factors matter, range and angle are right at the top: the need to be placed in the right position with respect to the fish is paramount. This is a little less obvious, and probably less important, on still water, where fish are cruising, but nonetheless it should invariably be a consideration (it is very easy to over-cast the range on still water). I think of all those times when I have advised guests on the river to use their feet, rather than a long cast, in order to close down the range and open the angle. If this is right, the cast and the fly are so much less significant. It is how that fly

Strongly marked wild brown trout from the San 'wilderness water' – the islands near Zaluz

behaves, its *presentation*, that matters, and in the river this is largely determined by range and angle.

I have long perceived that our sport has had an over-emphasis on casting, and also on the AFTMA rating of rods and lines. Too much value is attributed to the (classically observed) nature of casting, and it is almost a heresy to suggest that there are other factors at least as important. But there are. The fly-fishing instructor schools, such as the Game Angling Instructors' Association (GAIA), of which I am a member, have historically been concerned mostly with casting and this really sets the tone for fly-fishing at large. Our history in the river sport, stemming from casting upstream, has developed into something of a mindset from which it is difficult to escape, and in some (English) circles it is even taboo to consider fishing any other way. It is therefore challenging to question this, though I think we should, looking at the reasons behind it all. Why is casting upstream, particularly with dry fly, considered to be the absolutely correct way to go about things? Why does the consensus sneer, ever

A mountain stream in northern Spain where technique must be improvised

so slightly perhaps, when we go across the stream at a fish, and worse, actually cast down-stream? And if we put on a nymph, especially on the southern chalk, are we really blowing our fly-fishing souls to the Devil?

Of course, it is all a romantic, British notion that there is a right way and many wrong ways, and there is some derision and bigotry focused towards all those alternative ways. The truth of the matter is that fishing upstream, with dry fly, is usually the easiest way to catch a fish. Facing away, upstream, from a downstream angler, a trout is most unaware of a close approach from this direction. It is practically much more difficult to approach closely from any other direction if we are to avoid spooking the fish. Historically, there-fore, we have always tried to achieve an upstream cast, but we should not deride an angler for trying to approach from all those other directions which are actually more difficult; and there are many circumstances when an approach other than from downstream will be necessary if good presentation is to be achieved.

As for the dry fly; well, again, this has been perceived as the highest aesthetic level, though it is actually historic pragmatism: it is usually much easier to deal with a target fish – in reasonably shallow water on the river – with dry fly than with anything else. For most of any year, I would feel hugely constrained by being told that I could fish *only* nymph. I know that my catch rate, particularly of large trout and grayling, would crash. Finally, to hold upstream dry fly on such a pedestal is fine, because it is a gloriously

The translucent ghostly qualities of an alpine grayling; such 'clear water' fish are often so difficult to approach that even the touch-down of lightweight fly line can spook them

aesthetic and hugely effective way to fish, but we should not revere it for being difficult, because it probably requires the least skill of all the fly-fishing methods to catch trout and grayling (and many non-salmonid species). To see it otherwise is simply to give in to the romantic, prescribed doctrine.

What really matters out there is presentation and I have no doubt that this is where the real development is taking place, above and way beyond preconceived ideas. This is what fundamentally drove Sawyer and Cove, and other giant figures in the sport before them, and what should drive us if we are to have any real effect on how fly-fishing develops from our generation. Of course, we need not bother, and we might be satisfied with treading water rather than development. The single-handed fly rod and modern fly line are perhaps elegant enough, although the boundaries as laid down by former generations and those established doctrines

Magnificent wild rainbow caught by Lubin Pfeiffer of Team Australia off the Baca (Soca system) using micro nymph in the utterly clear waters

Wild rainbow going back into the Sava tailwater

Beautifully marked wild trout from the Savinja, northern Slovenia

become a frustration to many of us, and once we have glimpsed a better way, or an exciting direction, it is almost impossible not to venture further. We are drawn towards the other side of the waters.

So, our approach has been orientated towards the fly and the fly line. We have each gone on from the tenet of the conventional fly line, while relying on the imitative (or attractor) qualities of flies, to target our fish. Immediately, that sets limits as to what we can do and the resulting process is a contrivance within those limits. Instead, I think that we should be fish-orientated. Viewing the world as a trout or grayling, hovering in the stream, yields a better perspective and leads us towards the grail of improved presentation. This really is the key and I am sure that Arthur Cove, during his extraordinary development of nymph fishing from the bank of Grafham Water, saw it this way; imagining, or working out, how trout hunted along the shoreline, and how best to intercept their travel. I suspect that Frank Sawyer did the same with trout and grayling on the Avon, and possibly even Skues before him: because the nymphs that particularly Sawyer produced owed more to their behaviour in the water than adherence to imitative qualities. These nymphs were designed for the purpose of presentation, not imitation. The overriding features of such nymphs are their dynamics (motion and attitude in the water); and their general impression of size and shape of invertebrate food-forms (GISS) is good enough.

Placing a nymph at the right depth, for as long as possible in a drift, is the single most important aspect of its presentation. Usually, fish will not move very much up or down the water column to take nymphs; they take them at more or less the same depth at any particular period in the feeding cycle. Nymph-fishers are familiar with the feeling that

Tenkara and grayling on the Kokra, Slovenia

their flies are fishing either below or above optimum depth, because, for much of the time, they are, especially so with grayling! Sawyer's PTN owes much of its considerable success to its slim design and copper wire ballasting, both of which allow it to cut through the column quickly. Heavily weighted nymphs obviously do the same, *but that is all they do* – sinking quickly to the riverbed and not allowing the angler to hold them up in the water at any particular depth at which the fish might be feeding. Heavy nymphs can, however, be used sacrificially, allowing improved presentation of other nymphs elsewhere on a team. The brilliant Czech and Polish nymph developments of the 1990s further exploited this principle, with generally slim, sparse dressings, not necessarily heavily weighted and, particularly in combination in teams, they allowed all depths to be fished effectively. It is worth pointing out in this context that Arthur Cove disliked the use of lead, and preferred to exploit sparseness of dressing to allow flies to sink quickly or, conversely, hackling (in his versions of spiders) in order to slow the rate of fall.

This is the nature of the presentation-designed fly – what I have referred to in the past as tactical flies – and it is the approach, in terms of range and angle, that should concern us more. As discussed in Chapter 1, the previous two decades have brought in a welcome, general reduction in rod/line weighting on the river from a #6 to a #4 or #3, while the rods also tend to be longer, with 10 foot being the norm nowadays. This has allowed us an altogether gentler presentation, with finer tippets, with control out to the region of 10 metres.

This is already considerably more effective and elegant than hitherto, with dry fly all the way through the methods to heavy Czech-nymphing. Thanks to the European competitors, we have added the French leader which vastly improves sensitivity, presentation and control with small nymphs – but still firmly within that 10-metre range. More recently we have explored leader-only systems that can be cast without the aid of the comparatively high mass of nymphs and are finally beginning to push beyond the fly line-limited range for good control (10 metres), while also stumbling on benefits regarding choice of angle; all with minimal disturbance. Finally, there is the tenkara-style fixed line, right at the top of the tree in terms of presentation (at short range).

We cannot, however, immediately go to leader-only fly-fishing without learning the approach – including the casting – with conventional fly line (or fixed line). All the same principles, all the watercraft, apply. Indeed, the casting, without fly line, is more demanding and one has to be very comfortable with casting a modern lightweight fly line, such as a #2 or #3, really understanding both its casting excellence and its control limitations, before making the jump to a

Wojtek Gibinski on the upper Radovna with tenkara

leader-to-hand. Only when we have experienced the situation, repeatedly, when our approach has been exemplary and we have failed to catch that big trout or grayling for no reason other than the limitations of fly line based presentation, can we reasonably question the boundary and look beyond. This has been a driver for me, ever since the England team experience with Louis Perez in Spain, and seeing other European masters working with fine tackle, since 2008.

The starting point, therefore, is what can be achieved with the elegant tackle that the river sport has evolved towards. Much of my book *Tactical Fly Fishing* focused on the development of this approach, particularly the analytical, technical and tactical aspects which lead us to the all-important ideas of range and angle. As all of this is consistent with the leader-only approach it is worth summarizing briefly the key points here. As the majority of developments in the modern sport have stemmed from the river, the following refers to the approach here, though much of it is consistent with still-water applications.

CASTING ANGLES AND RANGE FROM DOWNSTREAM
APPROACH

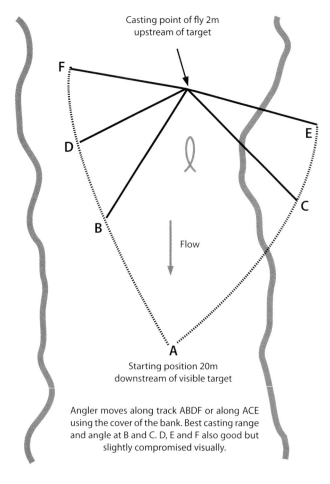

Casting point of fly 2m
upstream of target

F

D

E

C

B

Flow

A

Starting position 20m
downstream of visible target

Angler moves along track ABDF or along ACE
using the cover of the bank. Best casting range
and angle at B and C. D, E and F also good but
slightly compromised visually.

*The ideal range and
angle from the
downstream approach*

Armed with fly line we stand off from our target fish, preferably downstream, so that we can slowly work towards it, with as much cover as possible, particularly keeping off the skyline and avoiding throwing shadow towards the fish. Everything is in slow motion because we have learned that it is sudden movement that prey perceives, and predators avoid. As we begin to close the range we consciously and subliminally take in the environmental factors, especially the sun and wind direction. With dry fly and anything other than a down-streamer we are all right approaching from below, but we have to be careful even from this direction if the sun (including that shielded by thin cloud) throws shadow or shading in the direction of our target (or any water in that direction which might hold unseen fish). As we close the range we are also opening the angle so as not to be directly downstream, which will run the risk of lining the fish. Ideally we need to be somewhere about 45 degrees downstream: here we will be able to cast with a lead of two metres upstream of the fish, showing it no more than the fly and perhaps a little tippet. Even getting to this point requires painstaking stealth. A trout or a grayling is perfectly attuned to its habitat, and even tiny perturbations can cause an alarm response. Keeping everything low and slow, with soft footfalls, while also avoiding that pressure wave from the waders, nudging across the river, are all more important than the cast which is to come, because, frankly, if any of these are wrong, the fish is likely to be spooked and the cast is consequently pointless.

We really do have to get into this sort of range, and make a reasonable angle, because the currents on a river of any character at all – which means features and varied currents – are such that the more fly line is laid on the water, the more out of control we are. That water/line interaction is obvious with dry fly, because it very quickly results in drag, but is it also crucial to avoid this with nymph or spider *for which a dead drift is also nearly always necessary*. So we cannot stand off at even 15 metres and realistically hope to get away with a longer cast. Six metres (from hand to target) is ideal with a 10-footer, so that

not more than a metre of fly line rests on the surface with the rod held high. We can extend this range, thus keeping a reasonable distance from the fish, out to about 10 metres, though we are gradually losing control; beyond 10 metres the loss is exponential. There is simply too much line on the flow, bellying, snaking and either losing all contact with the fly or, worse, inducing drag.

This is not a casting issue, but a fly line issue. Even exceptionally good casters can extend the range at which there is reasonable control by perhaps only another 5 metres, and this only on a smooth, laminar river flow. In a complicated flow this distance is far less, and often even 10 metres in total is too much. We can mend line in order to put in slack to absorb some of that line/current interaction, but at best this will extend the drag-free phase of a drift by only a very short period and it also significantly reduces the contact with the fly. Being blunt, it is a crude necessity to attempt to overcome one of the main shortcomings of conventional fly line.

Having 'fished' our way in so as to adopt the best compromise of angle and range, we have acquired considerable information. We have an idea about the food-forms, the rate at which our target fish is feeding, its proximity to cover and anything that might shield the angler from view, such as broken water. We should have put in exploratory casts on any area which might possibly hold an unseen fish as we increasingly focus on the 'prime target', while also allowing our peripheral senses to glean information about the surround-

No matter what the angle to the flow or 'old school' doctrine, this is perfect presentation: Tom Speak with a zero-weight fly line on the Eden

The author hunting at the top of the islands on the San tailwater section with early leader-only technique

ings and potential target areas or fish elsewhere. It might be illuminating to consider that I pick up fish before the prime target more often than not and also, by the time any fish has been taken, I usually have a very firm idea of the next. Remember that the most important fish is the closest one, even if it has not been seen. If you catch it, it is a bonus; if you spook it you might also have lost the prime target(s) beyond. Old competitive reasoning, perhaps, but it is also good fishing practice.

All of this, so far, is consistent whether one is fishing dry fly or nymph, fly line or leader-only, including tenkara. The same principles of watercraft and approach apply. Similarly, if the wind is not a pleasant up-streamer, but the opposite, we would have to reconsider the angle of approach, and this is independent of the method used. It is from this point, however, that the most significant advances have been made, in terms of presentation. I make absolutely no apology for labouring what follows; in its deployment one finds an entirely improved presentation that really has changed everything on the river.

Consider, then, that we are out there in mid-river, having fished our way towards a prime target, whether or not we have picked up fish along the way. At the correct pace we have certainly packed away information about the immediate surroundings and conditions, all of which will guide us when we make the final delivery. The more we do this, the more we learn to be selective with the information, just as we learn better to adopt the correct position in the stream – but also the more painfully frustrated we become with fly

Choosing the correct approach and position in the stream: an idyllic section of the Wear in County Durham

line. We notice it first with big grayling. These fish are utterly the greatest challenge of all the salmonids. They adopt very precise lies on the food lanes, close to cover and, even when feeding on dry fly, tend to adopt a deeper position than trout. They are also enormously efficient feeders (though so too are *very large* trout), expending far less energy than smaller fish, particularly trout. We see this best with dry fly rather than nymph feeders, because we can see the number and travel of the duns, say, on the surface and watch to see how a big grayling reacts to these. Not only does the grayling rise to the same point on the surface, often within millimetres it seems, but it does so with a much lower frequency than trout.

As a consequence of its efficient feeding, and lack of energy expenditure, the grayling does not need to take every dun that passes overhead, or nearby. We might often count ten duns drifting by before one is intercepted. This is rare with trout, which will usually attempt to take every one that passes within range, even way off the feed lane, though often unsuccessfully. It is also worth noting that it is rare to see a grayling miss its target.

To many of us, one of the most beautiful experiences in fly-fishing is to be positioned down and across from a big grayling in clear water. It is poised there, typically perhaps at 60 centimetres depth, immediately beneath a concentrated feed lane. Duns pass overhead and finally the fish tilts, adjusting only its pectoral fins, so that it kites up against the flow to reach the surface while vertical, there to kiss the targeted dun away with the merest of

Where stealth includes merging with the backdrop: L'Aa, a wonderful hidden chalk stream in the north of France

disturbance, before reversing and sliding back to its starting position. It is a natural display of accuracy, efficiency and elegance, and almost always there is a rhythm in terms of timing or frequency of the rise to the duns. To be consistently successful with such fish, we have to be similarly delicate in our approach, with precision and minimal disturbance.

It is always a temptation to put a cast immediately at such a fish, but it is nearly always a mistake so to do. One needs to observe the exact position and the feeding rhythm of the fish and we can do this only by slowly manoeuvring into the correct range and angle. The closer we move, the better the understanding, and in so doing we should have resisted putting in an over-range cast which will either spook the big fish, or put us hopelessly out of control, or both. Even when in position we have to fight the urge to cast. It is always better to hold back and allow the fish to develop confidence in feeding in spite of our close proximity. Big grayling, and trout, are perfectly tuned to their environment and I'm sure that they usually do become cautious, if not actually spooked, for a short period even with the stealthiest of approaches.

We understand the grayling's rhythm and the point on the feed lane where it is rising, so it finally comes to the moment of the cast. We have already made extension casts, low and off-line, and have the fly in hand with degreased tippet, so it is a matter now of placing the whole such that the fly is delivered a metre upstream of the rise point, exactly on line. If the fly drifts drag-free, and the timing is good, all is well and we watch the fish tilt and rise to the ideal, text-book result. Realistically, however, there are so many things that can go wrong with this final phase of the delivery and presentation. Even with average-sized trout and grayling, there are so many components of this process which are demanding. There is nothing wrong with this, of course: it is all part of the wealth of skills in fly-fishing; but there is also nothing wrong with trying to improve the nature of the approach so that we spook fewer fish and achieve the desired result more consistently. Finally, it comes down to fly line and leader.

Even with a light conventional fly line, say a #3, and a delicate braided or furled butt leader and fine tippet, or alternatively that same fly line and long tapered leader and tippet – both of which are attempts to lower the disturbance of delivery – that fly line is giving us problems. The fly line is designed primarily for its casting function and for this it is superb; a delight to use and to watch being used. The very properties that make it a delight to cast, its thickness and its (distributed) mass, mean that it must either touch down on the surface with a degree of disturbance, or at least sag between rod tip and surface. Low-diameter silk lines improve the situation, and are a delight to cast in AA ratings (AFTMA #1 and #2), offering gentler touchdown than polymer lines, and this nudges us in the right direction. For years we have lived with a compromise between the ease of casting fly lines and their comparative disturbance value, but the more often you go for big grayling, and fail, while knowing that the only reasons are the disturbance from the fly line, or loss of control in the drift, the more frustrating it becomes. We can lengthen leaders and tippets only up to a certain point where casting and control become untenable, or soften the touchdown with skilled casting, while learning to achieve the best contact possible throughout a drag-free drift, but the boundary conditions defined by fly lines, even silk, conspire to be the single most important factor that holds back our presentation, and our effectiveness, on the river. And it does not end with big grayling. Trout, while seldom quite so demanding to the point of a successful take, will often adopt very 'protected' lies where the intrusion of fly line is detrimental to presentation, or will increase the alertness of the fish.

LINE DRAPE

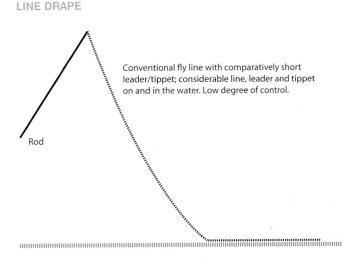

Conventional fly line with comparatively short leader/tippet; considerable line, leader and tippet on and in the water. Low degree of control.

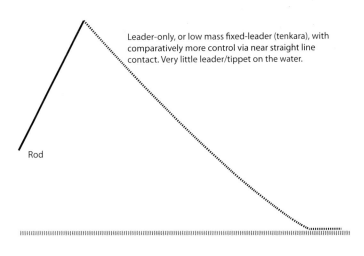

Leader-only, or low mass fixed-leader (tenkara), with comparatively more control via near straight line contact. Very little leader/tippet on the water.

The benefit of the long rod

Part of the 'turning point': a beautiful wild trout from northern Spain where the long leader was everything

And then, about a decade ago – well before the turning point of the Spanish European Championship – I finally reasoned that there was something intrinsically wrong with fly line presentation on rivers. All was well while we were streamer fishing – though not many of us did much of this on British and European rivers – and similarly with classic 'down and across' with wet flies or spiders. The problems started with the nymph, fishing these beyond the classical Czech-nymph range, which is very short, a matter of 2 or 3 metres out from the rod tip. As soon as we push this out further there is a marked drop in control. For a long time I was stuck with various incarnations of the French leader, striving to use these for more sensitive and improved nymph presentation on the river. I found I often reverted back to low AFTMA-rated fly lines, or, better, silk lines around the AA rating, simply because of their gentler touchdown and reduced interaction with surface currents. While this period was not exactly going backwards, since this was the time when Euro-style and indicator nymphing evolved, it was more like 'treading water' in terms of development; essentially just refinement of technique.

We need to go back to the beginnings, and to define the factor of control, related intimately to presentation, which is both an understanding of a fly's movement in or on the water and being able to alter this by subtle action of the rod and line. It is also the avoidance of adverse motion of the fly, known as drag. We should consider floating lines on the river, because this is where the issues discussed here are most obvious. While the act

Smooth water, late season conditions, where all aspects of control are crucial; Tom Speak with a big trout on the Eden

of casting is crucial, I will look at this in more detail later. What concerns us now is the fly line on the water, which is where our problems start, and quickly compound to put us out of control. With everything I say about fly lines, the situation is nearly always improved by using the comparatively lower diameter of equivalently rated silk lines.

Time and again I would find myself out there with a target fish identified, either nymphing or rising to dries. The temptation was, and is, always to cast at such targets, but in so doing this might involve a long cast. With the modern fly line this is not the problem. At 15–20 metres most of us can roll, Spey or overhead with a lightweight floating line, comfortably out to this range, with good turn-over and reasonable touchdown. On delivery, the fly, tippet, leader and line are all on the surface; and yet now there are mere moments, while tightening down on the fly line to absorb slack and gain reasonable contact with the fly, during which there is an element of control. Almost immediately the interaction of the water and fly line pushes us out of control (less so with silk), and this increases with the drift time.

Five seconds into any drift and the fly line will start to belly, and with rivers of any character the various currents on the surface will result in multiple coils and snaking, which significantly increase with range. Every single coil is slack line, and this loses us contact with the fly. Simply put, the longer the cast, the longer the fly line on the water and the greater the loss of control. I went to great pains in *Tactical Fly Fishing* to develop this issue and to stress the need for closing down the range on a target fish, which for the river angler usually means sub-10 metres and moving by wading, or at least along the bank. Indeed, this gain of control by closing the range is so crucial that it becomes the single most important factor that determines our success, and we learn, invariably by repeated failure, that it is so much more significant than excellence in casting.

The currents tug at the line, and the thicker this is the more pronounced is the interaction; but even on the smooth flow of the lower Test, say, before the ranunculus beds of mid-summer have swollen (which is just about as laminar as we find a river's surface), there is this effect. Here, and on many other chalk streams, the angler usually cannot wade (a protective measure for the substrate and the invertebrates that live there). He is confined to the bank, seeking whatever cover might be present, or kneeling well back from the water's edge, both of which necessitate long casting and the resultant excess of fly line on the surface, or on the riverbank among the foliage. We all live with this, while some develop strategies for minimizing the detrimental effect of loss of control: we put in line mends so as to reduce the effects of drag, or to prolong the drag-free period of the drift, but in so doing we are still losing control.

The harsh fact remains that, while a good caster can put in mends that look beautiful, the loss of control is bad practical fishing and, in any case on a river with the varied flow that adds character, line mends have a limited effect on minimizing drag. Such tactics are much better suited to still-water presentation, because here the only flow is the surface wind-drift, which is easier to deal with, even with a floating line. You might notice that top competitive anglers (at least on a rain-fed river) will rarely adopt a mended cast presentation and, for a fish which is 'protected' by varied currents, they will usually go for extreme accuracy. A very short drag-free drift will result – which is what demands the accuracy – with the fly touching down within centimetres of the target. This is one of the many aspects of the sport that competitive fly-fishing improves in an individual's performance, because although it might superficially look more elegant when an angler is able to deliver an attractively mended line, believe me, the resultant loss of control is not so obvious to the observer as it is to the practitioner, and this makes a significant difference in a competitive situation.

In 2008, during the European Championship in northern Spain, I felt that we had reached close to the limit of the presentation potential of French leader. That year, we were so fortunate to have Louis Perez as our coach, because he was an outstanding exponent of Euro-nymphing and he revealed and demonstrated to us a high evolutionary state of an indicator French leader rig (or, rather, how the Spanish had interpreted and developed this). I think it was even more sophisticated than the French were using at that time. Its use, however, on the wary, wild fish of the Catalunya Highlands, while effective, also revealed shortcomings. Again, all was well at very close range. Indeed, with a long, soft rod these nymph rigs made accessible trout that we were all certain would have not been catchable by any other method. At longer range (more than 8 metres), fly line came into play and not only did this bring about the above-mentioned, familiar loss of control, but also the casting issues which stem from having insufficient loading mass in the limited

Some of the most difficult water in which to maintain control: John Fisher of Team Australia into a big rainbow on the nymph in powerful flow on the Sava tailwater

fly line extended from the rod tip, and a long leader and tippet with very little mass: again, loss of control. We were also at that time locked into #4 weights as standard and were only dabbling with #3 and #2 weights for competitive purposes. I have suggested repeatedly that this actually held us back, because there is a problem with such heavily line-rated rods in terms of casting performance of low mass line/leader constructions. We were slow on the uptake, because we had all noticed that the top Europeans were actually commonly using long, soft rods.

After many failed attempts to make French leader constructions work satisfactorily with dry fly, I went back to first principles. These leaders were not properly loading the rod. A common feature was their taper, and everyone seemed to be following this general formula of a continuous taper over the whole length of the leader, with the aim of improving turn-over and presentation; but with low-mass flies – dry flies – the opposite was the result. It is a simple physics problem, specifically concerning momentum, the product of mass and speed (or strictly speaking, velocity). In order to load the rod during casting, the line or leader must have sufficient momentum. With conventional fly lines the mass is the dominant factor and the line does not have to move very fast in order to achieve the desired loading. With the much lower mass of a leader-only rig, the momentum has to be achieved by increasing the speed through the casting stroke. A gradual taper in that leader merely reduces mass and thus results in the necessity of an extremely fast power stroke, which is impractical.

Craig Coltman, captain of Team Australia 2012, here using a zero-weight silk fly line and long-leader technique – into a big grayling on the Sava

I had in mind the weight-forward or long-belly fly line construction (or even the level silk line, which I used a lot at that time), which places the mass further towards the line tip than a double taper. Abandoning French leaders, I assembled level running monofilament (experimenting with fluoro-carbon, nylon monofilament and copolymer) knotted to a steeply tapered section, which in turn was connected to a short braided monofilament section, to which the tippet was attached. All manner of hybrids followed before I settled on the form which is shown here; a 14+ metre copolymer leader, with all the features which made it both a casting and a presentation-orientated leader.

Since that period I have experimented considerably with all aspects of the presentation leader, but the only significant improvement has been in the replacement of the braided nylon section with a furled horsehair section of approximately the same length and mass as the old nylon version. More recently I discovered that some tenkara anglers in the United States were making braided and furled leaders which also had weight-forward or double taper profiles, both of which load mass away from the rod tip and make turn-over of the leader similar to my presentation leader, though obviously at ranges limited by the fixed line.

A breakthrough came when I started to use this leader on softer rods than hitherto. Escaping from the competition-based mindset (of the time) of #4 and #5 weights, I was fortunate enough to use some of the earlier models of lower line-rated rods stemming from Continental Europe, from Siman, Hanak and Hends, culminating in a Hardy/Greys prototype 11-foot #3 weight, which was to become the Greys Streamflex. Married to the presentation leader above, this changed everything in a single session.

It was on the Eden, in early summer, and several species of Ephemeridae were hatching simultaneously. These included olive uprights, *danica* mayflies, medium olives and spurwings. Mostly trout were up at them, rising non-stop, but there were a few big grayling also rising steadily in the most favoured drift lanes (and taking the smallest flies, as is typical). There was a gentle wind, slightly across the water, while generally upstream. It was sunny and this always makes close approach to the fish most difficult, tempting the fly-fisher to cast long, risking that loss of control which both spooks fish and loses accuracy. I tied on a 3-metre tippet of 0.12 mm copolymer terminating in a size 19 heron herl CDC plume tip. With the fly cast the entire length of the leader, plus tippet, this would give a maximum range, from my hands, of 17 metres.

I was on the tail of a broad glide, with a few clumps of water crowfoot and numerous boulders to give a complexity of currents; masses of feature which created a meshwork of holding lies and drift lanes. As I waded in on the tail, I counted four consistent risers within the 10-metre range of my position, and several others beyond. Of course, the hunter-fisher knows that the most important fish is not the biggest one, nor the easiest target, but the one that is closest – invariably. I stood, stooping, in the broken water at the tail, with the closest trout a mere 7 metres upstream. Any further and I would spook it. The damage done, in that case, would have been catastrophic, because an alarmed fish in such a position will always bolt upstream and spook almost every fish in the glide. Directly upstream, however, does not give the ideal presentation angle. You run the risk of lining such a fish, and with fly line this is almost inevitable; even the bulk of a gently touching down furled leader is detrimental in these situations.

The approach to accelerating water from downstream

But I was not using fly line, nor a furl. I peeled off about 10 metres of leader and sent the fly up the drift. With a shorter rod, the angler has a problem with accelerating water on a riffle, or tail, such as this: the current catches the line and while the fly is sitting in slower-moving water the faster-moving line and tippet quickly impart drag, which is always damaging to presentation and is alarming to any fish in the vicinity. A longer rod, like the 11-footer, can overcome this with the tip being kept high and holding as much line as possible out of the water. The adjacent diagram shows the difference in presentation between a short rod, and fly line, and a long rod and presentation leader-to-hand, which, note, is tending toward the ideal of the tenkara presentation.

The tippet fell almost directly over the fish, but it continued to rise. It missed the plume tip on the first drift, ignored it on the second, but nailed it on the third: a lovely wild trout that came hurtling to hand, where I slipped the hook to release the fish which immediately torpedoed into the cover of nearby crowfoot. Dealing with a trout this quickly is often easy in fast water so long as

LONG AND SHORT ROD APPROACH TO ACCELERATING WATER FROM DOWNSTREAM

Hidden by the fast water at the tail, an angler is usually invisible to fish when approaching from downstream. The accelerating water compromises presentation, producing almost immediate drag. A long rod and leader-only rig can usually reach beyond the accelerating water.

An alternative is for the angler to approach from the side, or upstream, though visibility is then often compromised.

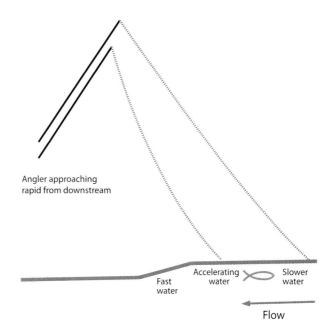

Angler approaching rapid from downstream

Fast water

Accelerating water

Slower water

Flow

Eden trout on the plume tip, leader-only technique

the angler is downstream of the fish. The trick is to keep up the pressure from the moment of setting the hook, turning the fish and keeping its momentum towards you so that it loses sense of direction and can't make its tail work at the water. It is a competition technique stemming from the need to maximize catch rate (while minimizing the disturbance of a hooked fish), but a by-product is fish very quickly released back to the water, which then have the best chance of rapid recovery. I suspect they do not even realize anything has happened once the initial shock has dispersed.

Fish elsewhere continued to rise, oblivious of anything untoward. As I dried the CDC, I took a few slow steps up into the tail, where the water was smoother. Even this small movement changed the tempo: it was quieter and I had a sense of the river opening out, being more aware of fish or drifting flies at greater range upstream, and even either side of me. This is very common and I think that many anglers rush too quickly to acquire this sort of prime position in a pool or glide, rather than more methodically 'fishing their way in'. I waited a few more moments to allow any disturbance of my movement to settle and to see that the fish were still confidently rising. This pause is tactical, always worthwhile (also in the competitive arena) because it helps the angler to build a mind map of the area, assessing the positions and accessibility of all the target fish. It also usually allows you to spot other fish, or high potential lies, which had not been visible earlier.

Again, picking out the nearest riser I laid out the fly, using a side cast rather than an

Wild Eden trout on the plume tip, leader-to-hand

overhead so as to reduce any possible disturbance, a metre upstream of the rise point. First drift and the fly was clipped away, resulting in another lovely trout, beached momentarily on a bed of water crowfoot, which subdued it instantly, before its release. Still the fish continued to rise all over the glide. I noticed that all *Danicae* were being ignored, with the spurwings and medium olives being the favoured food-forms, though some of the olive uprights were taken. Every single *danica* I watched take flight, however, was ambushed by pied wagtails. This, too, is very common, and one wonders how this invertebrate species can survive faced with such precision predation from above and below!

At this early point in using a leader-to-hand rig, I was very conscious of the casting and delivery. What really struck me initially was the ease with which a side cast could be performed. I mentioned earlier the long pause on the back cast to allow the leader to extend sufficiently so that the rod would be loaded during the forward power stroke. A by-product of the comparatively low mass of a presentation leader is that it hangs in the air – particularly in a slight side wind – much longer than a fly line. This has the benefit of avoidance of bank-side foliage. It might seem a small issue, but actually in practice it aids considerably with the delivery options. Moreover, a background of trees can be more easily negotiated than with fly line. With the latter, the most useful cast is the jump roll, utilizing the momentary drag of the tip of the fly line in the water, as in a single Spey. Thus the fly line is not extended all the way to the obstruction behind. With leader-to-hand a similar tactic is employed and only a part of the leader is allowed to extend and turn over behind the caster before the forward power stroke. In practice it is probably easier to master than the jump roll. Both casts suffer by being fairly inefficient, compared with a full-blown overhead, but they are incredibly useful in such confined situations.

That afternoon, taking fewer than ten steps up the glide, opening up the 360-degree river around me, I picked off almost every fish targeted, which included two grayling of over 40 centimetres. Exceptional fishing, for sure; possible only on a very healthy river. What struck me, forcibly, was the lack of disturbance – so little that I don't think a single fish was spooked during the two hours I spent there, and I believe that every feeding fish was subsequently caught. I knew all too well that this would have not been possible with a conventional fly line. Pragmatically speaking, four or five fish might have been caught, far apart on the glide, but the repeated presentation of the fly line touching down, the noise of it lifting off the surface during a new cast or tightening into fish, as well as its relatively conspicuous flight through the air during casting, would have rapidly increased the disturbance factor. It always does, even with fish that are particularly preoccupied with feeding, as that afternoon. This has nothing to do with matters of good casting or fly-fishing expertise: it has to do with limitations within the core of our tackle, the fly line.

As I climbed out of the river I found myself in a mixed state of elation and revelation. In a single session I had been overwhelmed both by the lack of disturbance caused by my presence there – apart from the capture of a dozen fish – and the ease with which I had been able to cast and present the plume tip on a leader-only rig. I felt as if I had cleared a giant hurdle, even reached up to a higher plateau in terms of the presentation possibilities on the river. I wondered at all the occasions, all the years, in circumstances such as that afternoon session on the Eden, which had been negatively affected by the use of fly line. No fishing time is exactly wasted, at least if we use the tools and skills available to us at any moment to make the best of the fishing process. We learn and move on, enjoying it all, which is the point. That afternoon, however, I began to appreciate that there was, after all, a different way of approaching the technical problems we have out there on the river, and that it had required going back to first principles, rather than relying on empirical ideas, or prescribed doctrine, set down by former generations of fly-fishers.

Finally, I was still presenting an artificial fly, casting in the conventional way with a fly rod, but with a newly designed leader construction in place of a conventional fly line. In a stroke, given the tools (the long #3 weight rod and the leader designed for casting purpose), I had stumbled upon presentation and control possibilities that had not been imagined at the outset. The aim had been to prepare a reasonably low-mass leader which could be cast with an overhead (or side cast) without the added mass of weighted nymphs, and which would touch down very gently. In practice, a construction had been discovered which could be cast beyond the 10-metre range and which, by virtue of its thin diameter and low mass, did not interact with the river's current to anything like the extent experienced with a fly line, and thus gave far superior levels of control during very long, drag-free drifts. Moreover, the extraordinary lack of disturbance meant that I could spend much more time on that glide than would have been practical with fly line, picking off fish which remained un-spooked until the moment the hook was set. Even the big grayling could be cast at repeatedly, whereas use of fly line, as any grayling devotee knows, would have demanded just a single, perfectly timed and accurate cast.

It was not all positive. There was, for instance, an accuracy issue. This is the tremendous advantage that fly line has over any leader-only approach. The comparatively high mass of fly line results – during casting – in it spending much less time in flight than any leader-only system and it is significantly easier to be accurate. There is compensation, however, in the much gentler touchdown and near invisibility of a leader. If one is inaccurate on the first, or subsequent casts, there is so little disturbance that the cast can be repeated, often many times, until perfect positioning has been achieved. As noted above, the fact that it is possible to get away with such repeated attempts even with big grayling, suggests pointedly that this minimal disturbance is being achieved. Nonetheless, I was initially somewhat disappointed by reduced accuracy, even at short range. The fact that big grayling were usually not put off by errant casts did not excuse this failing in the approach.

Tom Speak with Eden grayling, leader-only rig and plume tip

There were other issues. In my early leader-to-hand rigs, the material I used in the running section was too stiff, or worse, in the case of fluorocarbon, too thin for its mass and also required constant greasing to keep afloat, which is essential. Also, the taper I used was initially too long, at 3 metres, running down to the braided monofilament section which was too short (and thus too low a mass). All of these subtle nuances, once addressed, produced significant improvements to the leader in terms of casting, presentation and subsequent control during the drift. The version with the horsehair furl (stiffer than nylon braid) I consider to be currently unbeatable, though I look forward to inevitable improvements, perhaps in the running leader from hand to taper, or perhaps in the taper itself.

Two years had passed since the 2008 European Championship in Spain before that summer afternoon on the Eden; a lot of development from going back to first principles in my *ab initio* attack on the problem. Fine tuning has taken place since then and today,

The perfect water for developing a leader-only approach with dry fly and nymph: the Solinka, near its confluence with the San

at the time of writing, I cannot conceive of any significant change which would yield measurable improvement in performance; but then I had not imagined where we would be now starting from the nascent experiences with French leader presentation as it was in 2008. Fulling Mill have mirrored the design and through the mass market have made available the 'tactical presentation leader', while many individual anglers have echoed the development to come up with their own versions. I see this now proliferating among Western-style fly-fishers and cannot help but observe how this is converging our whole approach towards the Eastern tenkara style.

Fly line manufacturers have also addressed the problem by attempting to integrate line and leader and ideas of low casting mass coupled with feather-soft touchdown, finally (way overdue) escaping the anachronistic AFTMA system. Rio have led the field with the production of the zero-rated double taper, high-floating lines in the form of the so-called triple zero LT. Silk lines also help us to reduce the disturbance 'footprint' by virtue of their better diameter-to-mass ratio. It is all a compromise, not quite achieving some of the properties of a leader-only rig, but winning slightly in the ease of casting, which is much of the presentation process. Among others, Hends, Hanak and Greys have all produced top-of-the-range rods that are capable of casting and controlling the new generation of ultra-lightweight leaders (initially by default, because they were all designed essentially as Euro-nymphing rods). Proliferation of such rods and their becoming the norm is only a matter of time, and it will, as always, be market led. In any

A pristine alpine torrent

case, it remains tremendously exciting that there is still scope for development as we fly-fishers coincidently develop the necessary skills in presentation.

From early experiments on the Eden I made a commitment to use a presentation leader-to-hand rig on every river I fished, as well as on still waters when appropriate. I reasoned that the essential principles of excellence in presentation were consistent for any trout and grayling situation. Of course there were problem days (and these will surely continue) when conditions contrived to make any good presentation challenging, if not impossible. On other days we can be confronted with situations where we know that a fly line – and short leader and tippet – would be preferable: in strong winds, or upland torrents of pocket water, where speed of delivery with accuracy (a forte of fly lines), is of the essence. These assumed deficiencies of a leader-only rig are not, however, nearly as common as expected at the outset, at least on the river. In the summer of 2011, I spent two months in various European countries, fishing exclusively on rivers, and only with the 11-foot Streamflex #3 and leader-to-hand. The range of rivers was extreme, from the comparatively sedate flow of the upper Moselle, to snow-melt torrents at 2,000 metres in the Dolomites; from the awesome tailwater of the San River to the equally awesome Sava surging off the Slovenian Alps.

I cannot deny that there were moments when I yearned for a fly line. On the other hand, there were many more occasions when I experienced that same feeling of revelation as back home, on the Eden. Time and again I climbed out of the water in a state of wonder

The clear waters of the Baca, where I first discovered the effectiveness of very long leaders with small 'spot' nymphs

at the incredible presentation possibilities that could be achieved; simply catching trout and grayling that would otherwise have been considerably more difficult. Some friends pointed out that I might have been choosing the water that was most suitable for leader-to-hand. While this might have been the case in some instances, I actually chose, and continue to choose, water where, in the first instance, dry fly will be most effective (usually less than 1-metre depth), and this approach is certainly consistent with the best that leader-to-hand affords, because the best of it is most certainly with dry fly in shallow water.

The most obvious situation in which leader-to-hand was inferior to fly line presentation was for long-line nymphing on deep, fast sections of rivers. Such water demands heavy nymphs, and these destroy the delicate casting attributes of any leader-only rig. What normally is the most elegant presentation construction I have ever used, then becomes clumsy and ungainly – but then heavy nymphing with fly line rigs is hardly the most attractive method either to practise or to observe. Gusty, unsettled conditions are also not conducive to good performance with a leader-only rig. It becomes enormously frustrating working one's way into the river on a target fish, carefully developing the ideal angle and range, only for the wind to change and render one's position poor, necessitating either waiting for the wind to change more favourably or moving again, thus increasing the disturbance value.

It has been a surprise to discover that what stemmed from a European-led nymph approach, with French leader, has evolved on a tangent, into an astonishingly delicate

The Radovna, a clear, cold alpine river

means of delivery and subsequent control with dry fly. Moreover, because of the low mass of the leader, and the distribution of that mass, the peak performance is between 12 and 17 metres (from the hand), and this is considered long range when we appreciate that ideal performance with fly line delivery is sub-10 metres. This is leader-to-hand at its best, and from the Eden to the Moselle, from the Sava to the San, with CDC plume tips, this is what completely changed my appreciation of what is possible in this enthralling area of the sport.

Though I never claimed leader-to-hand was a panacea, I was occasionally misquoted thus, and in my promotion of leader-only technique in order to achieve improved presentation, I have even been vilified as the cause of the destruction of values in our sport – a rather unearned, though very funny, accolade which is now something of a party piece. Where I think any panacea, or ideal, might lie is in presentation itself. Anything that allows us to achieve this more proficiently (or elegantly) than hitherto is, surely, laudable, and I believe it is often the primary aim of the trout and grayling fly-fisher, at least those for whom nymph and dry fly are everything. All I have really claimed is that there are many situations, perhaps the majority, on rivers (of all types) when leader-to-hand offers improved presentation over fly line. Often this is marked; sometimes it is subtle. And sometimes it fails.

Fly lines are not obsolete, even for dry-fly presentation on the river; less so for long nymphing and much less for streamer on river or lake. And I doubt that there is any

Tom (and Ellie) with big grayling on the Eden; leader-only and plume tip

application at all for leader-to-hand for salt-water or large predator species (with 'fly'). Where the new generation of leader-only rigs (including tenkara) win is with presentation and control as outlined above, and here they are utterly supreme. It has now been three years during which almost all my fishing has been with a leader-only rig or, occasionally, a very light fly line tipped with a furled leader and long tippet. There have been very few occasions when I have found leader-to-hand wanting. I have delighted in its minimalism; its 'less is more' attributes. I have played Devil's advocate in approaching difficult river situations while suspecting that a fly line approach would have been better, only to find the converse.

Neither do I claim that this approach is for all. It is certainly not right for the beginner or the inexperienced caster. Here, fly line is essential, because the rudiments of casting can be learned only by having sufficient loading mass out of the rod tip. It is not for the still-water angler except in limited conditions, and it is not for the committed fly line aficionado who revels in the much-vaunted delights of specialist casting, such as Speys. This brings us, however, to the principles of casting with a leader-to-hand or with one of the new generation of ultra-lightweight fly lines, or the traditional, low-mass silk lines.

During early broadcasting of the leader-to-hand approach, many anglers suggested that I would be unpopular with the fly line manufacturers, at least if the idea caught on. Well, it has, rather, and the market force generated has meant that the demand for improved presentation has led to leader and fly line producers extending their efforts to fulfil our needs. I think this is the way any development takes place and to object to this is, in my view, merely blinkered. All of us are subjective to various extents, and resist change, particularly as the years pass; but to deny progress, unless for rational, objective reasons, is counter to the interests of the sport's development. I think back to all the many innovations in fly-fishing that I have initially disliked: the gold-head, the blob, duo technique, the bung, down and across, indi-style, and even the French leader ...

Finally, the experience is that we would be better to embrace all of these, use them, learn from them, and move on, if so inclined or inspired, in this enthralling journey of discovery. So far as the leader-to-hand is concerned, the biggest objections came from those who misunderstood the casting principles. It was a continuous source of frustration to me that even experienced fly-casters were trying to use French leaders, or similar, with dry flies. Finding this poor unless at very close range, they then dismissed the whole idea as unworkable, while many of the British contingent – perhaps because the whole idea stemmed from Continental Europe (along with the tenkara influence) – felt that there was something intrinsically underhand going on here; a dark art. Give that same angler the appropriate tackle at the outset, however, and invariably it is a completely different matter. I have friends who now say that, like me, they find it very difficult to go back to using fly line, finding this simply too crude (though there are exceptions with fine silk fly lines and even furl-tipped low-rated AFTMA synthetic lines).

With the appropriate tackle, as described here – the soft actioned rod and properly designed leader – we are not faced with learning a whole new casting style or regime, but merely extending the skills we have learned with fly line to compensate for the comparatively low mass of the leader. Also, some casts are simply not possible. Other than for short range, with low-mass flies, roll-based, or Spey casts cannot work because the low diameter and mass of the leader does not offer sufficient drag on the water's surface to permit putting enough energy into the rod and leader to allow turn-over or extension on the forward delivery.

When using nymph, or nymph/spider combinations, the constant tension cast (sometimes referred to as the switch cast) is most useful. With the leader, tippet and flies hanging downstream at the end of the drift, the rod tip accelerates upstream. As with all casting, the line and flies always follow the rod tip and the net result is that the flies are repositioned upstream. There has, in consequence, been an angle change of approximately 180 degrees, though with practice we tend to 'bend' the cast somewhat (sacrificing a little efficiency), by pushing the rod tip through a slight curve, so as to achieve more of a 140-degree change of direction, 'positioning' cast. This is a very simple and effective cast, used a great deal with French leader and long-range nymphing techniques on the river, and is

The immensely useful constant tension cast (in river nymph fishing)

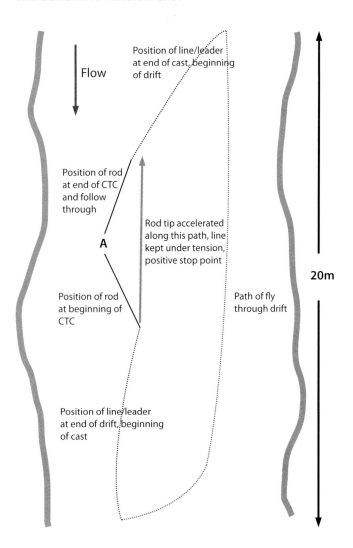

THE CONSTANT TENSION CAST

Flow

Position of line/leader at end of cast, beginning of drift

Position of rod at end of CTC and follow through

A

Rod tip accelerated along this path, line kept under tension, positive stop point

Position of rod at beginning of CTC

Path of fly through drift

20m

Position of line/leader at end of drift, beginning of cast

An unconventional approach in every sense: magnificent wild rainbow from a catchment lake in the Alps

eminently suitable for any leader-to-hand approach with nymph. It is just as easy with the latter as it is with fly line, and actually results in a consistently softer touchdown and low disturbance value.

It is with dry fly, however, that the most exciting casting discoveries are made. Several people have told me that this is the most daunting aspect of it all, like a writer bursting with ideas, but faced with the dreaded white paper scare; the empty page. Where does one start? Once you have started the process; have set down the first words, it all unfolds. None of us is alone. We fly-fishers share the journey, so you should know that we all make the mistakes, all share the struggle of going through casting and presentation issues. Only in this way do we develop as individuals and the sport develops as a whole. I will not pretend that the overhead cast with a presentation leader-to-hand will be as easy as fly line delivery for the new exponent, who will not learn it so quickly. It is essential that before we cast without a fly line we have become proficient (at the least) with low AFTMA-rated fly lines, ideally #2 and #3 weights. From this point, we find that we have already laid the foundations in the principles of casting fairly low masses and this is very good, indeed essential, preparation for dealing with the casting of ultra-low-mass leader-only rigs (including fixed line).

The fundamental principles of overhead casting with a fly line are entirely consistent with casting with a leader-to-hand. It is all a matter of momentum, which is the product of mass and speed (strictly, velocity). With a fly line, mass is comparatively high, so line speed is slow. There is much less mass in a presentation leader, so the speed, on the power stroke, must be higher. And this is the main difference. We still must observe the high stop points, classically referred to as 1 o'clock on the back cast and 10 o'clock on the fore cast. We must still pause on the back cast, but much longer, waiting for the leader to unfold, to give us enough mass to load the rod on the fast power stroke. Similarly, we must pause long on the forward stop point during the 'follow through' and delivery. The leader and fly follow the rod point exactly as does a fly line; this is inescapable physics, and the first pitfall is a profound loss of accuracy because the caster loses control, or becomes a bit wayward during the power stroke. With the very soft rods we are using, the rod tip can often dip on the stop points and throw the line off track. This is one of the sources of inaccuracy and can only be ironed out with practice – by having a particularly high stop point. Another is not compensating enough for the effect of wind, and this comes down to those long pauses after the power stroke. The light leader is more affected by the wind than a faster-moving and heavier fly line – its energy is rapidly dissipated and it will then simply be blown off track unless the angler has compensated for this during the power stroke. Again, one learns how to manage these subtle, but crucial, differences – it is only a matter of practice.

We quickly find that a side cast is often preferable to an overhead. The trajectory of the side cast is more comfortable and accurate for most practitioners, when putting in the fast power stroke. This has the added advantage of keeping the rod and leader low, off the skyline, and avoids spooking the fish; all part of the minimal disturbance approach.

Moreover, because of the low mass of these leaders, they do not sag as much as weightier fly lines during the pause, and so avoid ensnaring bank-side foliage or 'ticking' the water behind the caster. Small points perhaps, but actually they make a huge difference out on the river.

The wind is significant in all casting, including leader-to-hand. I had initially imagined that it would be a major constraint, perhaps even limiting use of the approach to calm conditions, or an upstream wind. In practice, however, I soon discovered that flat calm is not ideal; in fact it is about as problematic as the other extreme of a strong wind. Any sort of breeze in between offers no issue at all, particularly if it is generally upstream, once the fundamentals of leader-to-hand casting have been mastered. Indeed, we learn to use the wind, and a gentle side wind can be a delight. The crucial aspect which determines accuracy is making due allowance for the direction and strength of any breeze. In such conditions we find that we actually 'float' the leader across the wind. Immediately after the stop point has been reached the leader has the highest momentum, but this very quickly dissipates. As it turns over, the breeze carries it, like a kite's string. This is another reason why the side cast is often preferable to the overhead, because with the former there is less vertical distance for leader, tippet and fly to travel, and thus be blown off course. It is, in any case, a matter of compensation, and timing, with due deference to the prevailing wind conditions (as well as the range and angle of attack to the fish).

Another water where the competitive approach coincided with developments in leader-to-hand: lovely channels of water crowfoot on the Welsh Dee at Maelor

Upland river where either double nymph or dry fly with leader-to-hand defines the perfect approach: incredibly productive wild trout waters on The Tees above High Force

There are very few conditions on the river when I would nowadays prefer to be using a fly line. This is, however, fishing dry fly, with some nymph and spider, exclusively with #2 and #3 weight rods, and 5:5 and 6:4 tenkara rods. There are rivers where such rods would simply not be appropriate, mostly because of very powerful flows or a high average size of trout, including sea-trout and steelhead. Twice in 2011, I hooked very large trout; one on the Eden at Winderwath – actually, I believe, the biggest brown trout I have ever hooked on a river – and the other on the Sava in Slovenia; a rainbow in the region of 4.5 kilograms in weight in a strong flow. On both occasions I was utterly powerless to do anything other than hold on, rod tip held high, while these great fish just swam away with that indomitable surge of power that truly big trout possess. The only solace to their eventual loss was that the hook-holds gave, so I did not have the added ignominy of a break, in which case a more powerful rod would have made no difference; indeed the hook-hold would have given way even sooner. Many will suggest that it is irresponsible to fish with such soft tackle when the quarry might be expected to be so large, but this is not my experience. I believe that very fine tippets should not be used when big fish are targeted, but soft rods are another matter.

Many river anglers, and a growing cohort of still-water exponents, prefer rods with a low line-rating, believing that trout are aggravated and alarmed by the impact felt against a stiffer, casting-orientated rod. Fish can usually be calmed much more quickly by the softer touch of a #2 or #3 weight. The presentation leader also has a role in this context. When a fish runs, at speed, the drag of a fly line through the water is often too much for even fairly substantial tippets, and for the fragility of the hook-hold, particularly with fine wire dry-fly hooks. There is much less drag against the 0.47 mm copolymer of a leader (similar to a low-diameter silk line) and this helps considerably in gaining the edge over big trout; again it might seem a small point, but it certainly feels important when off-the-normal-scale trout are hooked. Since my emphasis on presentation-orientated leader-to-hand has developed, encounters with large specimen trout and grayling have increased, which is telling in itself – it is a direct consequence of both the improved presentation and the minimal disturbance. In the context of the earlier point about losing fish, the actual number of fish successfully brought to hand has also increased.

Contrast again, and a more difficult target than even large grayling: a dace from the San on caddis-style plume tip, leader-only

Given a soft action rod at very short range, up to about 6 metres, the casting process is trivial, with or without fly line. There is then a relative 'dead zone' with leader-to-hand, up to about 10 metres, when there is insufficient leader in flight to load the rod properly. This is where the angler must put in a particularly fast power stroke in order to achieve this loading and subsequent turn-over of a low-mass fly. The casting process actually improves at longer range – beyond the good control range of fly line. At extensions of a presentation leader greater than 10 metres, the loading is adequate, even on a #3 weight rod (better still on a #2), and the casting is as with a low-rated fly line, but every time with superior touchdown and that low interaction of leader and water surface.

Whether fishing the nymph or dry fly it is crucial to keep the leader afloat. This is why copolymer, rather than (higher density) fluorocarbon is used in the running and tapered sections. It is also the main reason why a braided monofilament or furled horsehair section is incorporated between tippet and leader. This section takes grease very well (a single application lasts all day) and serves the dual purpose of keeping it afloat and adding a little (but noticeably) to the casting mass (remember the weight-forward profile concept). The need to keep the leader afloat cannot be over-stressed. If it drowns it destroys presentation, just as a sinking fly line tip does, while also being noisy on the lift-off during re-casting, thereby spoiling the disturbance-free nature which is one of the fundamental, key attributes of a leader-only approach. Indeed, minimal disturbance, and superior presentation and control, are in combination the driving force of the entire leader-to-hand approach. As far back in my fishing life as I can remember, I have used the red labelled Mucilin (non-silicon) for leader and line application. It is the perfect material for dressing a presentation leader, including the braid or furled section. That said, you can use butter, margarine, lip salve or all manner of oils and greases you might have with you. The important thing is to keep that leader afloat, because if you do not, then your desire for improved presentation is futile and it would be far better to use fly line (the tip of which should also be greased).

Tenkara advocates generally recommend either furled materials or level fluorocarbon for the bulk sections of their leaders, but one of the key differences between leader-to-hand and tenkara is that, in the latter, all of the leader (and often the tippet) is in the air, with no contact with the water, and therefore no sinking and the subsequent spoiling of presentation. With leader-to-hand, beyond 6-metre range, the braid and tippet is on the water, and beyond 10 metres a substantial length of the leader is also laid on the surface.

Leader-to-hand will not make conventional fly lines obsolete, silk or polymer. It should, though, precipitate further development of these materials, and is actually beginning to have this affect in the form of ultra-light fly lines with improved presentation characteristics at short to medium range, such as the triple 0 rated line from Rio. What the leader-only approach has shown us is that there is considerable scope for improving presentation, and control, at both short range and medium range (6–18 metres) on the river, with nymph and dry-fly techniques. Some will go further, discovering the simply extraordinary delicacy and elegance that are possible, and even extending the scope away from ideal conditions (of a gentle upstream wind) to find that there are, in fact,

remarkably few limitations. Of course, the fly line, with its supple structure and signifi-cant mass, will always be the easier tool for the casting process, with accuracy, but then it is up to leader-to-hand exponents to improve our casting ability to the extent that we overcome such problems until they are no longer limitations. Then we really discover the breathtaking merits of the presentation leader-only system.

Except … many of us tend to be drawn back to silk and the very lightweight polymer lines because of their delightful versatility, including the rather nicer feel (than monofil-ament) in the hand and fingers. In fact and in practice, there is something of a renaissance for these low-mass lines, because in several ways they represent a workable compromise between the conventional mass and casting experience of a heavier polymer fly line and the extreme of the leader-to-hand. They satisfy the traditionalist as much as the presen-tation-orientated adventurer on the river. Moreover, there is an international flavour to the silk lines in that they are as popular with the traditionalist Englishman as the pres-entation-obsessed Frenchman, and their increased utilization is seen as far afield as the Antipodes and North America. We observe, even, an application in tenkara, where the low diameter and mass of ultra-fine, furled silk or horsehair lines makes them ideal for purpose, particularly as they have zero memory, which is a problem with monofilament-style leaders. Even the modern polymer fly line in low AFTMA ratings can be hugely improved by the careful deployment of suitable leaders, particularly in the butt section.

The country with the clearest water in Europe, where the value of leader-only techniques are enhanced: an alpine meadow below Triglav in Slovenia

Idyllic alpine flow, where the long leader allows a short-range approach to wild fish

For the last year prior to writing this I have taken to using a short horsehair furl (three or four strand) for silk lines and #2 and #3 weight double-taper floaters. The stiffness of horsehair, which yields good translational kinetic energy (finally, turn-over) coupled with its excellence in floating when greased leads to my choice of this material (as in the presentation leader furled section).

Leader-only techniques have developed alongside the Japanese fixed line technique which is similarly such a beautifully simple, minimalistic and disturbance-free method. I believe that leader-to-hand is where West meets East: a hybrid, between Western-style fly-fishing involving a fly reel, and the Eastern fixed line tenkara. There is currently a lot of debate, and controversy, surrounding these parallel approaches, and comparison between the two. Once escaped from the entrapment of traditional bigotry, all this is entirely healthy. Although my own background is in reel-based, leader-only and light fly line techniques, I also delight in tenkara. These approaches share many virtues, at the core of which are minimal disturbance and supreme presentation, which for an increasing number of us are the most important aspects of the sport. Indeed, with dry fly at short range (up to 10 metres), I believe that tenkara actually has a presentation edge over leader-to-hand, though there are problems with subsequent control and particularly dealing with a hooked fish, which give the reel-based approach an advantage.

The objections to both, however, stem from the lack of fly line, which many Western fly-fishers question (irrationally), and also the nonsensical claims that both are for small fish only, at short range. This is simply not the case. As outlined above, the softness of the rod for both approaches actually helps with subduing or dealing with large fish. The only real exception is for large trout which might run, fast, when bolting. Here, the fly reel performs its greatest service to us, yielding line, while the fixed line fisherman has no option other than to use his feet. There is a saying in tenkara: 'When a big fish runs, you run.' This should not be seen as an untoward fault or limitation of the method, however. In practice I recall very few fish that have been lost as a result of the fixed line, though one admits to the necessity of some deft footwork and wading technique in order to follow large running fish. The worst situation is when a fish is hooked in shallow water on the near bank and decides to bolt out into deeper water across a broad river. Such a fish is very difficult to turn around and because of the deep water we cannot follow it. In order to protect the rod from breakage, a fine tippet is essential, and frankly this is the only real issue that sometimes makes tenkara inappropriate on big trout rivers (or lakes), because it is irresponsible to break, leaving fly and tippet in a fish.

Another issue is the common situation of having a leader and tippet longer than the rod. The result is that a hooked fish, even a small one, cannot be netted or brought to hand

The beautiful and strange markings of an alpine trout, caught with fixed line (tenkara) and plume tip

Wild rainbow from the Savinja: the perfect 'scale' of fishing for tenkara

as comfortably as in the Western-style by-line retrieval. We could, of course, use a long-handled landing net in such situations, but as all river anglers know, these are extremely cumbersome, and completely ruin any attempt at minimalism or a stealthy approach. We thus have to resort either to beaching fish or to a mixture of extreme arm-stretching and grasping the line and tippet in order to bring the fish close enough to deal with – altogether an ungainly process and one which is prone to accident such as tippet-cut fingers or breakage.

Tenkara is perhaps best-suited to comparatively small fish and the small river, but should not be dismissed for medium to large rivers. For the pack-rod fisherman wandering among river valleys and upland streams, this minimalistic approach is outstanding. It is immensely satisfying to exist in a fly-fishing sense with such a sparse amount of equipment; the telescopic rod, fixed line, a spool of tippet and a dozen flies, and very little else in the way of peripheral tackle. Indeed the liberation of one's natural hunter soul is unsurpassed, even by leader-to-hand.

There will always be doubters and bigots, and perhaps most of us are subject to these traits from time to time, but this being the case, we are losing out enormously by closing down our horizons and being satisfied with the mediocre in what should be an enthrallingly expansive sport. At the heart of it all is, I think, the grail of improved presentation with minimal disturbance. It might be somewhere out on 'the other side of the water', in a conventional sense, and even a stage on from international-level competitive fishing; but all this, too, is for many of us not so much a dark art as a giant leap in the natural evolution of fly-fishing.

I am now in the region of 3,500 fish into leader-to-hand technique, which includes tenkara. I am utterly overwhelmed by the minimalistic and *minimal disturbance* approach to fly-fishing, quite apart from its enormous effectiveness. This has been achieved since 2008, during which time I have increasingly drawn away from the Western line-based approach, with the limited exception of horsehair-tipped, low-mass fly lines in certain circumstances. I admit to this being river-centred, though with applications on still waters. I have absolutely no time whatsoever for those who try to undermine this exquisite approach, for whatever reason. They are simply wrong, ensnared by bigotry and prescribed doctrine. The level of presentation possible with any leader-only technique simply exceeds what is possible in the 'traditional' Western style.

I think there is a Tao in fly-fishing, a unification of ideas and practice: what we in the Western world will recognize as an advanced state of technical development, while in the East, perhaps, it will be seen as a more instinctive or holistic approach. In this sport there is the common ground of presentation: what I have described as a fish-orientated approach, rather than the easy reliance on whatever fly-fishing school has nurtured us. We can escape this, and find a liberation that is absolute freedom to express ourselves and enjoy our own approach without constraints.

CHAPTER FOUR

Presentation Flies

Presentation by design ...

I have laboured the need for being fish-orientated in our thinking if we are to produce effective flies, via the consideration of presentation. It was Arthur Cove who told me: 'Any old bit of carpet wrapped around a hook will catch a trout, it's the behaviour of the fly that matters.' Although he was being typically provocative in order to make the point, I happen to know that Arthur put considerable thought into the design of his flies to the extent that he could alter their 'behaviour' to meet particular needs, always geared to presentation.

There are three main schools of thought concerning trout and grayling flies. There is the aim of exact imitation and another for the attainment of general impression of size and

Bibio snatcher-style: a contemporary wet fly for still-water use

shape (GISS), while the third is focused on the tying of flies with certain trigger points or by prescription, relying on successful designs handed down through the years; for example, traditional wet flies. I think that most of us subscribe to the third category in our early years, but then gradually become more interested in imitative qualities. Some go on to produce outstanding examples of imitation, but for most, GISS is as close to imitation as we choose to go, and with good reason. Fly-tying is a craft, and as such has varying impact on the business of actually catching fish. We have only to look at the incredible intricacy of a fully dressed traditional salmon fly, or the spookily life-like 'caricatures' of various trout food-forms that are produced by expert fly-tiers the world over, to appreciate this.

Lake trout on the bibio snatcher

The delightful efficacy of the simplest flies: wild lake trout on the Diawl Bach

What interests most of us is that nebulous centre ground, where our flies have some imitative features, as well as other triggers, and yield dynamic qualities that make them most suitable for practical fishing purpose. GISS describes some of it, but colour should be added and, crucially, that most difficult concept of all to learn, and to build in – the behaviour of the fly on the surface or in the water column. Only in very simple terms, for example, is a dry fly one which sits *on* the surface. There are many ways in which a dry fly interacts with the surface, as does a live invertebrate. So, imitation is not just how a fly looks in a static, visual sense, but how it moves; its dynamics.

Presentation is vastly affected by matters other than the fly itself, but the more we fish and the more we tie flies for fishing purpose, the more we discover that the built-in characteristics of the fly itself can be an important part of the equation. Fly-fishing is

The most universally adaptable nymph pattern of all: wild trout on the tungsten beaded PTN

much less about the fly rod, and still less the fly line; it is about the fly itself, however it is delivered (recall the definition set out in the introduction). Most very experienced fly-fishers have a limited number of patterns. This is partly to do with our learning to choose certain types of water, or circumstances and conditions, with which we are most comfortable, and partly because we make discoveries about common features of most prevalent food-forms that can be built into our flies, remarkably consistently, thus reducing the number of different patterns that we actually need.

My great friend Lawrence Greasley often teases me about my predilection for the CDC plume tip: 'Doesn't choosing a fly become boring for you?' Well, it is not boring in the least. It might, at most, be an over-reliance on a single pattern: simply because it is so effective, it might actually reduce my need and will to explore. For much of the year, the choice is easy in the form of this generic dry pattern. There is enough going on out there, enough to consider, without having to fuss about fly choice. I like to reduce the variables to a minimum. It comes of being a scientist, I suppose. Lawrence also says, following on from his statement above concerning my 'dependence' on the plume tip, that this chapter of the book will be very short, but it isn't! We experiment with numerous tying techniques and development of patterns: we discover more about our environment and our pursuit that way, and over the years one learns to exist with a very few fly patterns. On the river, the plume tip is right at the top of the list, and the Sawyer-style PTN, or variants thereof, are essential in the nymph category, but beyond that the list dwindles away rapidly into patterns that have limited or occasional use for particular circumstances. It is not, there-fore, a choice between patterns, so much as a choice of size, and, in the case of the nymphs, their weighting and other dynamic considerations. I have uncomfortable memo-ries of earlier years when it was not always so. I remember having numerous fly boxes, all crammed with a multitude of patterns and sizes, and know that most of them were never used. There were always areas of a box which were used constantly and replaced, while the majority were just there, as wallpaper or decoration.

For me, the most influential book on fly-fishing ever written was *Nymphs and the Trout*, by Frank Sawyer, the two most enthralling chapters being 3 and 4, in which the design of nymphs in dynamic terms is described in detail. I read this book back in the 1970s, auspiciously during the same period in which I was fishing with Arthur Cove at Grafham and other East Anglian waters. Perhaps the strongest understanding that came across was the behaviour of nymphs in the water column, and in the act of eclosion, and how each man built characteristics into his flies to best simulate the naturals. Although Sawyer was primarily interested in the nymphs of the Ephemeroptera on English chalk streams, while Cove was very much focused on the pupae of Chironomidae species, the fundamental principles were common to both. Interestingly, they both abandoned the traditional doctrine regarding fly design and approached the problem from the viewpoint of the trout, which I believe is the only sensible way of finding a solution. Long observa-tion of the nymphs (and to an extent the relevant adults), and the way that trout fed on them, allowed both men powerful insight.

I remember, after we met one evening on the north bank of Grafham to find swarms of grousewing caddis on the water, Arthur saying to me: 'When you come down to the shore and find all these caddis about, if you see a single buzzer, put a buzzer on (by which he meant either a black spider or a PTN), and if you don't see a buzzer, then still put one on!' Again, typical Cove and the message was clear: *trout will always focus on the easy targets*, the most vulnerable state of their various food-forms. Buzzers (or their pupal stage) are much more vulnerable than caddis. If fish have a choice between the two, they will not turn down the easy alternative. The same applies to the river, in my experience, except that here the Chironomidae are mostly replaced by the Ephemeroptera (olives), these favoured food-forms of both trout and grayling being comparatively slow-moving and soft targets, particularly when in the surface film. Of course, readers might be surprised at this, knowing how important the various caddis species are as food-forms. All Cove was suggesting, as I am repeating here, is that if there is a choice, the easier targets will be preferentially taken. Think of all those northern rivers where caddis are prevalent: here they are at the top of the menu. It is on rivers which also have strong populations of various olives that the fly-angler is generally better off with imitations of the latter.

When I first visited the magnificent San River, in Poland, I went expecting the caddis to dominate the fishing approach because the San was, and is, known as a classic caddis river. What I found, however, reinforced in all the subsequent visits through the years, were olive hatches that were breathtaking, particularly in the summer months, culminating in the super-prolific blue-winged olive hatches in the autumn. The caddis are there, right enough, in great diversity and abundance; but the olives are always fed upon by the trout and grayling, often selectively, even when good numbers of caddis are active. It was the San, every bit as much as the Eden, where I fine-tuned my CDC plume tip, and this is primarily a generic olive dun imitation (while also being passable in terms of GISS for a hatching midge).

Perfection in dry fly: the quill plume tip (note the Coq de Leon tail)

The main point of all this is that we need to identify the prime target prey item and to understand its behaviour – its habit within its environment – and then to build our artificials to best simulate this. The fish observe their prey better than we do, so we must attempt to see the flies from the fish's viewpoint. Sawyer wrote: 'Perhaps you will have noted the phrases I have used to convey the fact that the patterns have been constructed from what I think is the view of the fish, not that of the human.' I think this is at the very core of fly-fishing (or tying) for trout and grayling, and is certainly the driver for my interpretations of the flies I tie and use.

Let us start with the single most important fly of all, the plume tip. As mentioned, this is a generic, ephemerid emerger or dun imitation (and, at a push, a spinner too). There are several variations, but the central theme is consistent. The *core pattern* is dressed as described below on the outstanding Tiemco 103BL in sizes 21, 19 and 17. This hook is the perfect compromise between fine wire (essential for a lightly dressed dry pattern) and strength (resistance to bending or breaking), with an appropriate shape, together with proven hooking and holding performance. I use this hook for almost all my dry flies, other than a few still-water patterns such as the hopper.

Benecchi Ghost thread is wound as an underbody from eye to bend. Two strands of heron primary or secondary feather are tied in by the tips. The thread is wound back to just short of the eye. One or two CDC plume tips are tied in facing forward, shuttlecock style. The stubs are fixed by several turns of thread and then trimmed flush. This process forms a slight, but distinct, swelling for the thorax region of the fly. The heron herl is wound almost up to the base of the CDC and fixed into place with thread. The thread is then wound with two very open turns to the bend and then returned, again with just two turns, to the thorax. This can only be done with very fine thread such as Ghost. Its purpose is to prevent the feather fibre unwinding in the event of being cut by a trout's teeth: it should be invisible. The thorax consists of a little dubbed CDC (taken from the discarded butts of the plume tips). This adds improved buoyancy and also a lovely effect as if of legs struggling free of the nymphal shuck. With the thread then passed to the eye side of the

My most successful pattern ever: the heron herl plume tip

CDC plume tips, a whip finish, or preferably a double whip finish, is executed both to finish the fly and also to partially lift the wing out of the shuttlecock position, even to fully upright.

Ghost thread is a wonderful material; essentially ultra-fine nylon monofilament, it is strong for its diameter while being invisible, and even with multiple turns does not build in overmuch bulk to a fly. It takes some getting used to, not taking a dubbing quite so readily as a multi-strand thread, but one learns to make up for any problematical issues like this by exploiting its benefits.

The plume tip is a blend of several other patterns in a similar vein. It is an evolution, with many virtues, quite apart from its fish-attracting properties. It is perfect for the tying which I enjoy the most: speed tying. I have always hated labouring on a fly with intricate tying techniques and too many materials – I like to minimize both. In so doing, and exploiting the experience of thousands of trout and grayling to the dry fly, I believe this evolutionary process is pretty near the climax state. I can be on any European river and not really have to think too much about what might be hatching. If the fish are focused on the surface, then the plume tip is very rarely refused. The starting condition is usually a 19, and if that is rejected I go to the 21, unless there is a very powerful flow, or substantial depth (greater than about a metre).

CDC itself is a fantastic material for those who fish the dry fly. I don't think there will ever be a material, either natural or synthetic, which will compare to it for the general representation of invertebrate wings. Contrary to popular belief, it does not float because of the oils it contains, but because of its delicate, filigree structure. It is essential that it is kept dry, and *not* oiled. If it becomes wet (or oiled), it is useless. It is very easy to manage CDC, however, and this simply involves drying it on cotton, which is very absorbent. Tied as above, the fly can be held firmly between forefinger and thumb so that only the CDC wing is exposed. This should then be rubbed vigorously on cotton (I always wear a cotton shirt for the purpose) until the original dry structure is restored. The whole practice takes perhaps fifteen seconds and, by repeating when necessary, one can use the same fly all day. It is remarkably robust.

In the early days of perfecting the plume tip, for competition use, I used to test how many fish I could catch on the same fly before it was ruined. My record was on the San River, with a three-hour catch of more than fifty grayling. I even put on the same fly the following day and continued catching! Those who claim that CDC produces 'one-fish flies' simply do not manage it properly or tie it in properly in the first place. Moreover, the use

of amadou or even silica powder floatant material, while also effective, is unnecessary. All that is really required is dry cotton. The only difficult conditions for CDC are during heavy rain, particularly when the fingers become wet –or worse, your cotton does! One little tip to help here: fast, almost whip-like, false casting, while rather inelegant, has the effect of blowing water off a fly in the form of a fine spray. Indeed, even after the cotton drying process outlined, I frequently use rapid false casting to blow any last vestige of water off the fly before repositioning for another drift. The plume tip is at its very best when all the CDC is in the air, above the surface, 'high and dry' as it were.

On the heron herl plume tip

I should stress the use of only the tips of the CDC feathers, or plumes. Formerly, I tried to maximize the CDC by stripping the flues from the quill of larger plumes and using this, but the final wing effect is poor. *The plume tips are what are required*; a single in the 21 (or smaller), and a pair (ideally placed concave to concave) for the 19 and 17. The best are from the mallard, though I have used other species of duck and even goose. If you find that it looks bulky on the size of fly you are tying, then it simply is. The aim is for a delicate structure, as in the wings of Ephemeridae we are imitating.

I am so comfortable with this core pattern plume tip. It is with me everywhere, on any river I visit, and is my 'go to' dry fly. Yes, I might see those caddis on the water, or other non-ephemerid species, but the plume tip never lets me down. I always remember Arthur's words about the most vulnerable targets, and the dead-drifting plume tip represents just

San trout on the plume tip

that. In recent years I have discovered many rivers where midges (Chironomidae) are far more significant food-forms than we had previously suspected, and this plume tip is ideal for fish feeding on these species as well. Managed as above, it has exactly the attitude on the water's surface that we want, with the hook point and bend, and perhaps a little body, sitting in and below the film, with the thorax of straggling CDC a chaos in the film itself, and the wing dry in the air above. So, we dress it sparsely, manage it by keeping it utterly dry, place it to dead drift, and never take our eyes off it throughout that drift. Lose sight of the fly and it can be difficult to find again, and if you cannot see your dry fly, your confidence is lost and every time that happens is a wasted drift. If you have difficulty seeing the fly touch down because of inclement light conditions, then shift your angle and/or range and reposition the cast: you need to be able to place the fly accurately, visually picking it out from the start, and manage it throughout the drift so as to maintain contact. That, primarily, is good dry-fly technique.

The plume tip described was developed from one which had a body of dubbed mole fur on yellow thread. This was (and is) also a superb pattern, with a lovely dark olive effect when wet, but thread and mole fur are a little difficult to keep dry and tend to sink the fly too quickly (and bed down too deeply into the film). I still find mole fur versions of the plume tip in old fly boxes, and am happy to use them, but I do notice that long-term buoyancy is a little compromised. Also, this earlier version was tailed, either with micro-fibbets

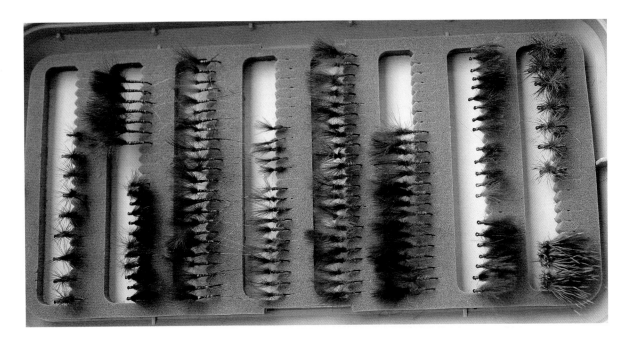

or a coarse hair such as badger. The tail actually changes the attitude of the fly on the surface significantly, because a split tail has enough surface tension to suspend the fly along the axis of the tail and the body of the hook. Tails as such are also reasonably representative of those of ephemerid duns and spinners.

During the early years of this century I discovered Coq de Leon (CDL), of course from the French, Spanish and Italian river masters who had already long exploited this beautiful feather in their dry flies, most usually with CDC. I had always disliked the thickness of animal hair or synthetic fibbets on the smaller, delicate dry flies, such as the plume tip. These are simply too thick when compared with the setae of duns up to the size of, say, a medium olive or a large dark olive. They seemed only in proper proportion when dressed on larger patterns such as *danica* mayflies, or olive uprights. A tail tied with such materials is out of proportion with the rest of the fly and tends to dominate the visual effect. In many cases this might be a valuable trigger, so may not be a problem; but nonetheless it jarred with me for many years before my discovery of CDL, which provides a stiff fibre that is very thin – close to the thickness of dun and spinner tails. These feathers are also beautifully mottled, so closely resembling the setae of the March brown or brook dun, for example.

During this same period, I also began to use stripped peacock quill in order to better represent the segmented abdomen of olives (and midges). When wound over a pale thread underbody, the overall colour effect can be manipulated. At the time I used the natural quill mostly over yellow Pearsall's Gossamer and this gave a good general olive effect. More recently I often opt for a yellow dyed stripped quill, still over the yellow thread, and the olive colouration is more pronounced.

My river selection of dries: plume tips with a few Mullers and Oppos

There is a neat and quick way of tying in the tails, shown to me by Pat Stevens, who is one of the most skilled all-round fly-tiers I have ever known. When winding the thread underbody, leave a short tag at the bend. Tie in two CDL strands and bed in with perhaps four turns of thread. If you lift the CDL it then tends to split. This split is fixed into place, and exaggerated, by bringing the tag up between the strands and bedding down along the hook shank. The CDC is then tied into place, as in the heron herl version above. The quill is then wound from the tail right up to the wing, with a single turn taken in front of the wing (to the eye side) where it is immediately whip-finished. This has the effect of cocking the wing in the upright position.

This variant is almost as quick as the heron herl version to tie, with the slowest process being the setting of the tail. I usually tie in the CDL rather long (about twice body length), as are the setae of spinners rather than duns. As such they further aid the buoyancy of the fly, sitting it flat on the surface film, and also provide a trigger feature. One can never know, of course, but the beautifully pronounced segmentation effect of the quill body is probably a further trigger. I often catch myself thinking that if I were a trout, watching one of these quill plume tips dead-drifting down the feed lane, I would take it for sure. The combination of CDC plumes, quill and CDL tail yields the perfect impression of the soft target of a sub-imago or imago on the surface. I have noticed that some tiers spend a lot of time making sure the tail is in perfect proportion to the body (for either the dun or the spinner) and also nicely, evenly split; but I do not worry about this. Sometimes the tails, though of even length, are fixed at rather extreme angles to the body, even standing out at 90 degrees. As such, they represent the accidents in nature, which are very common in a hatch, and perhaps these become the easiest targets of all.

Plume tips are best fished singly; that is to say that they are not duo flies. They will not support the mass of even an un-ballasted nymph and such will ruin their presentation. They are approach-independent and can be fished with conventional fly line, tenkara fixed line or leader-to-hand (my first tenkara-caught trout was on a yellow quill plume tip). Although developed for river use, the plume tips give perfectly good service on the lake where, after all, we have numerous ephemerid species such as lake and pond olives, and caenis, as well as the ubiquitous midges, for which the heron herl variants are representatively ideal.

One can become over-prescriptive when it comes to fly-dressing, and having something slightly 'different' in a fly can destroy confidence in it; but this is almost always simply an insecurity. Of course, there are the special nature and characteristics of certain materials like CDC, CDL or stripped quill, perhaps even heron herl, but so far as the last-named is concerned, I have used cock pheasant tail, mole fur or variously coloured sheep wools (particularly olive and black) as perfectly good, and often preferred, alternatives. In fact, I had not used heron herl at all until introduced to this material in the 1990s by my team-mate and godfather to my son, John Lindsey. Until then I had a leaning towards pheasant tail and lamb's wool for the bodies of dry flies (and seal fur for hoppers). Today, if I had no quill or heron herl, it would not trouble me in the least to revert to pheasant tail, tied-in exactly as described for the heron herl plume tip, above.

San tailwater trout on the plume tip

So, the plume tip in the heron herl and quill forms completely dominates my dry-fly selection, especially on the river, rendering all other dry patterns for occasional use only. These include the F-fly style of tying-in CDC – flat over the back – with all other materials and tying features as in the plume tip version. CDC tied in this way, however, completely changes the form of the fly into a caddis-like or hatched midge profile, and this is indeed the intention. Also, if black sheep wool, or black feather fibre (such as black cock pheasant tail, or crow), is substituted for heron herl, then we have excellent representation of the black gnat and, in the larger size (17), of the hawthorn. For the latter, I use very coarse sheep wool (from the sheep on the Pennines hereabouts) which, when loosely dubbed, gives a pronounced leg effect. Black gnats should never be underestimated as important food-forms for both trout and grayling. Many a time in the late spring and early summer, in the absence of a strong hatch of one or other of the Ephemeroptera, I have found fish completely preoccupied with gnats, even though these can be difficult to see on the surface because they sit so low to the film. Like any dun emerger, or most windfalls, black gnats represent easy targets for the fish.

For imitations of the small midges of the river, which are hugely underrated food-forms, the plume tip is simplified further on sub-size 20/21 hooks. Choice of hook is important (as in all fly design), as is the use of Ghost thread, or very fine thread of 12/0 maximum. The Varivas Ultra Midge 2300 is excellent, though perhaps just a little too fine

The championship caddis

in the wire and is also micro-barbed. These are available right down to size 30. I have never, however, found a situation which necessitates such a small fly and have managed to cover such situations with a 26 or larger; most commonly a 22. For this purpose the Varivas 2200BL curved shank hook or the TMC 100 are excellent. The dressing itself involves only the thread and a single CDC plume, which is tied in with the tip facing away from the hook eye, over the bend. This is then pulled up over the back of the fly and tied in at the head so that the plume tip is now facing over the eye, shuttlecock-style, and about equal to the overall body length. Bringing the thread between eye and plume tip, the wing is then partially cocked while a double whip finish completes the process. This simplicity and minimalism produces excellent GISS for the various small midge species.

A possible improvement involves the use of pearl mylar wound from the bend right up to the thorax. The effect is very much of the silvering that occurs as midge species are in the act of ecdysis, as the emerger prepares to shrug free of the shuck. Again, this might be an unnecessary embellishment, and I cannot honestly say that this version is any more effective than the former, although visually, to the angler, the effect of realism is certainly enhanced. If this leads to greater confidence in the pattern, then so be it.

While the flat-over-the-back style of heron herl plume tip is perfectly good as a general representation of the smaller caddis (and midge), the following has been an outstanding generic pattern for the larger caddis. Dubbed hare fur replaces the heron herl body and the wing is made more robust with deer hair. On a size 15 TMC 103BL, an underbody of thread is laid from eye to bend (again, the yellow Pearsall's Gossamer is good, but in any case not too fine a thread should be used, or there will be problems in tying-in the deer hair later, because fine, taut threads cut through deer hair fibres. The hare fur is dubbed and wound from bend to thorax region where a pair of CDC plume tips are tied in, flat over the back. A bunch of deer (or elk) hair is tied in over the CDC and kept reasonably tight (rather than splayed) over the back. Several turns of thread, gradually tightening towards the eye, should be made here. The butts of the deer hair are now trimmed so that there is a little stub of this exposed, sticking out over the hook eye. Some of the waste CDC is dubbed in to cover the thread at the head (or this can be replaced with hare fur). An excellent substitute for hare fur is squirrel, which is spikier and certainly adds to the buoyancy of the fly, when greased lightly.

Tied in the form above this pattern has been excellent for caddis feeders. You can play around with the materials to an extent, while still maintaining the profile of a caddis. For

Fished on duo rig: Eden trout on the Oppo

instance, a short tag of orange or green wool (lovely in a closed-end plait) can be added to simulate the egg sac. In fact, the orange-tailed version came into being in World and European *FIPS* Championships, strangely simultaneously in almost exactly the same form from various teams, and became known as the championship caddis. This is a particularly buoyant fly and as such it has great use for lively, bouncy water – what my Australian friends refer to as 'gnarly' water. It is not easily drowned and fish can pick it out. While a dead drift is nearly always the best option, one can get away with a bit of movement with this fly. Newly hatched caddis, or the egg layers, often cause quite a lot of disturbance on the surface. The buoyancy and bulk of this pattern also make it very good as a duo fly, because it will support up to a 2.4 mm tungsten-beaded nymph, or even one a little heavier. For this purpose, however, or for particularly lively water, it is worth considering replacing the CDC with an off-white polypropylene yarn, which takes a light oil and remains buoyant for prolonged use with no more treatment than occasional drying. For smoother water, and as a singleton dry fly, I would opt for CDC every time.

For duo use, however, I designed the Oppo, the orange polypropylene-winged paradun. This pattern has the combination of buoyancy and excellent visibility (for the angler) in the form of the orange wing post. In the larger sizes it can support a reasonably heavy nymph, or even two of these in the trio style (dry and two nymphs). As a 19 or 21 it is a good dry pattern accompanying a micro-nymph. The Oppo is rather of the Klinkhammer

Brown trout on the Oppo

style, sharing similar buoyancy, though not quite so bulky. While the Klinkhammer is obviously very popular, justifiably so, I was always suspicious of this pattern because I found its bulk a problem on smooth water – with frequent rejections particularly by big grayling – and also the hook that this fly is usually tied on commercially is simply awful in terms of hooking and holding ability. The fly improves if one is careful with hook selection. At the outset I used the Fulling Mill all-purpose fine wire barbless for the Oppo. Initially, also, I set in a small kink one-third down the shank from the hook eye, with needle-nose pliers, in order to acquire the right shape. Nowadays I use the TMC 103BL in 15 down to 21 for this pattern, and usually dispense with the kink.

Ghost thread is laid as an underbody and hare fur is dubbed and wound to form an abdomen, along two-thirds of the shank from the bend. At this point, where there can be a kink in the shank, a wing post of dull orange polypropylene is tied in, together with a genetic red game cock saddle hackle, short in the flue, by the stalk. Before winding the hackle, parachute style, a dubbing of hare fur makes the thorax (remember that this can be over-wound with Ghost thread, which is invisible). The number of turns of para hackle depends on the hook size, ranging from one or two turns in the 21, right up to eight turns in the 15. It is important that the flue length is short, as can only be found on good quality genetic saddles. Do not be hidebound to matching hackle size to hook size in the conventional way, as some saddle and cape producers recommend. For a size 15 hook, I prefer

Another on the Oppo:
wild trout from the Eden

to use the size of hackle which is more commonly suggested for a size 16 or 17. Always err towards a short-flued feather (ideally from a saddle, because these are of more even length throughout the feather), which is a good way of avoiding making an over-bulky fly, as is keeping the hackling turns to a minimum. A preferred hackle for the Oppo is actually a genetic Cree, but these are now very difficult to obtain, being used, I am told, by fashion hairdressers and hat makers, which give rather more profit to the selective-breeding hackle businesses than does fly-tying! Red game is perfectly suitable, however, and grizzle is also a good alternative.

A related pattern is the Muller which, though a good duo method dry fly, was designed more for use as a singleton for summer grayling, which have a way of sipping in and ejecting a dry fly very quickly, resulting in poor returns on risen fish. In actual practice, there are other ways of achieving a more positive or confident take from grayling (particularly with a plume tip), but the structure of the Muller illustrates how we can tackle this problem using the features on the fly itself. While the Muller served the purpose of more consistent hook-ups very well indeed, it soon became clear that this was an exceptional pattern in a much broader range of circumstances. It is equally attractive to trout and grayling, and I have even had sea-trout and salmon take it. Also, it has been remarkably effective on still waters during buzzer hatches.

Hooks are as for the Oppo, with or without the kinked shank. The purpose of the kink is to push the hook point and bend below the surface film, while the main body of the fly, other than the abdomen, is dry, supported by the parachute hackle. A fish might then be hooked even if it does not take in the whole fly. In practice, I doubt that this is a consistent consequence and believe that the kink merely gives the fly more of an emerger profile on the surface; which in turn provides a feature triggering a more urgent or confident taking response from the fish. The body and thorax are dubbed hare mask fur, again as in the Oppo. The wing post is a single plume of CDC, but looped, and has the appearance of an opening wing or an emerger shrugging free of the nymphal shuck. The para hackle is a tightly wound, very short-flued genetic cock in a dark purple or burgundy colour. The original hackles were from a Whiting mini cape, but these are not currently available, and the particular colour is difficult to find in the small, genetic hackles necessary for this fly.

The value of this fly is indicated by how it derived its name. I was fishing on the Lake of Menteith during a practice session prior to a loch-style international. Several of my team-mates were out in various boats around the lake. I was fishing a pair of dry flies; a black hopper on point and one of these new flies, in a 14, on a dropper. Rainbows were occasionally showing, and cruising slowly upwind. For a two-hour period I had fantastic sport and every fish bar one came to the dropper. When we all met up in the evening I discovered that my catch was way more than anyone else had achieved. Simon Robinson asked me what I had been fishing and I told him that I had been using dry fly, just as he and most others had been doing. 'Well, that might be', said Simon, 'but you were mullering them!'

So, I do think it worthwhile to acquire the suitable hackles for this fly. It has turned many a day completely around for me, on river and lake. It is an all-rounder and at least provides a great change pattern for the Oppo when using duo rigs.

The hopper came out of the heyday period for loch-style fly-fishing in Britain, back in the 1990s, and remains to this day my number one still-water dry-fly pattern, in spite of what I have written above about the Muller and plume tips. The hopper is really the evolutionary culmination of many patterns before it (are not all flies?) and I cannot yet see how it can be further improved. It is such a versatile fly, being effective even when drowned and falling slowly through the water column, on the drop, or on a slow, nymphed retrieve. It is at its best, however, dry in the surface film.

The favoured hook is the Fulling Mill all-purpose light, in 14 and 12. Ghost thread is good, but appropriately coloured thread (as described below) is also useful. This is laid as an underbody and taken to the bend. Seal fur or coarse sheep wool is dubbed and wound three-quarters of the way to the head, which leaves enough room to complete the dressing. I used to tie hoppers in a very broad range of colours, but over the years have narrowed these to black, pink and orange as the essential colours; with claret, fiery brown, insect green and red sometimes being worthwhile. Four legs made from single-knotted cock pheasant tail are tied in before a non-genetic red game or furnace cock hackle is wound with sparse turns at the head. Again, we have here a simple fly, with the most complicated tying procedure being the legs, which are time-consuming. One should take care in

Feral rainbow on the pink hopper

the positioning of these, because they are ideal when they are curving in towards one another a little beyond the bend of the hook.

A variant sometimes used involves the addition of a pair of CDC plume tips, tied-in flat over the back, up to the hook bend. In this version, the hackle can be dispensed with and the thorax/head region just built up with a little extra seal fur. The result is a rather more delicate fly, more closely resembling buzzer emergers.

Readers might be surprised that I recommend pink as one of the top three essential colours for this fly, and I should qualify this. The first to popularize the hopper style of dry fly, in Britain, were the Grafham Water Fly-Fishers' team, in the boom years of loch-style competitive fishing. They always used to say that the body dressing should be matched to the colours of the buzzers prevalent at the time. Pink did not really feature! In this period, however, some top loch-style anglers, including double World Champion Brian Leadbetter, were achieving success with predominantly pink flies, including dries. Brian often said that pink was probably the most under-rated colour for reservoir trout patterns, and he even suggested that it had considerable potential application for wild fish, including on the river. Of course, many of us experimented broadly with the range of pink materials available, in patterns from streamers and boobies to dry flies. I believe we went much too far with this, however, in that most of the very bright pink flies produced only really had application for stock fish. Out there on the wild waters they were just too much and one suspects that more trout were spooked by these offerings than actually took them.

Late one season I was sharing a boat on Stocks Reservoir with Kate Royce, then captain of the England Ladies' team. The lake ranged from flat calm to a very gentle ripple and there was a hazy, heavy sun. With occasional fish showing, obviously multi-directional in their feeding paths, conditions were ideal for dry fly. We cast generally out in front of the boat, and a little to each side, leaving the teams of hoppers static, in the hope of intercepting some of the irregular risers. It was very slow fishing, but Kate managed four big rainbows before I had even had a take, every one to a pink hopper which she had on point. She gave me one of these and I naturally used it to replace the orange hopper I had on the point position. Only then did I start to catch fish, again all coming to this pink hopper. It was a remarkable experience seeing such selective preference for a particular colour. I sensed, also, that it was not just one of those occasional phenomena that all of us have experienced with a particular fly, and so it proved – and it hinged on the shade of pink and the amount of this used in the final fly.

I noticed that this pink was almost identical to that I had derived for the tup bug (see later) for winter grayling fishing. This is not as subtle a pink as was the Chadwick 477 used by Sawyer in his hugely effective killer bug, but it is far from being a bright pink, and it is also non-fluorescent (which is usually better to avoid where wild fish are concerned). Determined to test the long-term efficacy of this colour in hoppers, I tied a lot of 14s and 12s and used these on a whole range of still waters, from Rutland to the lochs of Scotland and lakes of western Norway. Sometimes as singletons, but more often as a pair of flies between 1½ and 2 metres apart on the tippet, I tend to opt for a pink hopper (in either point or dropper position) accompanied by either a black hopper or a Muller. This has become my usual starting dry-fly option for still water from bank or boat and it has been hugely dependable.

It is noticeable that the pink hopper is most effective in sunny weather (Brian Leadbetter always associated pink with bright conditions), and this particular shade of pink should never be underestimated for wild fish. Also, unlike the Muller, all the hoppers work well if they become drowned. I have had hundreds of rainbows and browns when the flies are sinking slowly, or even nymphed. They must represent very soft targets for cruising lake trout. In consequence, I seldom bother to re-grease a hopper after unhooking a fish. I like to 'dry' them in the same way as CDC plume tips; by vigorous rubbing on cotton (taking care not to break off the pheasant tail legs), with just an occasional application of a light oil or smear of Mucilin through the day (none at all on the CDC variants).

Nymphs are unashamedly considered after the dry flies, because for spring, summer and autumn months, at least, nymphs are secondary to my fishing approach. This, too, is simply pragmatism: natural invertebrate food-forms are at their most vulnerable on the water's surface, when the emergers are struggling free of the nymphal shuck, or when drying their wings prior to flight, and also when returning to the water during egg laying, and of course there is the spent fly itself, as well as the myriad of windfall casualties. The possibilities for easy pickings are legion to the fish, particularly so in the warmer months. There are periods though, of each day and each season, when the nymph is more important. There are many variables, including wind conditions and water height, which make it so. Sometimes it is more effective simply to drop a nymph through the water column, perhaps to the level where fish are obviously feeding and reluctant to lift up to the surface. This is very common and river fishermen are well acquainted with the need for long hours of nymph fishing on a quiet river until there is the sudden, magical switch effect of a hatch or windfall triggering a rise.

In the same way as the plume tip dominates my dry flies, so the pheasant tail (PTN) dominates my nymph selection. In the 1980s my top river nymph was the Sawyer-style PTN, the version as tied by Sawyer himself, with fine, red-coloured copper wire and cock pheasant centre tail. I still use this 'retro' pattern today; as effective now as it was then (as is the Cove-style PTN on still waters),

Copper/tungsten beaded PTN

though I have to admit to variants which are often more suitable, discussed here. Right at the top of the list is the copper tungsten-beaded version with rabbit fur thorax, both with and without a pearl mylar 'wing case'. This nymph was developed, from the generic Sawyer-style, by river competition anglers in several countries, including England, and this was not accidental. It can be 'tuned', principally in terms of hook size and shape, and bead size and colour, to particular requirements, and is also a pattern which possesses excellent GISS features for a broad range of invertebrates. Tungsten itself represents a leap in application in fly design, much more than brass or copper, even lead, because it is so dense. We can more easily obtain the required mass with comparatively little bulk, and this is crucial.

Again, hook choice is key, and now we must add bead size to this. The Fulling Mill grab gape hook is currently my first choice, closely followed by the Tiemco 2499 SPBL (the latter being also outstanding for spiders). An alternative is the Knapek nymph in-point hook. On a size 14 a 2.4 mm tungsten bead is threaded and held in place by three or four turns of fine lead wire (copper wire can be substituted here). Ghost (or other fine) thread is used to form an underbody, along with a dab of varnish, which locks everything in place. With practice, the varnish can be dispensed with as one learns how to tension the tying thread sufficiently to prevent slippage of the bead along the hook shank. Also, traditionalists might like to dispense with thread at all and simply use very fine copper wire to lock the bead into place and indeed to complete the dressing. The copper wire is tied-in at the tail, along with four or five strands of cock pheasant.

Sawyer-style was to weave pheasant tail with the copper wire and wind these together up to the thorax. I prefer to wind the pheasant first and then counter-wind (rib) with the wire. The result produces a more robust nymph body and also more clearly shows the

Grayling on the PTN

segmentation effect; a clear trigger feature. Dubbed rabbit fur forms the thorax, and this too can obviously be replaced with all manner of materials, including the same material as the abdomen, or hare, squirrel and peacock herl, for example. I like all of them, but rabbit, with plenty of blue under-fur showing, is my favoured material. This is subjective, but it has caught me thousands of trout and grayling. In the fundamental fly – the core pattern – the pheasant tail forms the wing case and the fly is tied off with a double whip finish (or four turns of copper wire if this is used instead of thread) immediately behind the bead.

As well as the materials for the thorax, variation potential is enormous in this nymph, which itself is only an adaptation of Sawyer's and Cove's own versions. Instead of the pheasant tail fibres forming the wing case, a single strand of pearl mylar can be substituted and, in this form, most anglers prefer it, as I do unless in very low, clear water. Also the bead colour is highly significant. In conditions as above, it is probably best to avoid brightly coloured beads, such as gold or silver, and certainly the fluorescent-coloured beads that are available. My starting colour is copper, but if this fails I tend either to go for black, or to dispense with the bead altogether. Brightly coloured beads might best be limited to coloured water. I have seen too many big grayling spooked by flashy beads. The hook size determines the bead size as follows: hook size <18, bead size 1.0–1.5 mm; 18, 1.5 mm; 16, 1.5–2.0 mm; 14, 2.4 mm; 12, 2.7 mm; 10, 3.3 mm. This might seem a little over-prescriptive, but it does work well. At least try to avoid a bead which visually over-powers everything else in the nymph. Remember that fine lead or copper wire can be added for further ballasting, as described above, and here the aim is to add this weight without overmuch bulk, particularly in the abdomen of the nymph.

Generally, if not invariably, the sparser the fly, the more effective it is. Moreover, I always try to get away with the smallest fly that the conditions will allow, and this is mostly determined by flow rate and depth. If I can get a size 18, say, to the feeding depth, then that is what I will use rather than a larger fly. Never doubt that a trout or grayling can see your fly in water of even marginal clarity. What they can pick out is nothing short of incredible.

Tungsten beaded Czech-style PTN

The Sawyer-style of PTN is beautifully minimalistic, a factor which has not gone unnoticed by the new wave of tenkara specialists around the world, and is consistent with another of Sawyer's wonderful patterns, the killer bug. The variants above are also delightfully simple, with a limited range of materials and required tying time. I admit, however, to a variation which is much less simple; in fact probably the most complicated

Czech-style PTN

fly I ever tie nowadays. All is as above until the thorax, where the stubs of four pheasant tail fibres are laid-in across the top of the thorax, before being bedded-in and locked into place by the rabbit fur dubbing. These stubs are prepared simply by peeling them from the feather stalk. Tied-in as above they serve two functions. First, they appear so life-like in representing the legs of all manner of sub-surface invertebates, especially the prominent legs of stone-creeper (Ephemeroptera) and stonefly (Plecoptera) nymphs. Second, and possibly more importantly, is that tied-in thus, across the top of the shank, they act as a brake to the rate of fall of the nymph through the water column (as does the tippet) and keep the fly on an even keel, with the hook point below the

As tied by the great man himself: the Cove-style PTN

The olive quill nymph

shank. If we are departing a little from minimalism here, we are at least delving into innovation of design in terms of dynamics and we might even be developing an incremental presentation advantage. Initially, I perceived mostly the benefit of the visual trigger of invertebrate legs; I am convinced now that these give me an element of control over the drifting nymph.

I have also used this technique in Cove-style PTNs for still waters. I am less convinced of any increase in efficacy; but that leg effect certainly is pronounced. This style of PTN does away with the tail, and instead the pheasant fibres are wound from well around the bend of the hook, giving the abdomen a pronounced curved shape, rather like (our impression of) chironomid pupae. No bead is used on this nymph; only copper wire, wound under the thorax if necessary, yields necessary ballast. Arthur was always keen to extol the virtues of the rabbit blue under-fur, 'with just a few guard hairs showing', wound to form a rather ball-like thorax, all finished off with the dark stubs of the pheasant fibres drawn over the back to form a wing case.

We can also incorporate more brightly coloured dubbings in the thorax; these are useful in coloured water (as are small, fluorescent beads). Alternatively, we can tie-in a collar of brightly coloured thread, between bead and thorax, with orange having been a personal choice. Collars as such can also be effective in very small PTNs when fished singly on French leader or leader-to-hand rigs (Euro-nymph style) in clear water. For this purpose, however, dense, small patterns such as the quill nymph or new generation of ceramic nymphs have been specifically designed and are eminently suited to purpose. Almost ten years ago we noticed some of the top European teams using very long leaders with nymphs variously termed: 'French', 'varnished', 'spot', 'micro', and 'ceramic' or 'preformed micro' (see later). All possessed the common feature of high density in a very small pattern, typically sizes 18–22, with smooth surfaces. Dubbed materials and even feather fibre have a high surface area, causing drag in the water, which slows the rate of fall. In a small nymph, however, the idea is to achieve the required depth as quickly as possible after delivery. Czech nymphs, which are generally larger, achieve this by a mixture of weighting and slim design.

The quill nymph is tied in sizes 16–22, with a 1.5–2.0 mm tungsten bead, typically in black or copper finish, though this is one of very few patterns in which I use a gold bead, particularly in sunny conditions, with locking turns of fine lead or copper wire (as in the PTN above). A few fibres of Coq de Leon are tied in at this stage to form a tail. A stripped peacock quill is tied in at the tail before a tapered thread underbody is wound, thickest at the bead (over the lead under-body).

On the olive quill nymph

The quill is wound in touching turns right up to the bead, where a double whip finish is performed, revealing some of the thread. A very light dubbing of hare fur or even wisps of CDC is optional at this point. Thread colour depends on the effect required. I nearly always use yellow Pearsall's Gossamer, with either natural or yellow dyed quill. The overall effect is olive. Varnish is optional, but for a smooth, resistant and fast-sinking nymph, one can apply several coats of cellulose nitrate, though the finishes obtained with contemporary epoxy resin, or Bug Bond, look even better. Again, this is a generally imitative pattern, mostly of the Ephemeroptera nymphs, and I am sure it owes its main success to its rapid rate of sinking which makes it viable for fast water (in slower water, one might opt for the slower-sinking PTNs, above). The quill nymph, like the PTNs, meets all the criteria for the approaches indicated above, and also for the nymph under dry or duo style, married with an Oppo, Muller, or championship caddis as the dry fly.

Now we are in what I consider to be the second tier of nymphs; those that have more occasional or specific, rather than general, use. I have already mentioned the Sawyer killer bug, which has seen something of a renaissance in recent years. I still love this pattern in a simple size 14, tied exactly as Sawyer described. The Chadwick 477 wool which he so strongly recommended is no longer produced, but this is not a problem. There are many substitutes that really are very good, with one that is perhaps closest to the original being marketed by Lathkill. The colour is a rather natural-looking pale brown, which has a pinkish glow about it when wet, and this is enhanced if red or pink copper wire is used, again as stipulated by Sawyer. This pattern is excellent as one of a team, or pair, for winter grayling, and I have often enjoyed using it as a singleton on a leader-to-hand or tenkara rig for fishing in small, summer streams. Sawyer recommended it strongly for still-water use, even though it was designed primarily as a grayling fly.

Winter grayling on the tup bug

For fishing deeper in the river, a tungsten bead can be added at the head, and copper or black finish on the bead (2.4 mm on the size 14 hook) is recommended. Departing further from the original I used to rib the wool with various coloured copper wires, but no longer do so. One can never really know for sure, but I don't think the rib made any difference to the efficacy of this fly, even though the effect of segmentation was more realistic to the human eye. A variation of the killer bug is the tup bug, which differs only in the wool used ,which is a dull pink (roughly as used in the Tup's indispensible) and is dubbed rather than wound. This is the same wool I use in the pink hopper.

For really deep fishing, however, the killer or tup bugs are not ideal, and neither are the PTNs. In my competitive years I often found the need for dropping a nymph down to depths up to about 2 metres in the river, sometimes as much as 3 metres. In practice such fishing is hugely demanding in comparison with near-surface nymph fishing, or dry fly. However, when faced with depth, and fast flow, we need the nymphs to drop at least to the feeding depth. This is often not as deep as many suspect, with a metre being deep in most European rivers, but there are circumstances on tailwaters and free-stone rivers where grayling and trout will spend much of their time at 2 metres, and unless there is a hatch to lift them, we have to go down to where they are holding station. Double nymph and Czech-nymph rigs of three can better exploit the possibilities throughout the water column, while sometimes, because of national rules (as in Slovenia), we have to fish singletons.

My standard pattern for depth was always the tungsten-beaded caddis style of nymph on a size 10 hook, with the TMC 2499 SPBL or Fulling Mill grab gape again being the prime choice. A bead between 3.3 and 4.0 mm (in whatever finish one prefers; black, silver or copper being my choice) is threaded on the hook and locked in place with fine lead wire, which is also wound the full length of the fly, perhaps in a double wrap, for extra ballast. A layer of varnish is applied and tightly dubbed hare mask fur is wound the entire length of the body to the bead. Again, thread can be left to show as a collar, and I usually choose yellow or orange for this. Also, a short piece of pearl mylar can be tied-in as a wing-case effect over the thorax region.

Slim profile, jig-style nymphs are also excellent for depth. This design affords rapid sinking, while also flipping the hook so that it sinks head (bead) first, trailing an upward-facing hook bend and point. Both these properties work together to allow the nymph to trip along the riverbed without the hook point catching more than occasionally in the stones or weeds. The idea is sound, though it should become clear to deep water nymph-fishers that it is frequently not the hook point that catches in stones, rather the tungsten bead itself. In any case, hook-ups on the riverbed are less frequent with jigs and this innovative design does consequently allow greater control, at depth.

A pattern that has been hugely successful, again emanating from the Euro-pean influence of *FIPS* internationals, is a jig version of the quill nymph, above. A Fulling Mill or Knapek jig hook is used, typically in a 14, though a 12 or even 10 might be required for extreme depth and fast flow. A tungsten bead is essential on the kinked neck of the nymph. Slotted beads are designed for this purpose, but the slots are usually much too large (thus reducing the overall mass) and one can nearly always use an unslotted bead. Size of bead is chosen to match the hook size, further allowing for the depth required. Silver is my first choice of finish on trout and grayling rivers throughout Europe, including Scandinavia. Extra weight can be added in the form of a small 'locking' bead at the collar, or turns of lead wire, varnished. All other dressing is as for the quill nymph except in the thorax or collar region. Here, the hare fur can be replaced by a mixture of squirrel and sparsely dubbed strands of CDC. The overall effect is of no particular invertebrate, but it is nonetheless generally imitative, with trigger features and those all-important dynamics that put the angler fishing deep nymph in control.

I have caught so many thousands of trout and grayling on spiders that to consider them in the 'second tier' of flies is not really accurate. Neither dry fly nor nymph, the spider represents the middle-ground and performs a great service for us when searching shallow water and for speed-fishing situations; often when we do not really know exactly what the fish are feeding

Tungsten beaded hare fur bug

Euro-jigs

Winter grayling on tenkara: this time on a tup bug

on, lacking any visual evidence. Fundamentally patterns that are generally rather than specifically imitative, they simply ooze the qualities of aquatic invertebrates. They are most effective fished as pairs or in teams of flies, often with a nymph such as a PTN on point and a spider on the dropper. Arthur Cove commonly used a spider, usually black, on the top dropper position for lake fishing, though curiously Sawyer wrote little about spiders on the river. One suspects that the lightly ballasted PTNs he used (dressed without lead, remember) served the same near-surface function as that we associate with spiders. I believe, however, that it is simply not ideal to fish this narrow region of the water column with either dry fly or nymph.

At about the same time as Western-style anglers were enjoying a renaissance in spider fishing, again particularly on the river, so the use of 'reversed hackle' spiders (*sakasa kebari*) was being popularized by an avalanching interest in tenkara. The *sakasa kebari* is indeed the definitive, recognizable tenkara fly, brought about by virtue of its shuttle-cock-like design which affords ideal touchdown and presentation on the surface, even to the extent, often, of keeping tippet off the water. It is not really surprising that I have found my plume tips, which also lean towards the shuttlecock style of tying-in the CDC, utterly perfect for the fixed line approach. In any case, we should not dismiss spiders as part of old-school fly-fishing. They allow presentation of a near-surface fly as no other design.

Cove's black spider needs no reminder in terms of the history of our sport. Perhaps, however, we should recall the need to choose the hackle carefully, from either a hen or a cock feather, with an appropriate number of turns in order to drastically alter the behaviour of the fly in the water. The stiffer the hackle, and the greater the number of turns, the slower will the resulting fly penetrate the film and then sink. The choice of hook and even the number of turns of silver wire ribbing also have a dynamic effect, of which we should be aware.

In the days when I loch-styled a great deal, spider variants were often used on the top or middle dropper positions, though seldom on point because it is important to have a heavier fly in this position in order to help with turn-over and also sinking to reasonable depth, so that the team of flies is 'stretched out' to give an attractive presentation as they are retrieved towards the raised rod. Variants were rife, but favourites of mine were silver or pearl mylar bodied versions which are so imitative of the silvering effect manifested by many insects, particularly the Chironomidae, as they begin to shed their nymphal shucks. I also used to vary the hackle from black, with dark claret or a rich red game being successful on peat-stained waters throughout Britain and Scandinavia, including for sea-trout.

I will never forget a day on a remote lough in County Mayo when I was left to fish by myself, from a boat, while the crew were off filming Arthur Oglesby fishing for salmon on Beltra. I had the luxury of approaching the water exactly as I chose, rather than what was ideal for the camera. I drifted among a cluster of islands to find fish rising to black buzzers among the wind lanes there. I assumed them to be brown trout, of course, so I was very surprised to boat seven magnificent sea-trout, and two fat brownies, all disgorging buzzers, and all taking either the silver spider on the middle dropper or the black spider on the top dropper. The boys could hardly believe it back in the hotel that night. They had spent all day with the cameras trained on Arthur, for a single salmon, while I had enjoyed spectacular sport on buzzer-feeding sea-trout to the classic loch-style with spiders.

Nowadays, I use the TMC 2499 SPBL for spiders, and the 18 and 16 can be tied so that they remain in that all-important just-sub-surface region, and even the 14 and 12, with suitable hackling, sink very slowly. Coupled with that is the benefit of this hook being the best hooker and holder among wet-fly hook design. I believe that the spearpoint barbless, especially with a slightly in-curved hook point, are actually more reliable 'holders' than a barbed hook.

The delightful simplicity of spiders, like the plume tips, leads by default to their uncluttered, sparse, ephemeropteran form. A coloured thread underbody over-wound with quill and wispy, hackling turns of grey partridge, either in the Western style or *sakasa kebari*, is about as suggestively imitative of a hatching fly as one would seek to conjure. Yellow and orange quill versions are almost unbeatable in my view, unless, occasionally, by a hare fur variant, particularly at caddis time. And these are, indeed, magical in what they do out there on the river. How many times have I fished and lost that 'engagement' with a fly too high (dry), or too deep (nymph), frustrated, not reading the signals, or reacting to them, until … the spider is in the flow.

I think there is something of a healthy hiatus with dry fly and spider design. I dare say that we have developed the fundamental structures of these to a degree at which experimentation with new materials and any other fine-tuning is merely just that. Given the incredible effect of CDC in the dry fly, and invertebrate leg effect of grey partridge in spiders, for example, it is difficult to imagine where improvement can come. Of course, we *will* improve them, but this might be marginal (I just cannot see beyond, to where the CDC plume tip is bettered), whereas the scope for nymphs is greater. Not that there is a pressing need for improvement in any way; as discussed earlier the outstanding incarnations of PTNs and quill-bodied nymphs, for example, have reached a pragmatically effective state of development – and, can the quill spider really be improved?

Some years ago, emanating from the *FIPS* Championships, we began to hear word of *les ceramiques*, deployed by the world-beating French national team. Having already made the jump from lead and copper to tungsten-beaded flies, in order to achieve depth without overmuch bulk, and having assimilated the Czech and Polish designs of ultra-slim profiles in their nymphs, the logical step to ceramics in order to achieve density without bulk, has started yet another exciting avenue of exploration. This has not been a mere step, but a leap.

A shaped underbody is formed, usually with fine lead wire (but where lead is banned, as in many American rivers, for instance, then tungsten wrap or even thread) and then coated with ceramic or 'glass' paint. On baking or drying, this is painted, though the applied liquid ceramic itself can be coloured, as appropriate. I have heard of the usual objections about this not being fly dressing, or 'proper' nymph fishing, but this is the same, typical bigotry, mostly emanating from American or British old-school circles. Take it from me, the construction of these ceramic masterpieces is more demanding than more conventional techniques – with which we are comfortable – while their fishing, their deployment, is right up there at the frontier. The criticism is just a regurgitation of the old upstream dry-fly nonsense. *Les ceramiques*: if they are not the future of nymph fishing, they are at the very least a part of it.

The following represents a guide to the river nymph-angler's choices for varying water types. It is based on a variety of rivers throughout Europe and has worked well for me. For water up to a metre in depth with anything other than very fast flow, then the range from single nymph and double nymph to duo, using ceramics, PTNs, killer bugs, quill nymphs, as above, all offer standard procedure. Bead size, if used, will probably need to be no greater than 2.4 mm, but for the deeper end of this region, then lead under-wraps as well as tungsten beads are required. In shallower water, then, all the above applies, though with less ballasting, and now we must consider spider, particularly in broken and fast water in summer conditions.

If the water is very clear, with good visibility, then ceramics or the brightly coloured tungsten nymphs, such as the yellow quill, as singletons, can be fished effectively, even in depths up to 2 metres (with a lot of upstream lead on sighted fish and long casting with long tippets). With increasing depth, turbidity or colour, where we can see neither the fish nor the nymph, we need to rely on the heavier patterns, at least on point. Where more than one fly is permitted, however, then it is nearly always preferable to make the dropper(s) very sparse patterns, such as PTNs or quills, and moreover to present these on finer material than the remainder of the tippet. This has been one of the great nymph discoveries of recent years for me, having stumbled upon the idea on the San among crack local anglers. The idea is an extension of the sacrificial heavy nymph on point with an imitative pattern above. The latter, however, is the merest wisp of a fly, such as a tiny PTN on copolymer tippet diameters of 0.08–0.10 mm (whereas the sacrificial pattern is attached to 0.14–0.16 mm). It is absolutely crucial that there is no ballasting whatsoever in this pattern. The quality of truly big grayling caught from deep, turbulent water with this combination (almost all coming to the un-weighted dropper fly), is remarkable and completely impossible to achieve by fishing heavy nymph alone. This, surely, is supremely elegant presentation-based fly-fishing, well removed from the classical approach.

Throughout this chapter, and actually this entire book, I have promoted the need for simplicity, minimalism, and a fish-centred approach. We can be casting-orientated – most of us are – or focused on any or various aspects of our sport, becoming distinctly subjective and personal. And this is natural: we are individuals and none of us immune from the demands of our own agenda and needs in this fantastic occupation in which we immerse ourselves. I am aware that for much of my life I have been at odds with the conventions and the dogma: I have questioned it all. While delighting in the purity of upstream dry I have gone beyond to the very tenets of presentation. I have perhaps turned away from, or lost interest in, the manicured chalk streams and stocked, small, still waters. What has become the overriding issue is a means to improve presentation and, by extrapolation, control. The structure of the fly itself has been a crucial component of the journey; a way-point. It is a mixture of surprise, wonder and frustration at what sometimes seems like countless wasted hours (but in reality was all just development and experience) that leads us to a state of fly design – intrinsic to the entire process – that is so refreshingly pragmatic and simple. 'Any old bit of carpet wrapped around a hook …' Yes, but we can do a great deal to make that carpet into something which finally yields engagement with wild fish.

I want to leave the impression that dogma is to be avoided, that prescriptive fly-tying should be abandoned. We should, rather, put ourselves in the place of the trout or grayling, observing the world from a perspective of survival. Face the flow: remember, three things are then important, and only these three things – cover, oxygen and food. All are instinctive fundamentals. Given the first two, overriding, requirements, then the food-forms are what matter. And if these arrive in the vicinity of the predator as the currents deliver them, then inevitably they will be accepted. The angler's aim, therefore, is merely to engage with nature to the extent that our delivery allows this. Fly construction is as important as the cast, the retrieve, the dead-drift, the hold, the hang, our angle and range, our movement in the water, setting the hook … If you are surprised that the fish has taken, you have not engaged it all, including the fly's construction. If you are surprised when the fish has *not* taken, well, you are getting there.

There is a first, a second and a third law of Newtonian mechanics, and this physics decides the boundary of what we can do, and what we should do, with the way we cast. But are there laws that govern the way we place a fly, or its fundamental construction, to a trout? For sure there are rights and wrongs, good practice and bad; but they are not laws as I recognize them, as a scientist, as a writer – as a fly-fisherman. In which case, all I really demand is a fly and its presentation that are part of my engagement with water, fish and the natural forces and constraints that exist. This is the place towards which I have journeyed for fifty years.

CHAPTER FIVE

The Tarn

From a classical English still water approach ...

High up in the Howgill Fells in eastern Cumbria is a little tarn fringed by reed, greater spearwort and densely overgrown bordering meadow, which is a conservation area administered by Natural England. It is a very special place to me; on the edge of the national park, the European-designated wilderness area of the north Pennines and the European Special Area of Conservation which is the entire Eden system. This precious pool has survived, so desperately close to the agricultural abyss that has destroyed most of the Cumbrian and, indeed, the British landscape. There are wild brown trout here and the only non-indigenous species present are rainbow trout, probably now numbering in single figures as they are the result of an experimental stocking (of thirty) a few years ago. When they finally disappear they will not be replaced and the tarn will be left for the brown trout and the numerous other creatures for which it is home.

We have come up here because I want to show you something that is an exemplar of the nature of wild trout fishing in high country (notwithstanding those few rainbows).

The tarn in the Howgill Fells

Just as on the river in the valley, wild, or naturalized, trout will always demand good presentation. You could fish here as we used to fish the lochans in the hills of northern Scotland, or similar lakes at high altitude in Scandinavia: cast and move on, repeating until it seems that all the possibilities are exhausted. You can cover a lot of ground and there is a significant disturbance value to this sort of fishing. Some fish might be caught, but many more spooked. Here on the tarn we could be around it in half an hour, putting a fly in almost every likely spot, but then whatever we caught in that process would preclude any possibility of further sport for several hours. This would be crude, inelegant fishing, and poor style.

Choosing a more focused, efficient approach, you will have to think it through. We keep well back from the water's edge at first, off the skyline among the long meadow grasses, from where we can observe the tarn for signs of feeding activity or promising-looking casting areas. When we arrived a flock of mallard had noisily taken flight while a golden-eye duck had paddled her brood of five chicks to the far side of the island. The surface is settling, but there are no signs of trout.

We can see the shore-side reeds and thick beds of milfoil beyond. In the more acidic upland waters further north, in Scotland, there is usually less plant life, but here in this

Our view as we stalked the tarn

limestone region there is a proliferation of flora, with invertebrates to match. Although nothing is hatching now, you can be certain that there is a plethora of underwater activity, particularly of gammarus shrimps, corixae and various caddis and midge larvae. There is a strong population of damsel flies in this tarn too – typical of such alkaline waters – and trout are often seen foraging for these right up among the reeds. It has been twenty minutes since we arrived, and the disturbance of the wildfowl. The tarn is peaceful, marked by a slight ripple, but calm under our bank. We spot a rise over off the point of the island. You suggest it might be a caddis feeder, but it looks to me more like a rise to a damsel nymph swimming near the surface. We have not seen any caddis other than a couple of mature cinnamons resting in the meadow grass.

You have hurriedly set up the 10-foot #4 weight with a floating line and are eager to start fishing. I suggest that we are already fishing; watching the water, reading the weather conditions and generally observant of anything that will have a bearing on what is to unfold when you actually do begin the casting, and presentation, process. 'Let's just hold off a little longer and get to know the situation better. It will make all the difference. If you cast now without working out the best approach, you will spook the fish in this half of the lake.'

You are looking through the fly box and are leaning towards the nymphs, but a little confused as to which to select. Perhaps it is more important to consider at what depth you want the nymph to fish. This is a shallow tarn, nowhere deeper than about 2 metres, and thick with weed as we can see. There are a few marl patches, but nonetheless any fly that sinks very far will inevitably catch on the milfoil. You wonder, then, if dry fly might be a better option. Even as we quietly discuss the options, another fish picks off a nymph just sub-surface and only a matter of 2 metres off the bank near where we are hidden. Just think; if you had immediately gone for the fish we saw by the island this closer fish would certainly have been spooked. My very good friend Stuart Crofts once said to me that we should never, ever, move through water (with a cast or by wading) before first putting a fly on that water.

Perhaps the best 'percentage option' would be to fish duo, nymph under dry, with a midge pupa suspended a little beneath a dry fly such as a CDC heron herl shuttlecock (which, as you know, is a great midge imitation). You could cast this out into one of the holes in the weed and, with the breeze so slight, if you choose your casting direction carefully you will be able to leave the duo rig out for as long as you like, or until a fish takes one or other of the flies. This would be efficient, avoiding overmuch casting, which is always detrimental on small waters such as this. It is, however, as you mention, just a bit of a 'cop-out'; a little bit too much like float fishing, using that dry fly as both a means of take detection and supporting the nymph at the right depth. It might indeed give you ideal presentation, at least of the nymph, but that is not quite all the point. You would rather be more accurate, more specific, so this will require either a single dry fly or a nymph, pitched within the region of an observed feeder.

Dry fly will be easier, as always, because you will not have the weed problem and will know exactly where the fly is at all times, by sight. We talk a little about all the nonsense that surrounds the classical dry fly; about it being the 'best' way to catch trout. You point out that it is usually the easiest, and often the most appropriate method. I completely agree with this observation, and add that it is also usually the most visually exciting and satisfying approach; but, again, this is not the whole point of what we set out to do when we go fishing. The aesthetic comes from achieving something beyond the capture of the fish, which involves more than easy presentation with dry fly, or duo for that matter.

Nothing more has risen, or shown. You have more or less committed to nymph now, so you have to go more three-dimensional in your thinking. How are you going to target individual fish, keeping casting to a minimum with a nymph – a sinking fly – and keep it from catching on the weed? Apart from duo, I remind you of one of Arthur Cove's tactics, which he taught me back in the 1970s on the shores of Grafham. There used to be huge beds of silkweed with large, clear holes or pools, rather like we can see here among the milfoil. Arthur would fish a team of two, or more usually three, nymphs with the one on

Flag iris on the tarn in late spring

point being a heavy pheasant tail which he would allow to catch up in the silkweed. Gently drawing tight on the line would hold the other nymph(s) in the open water where cruising trout would happen upon them. It was one of a catalogue of tremendously effective, presentation-orientated tactics that this radical fly-fishing mentor came up with, and so it remains today.

You think about trying this, but want the greater freedom of a singleton nymph, cast into all those areas where fish might be hunting, or holding, and I think I agree, if only because such an approach will be rather less static. The trick, then, will be in keeping the nymph out of the weed. You could use a pheasant tail, of course, as a great generic pattern (midge, caddis, corixae ...), but perhaps a better choice would be a Diawl Bach, which, I suggest, covers all the above as well as damsel fly nymphs. An unweighted size 12 should do it; one with a long red game hackle tail to simulate a shuck, or damsel fly tail. On a medium 'nymph' wire hook there will be enough mass in this to penetrate the surface film and sink slowly, so that you can have a bit of control over it with a measured retrieve. If you grease the tippet to within about half a metre from the nymph, or perhaps even closer, you can further control the sinking rate, and this will be important today.

I further recount how Arthur used to put great value in greasing or degreasing the leader in order to have greater control over nymph presentation. It has stuck with me all these years, and it should with you, because it is important. You appreciate this and tie the DB to a long tippet of 0.14 mm copolymer on a short, furled leader. With up to 5 metres of fly line out of the rod tip, you will be able to fish up to 10 metres off the bank, casting slightly across the breeze, using the slight ripple to disguise the touchdown. And with the 10-footer you will be able to stay on your knees and have good clearance of the reeds and all those thistles along the tarn's edge. You will need to be aware of all the obstructions, because if fly or line becomes snared, you are likely to have to break cover and risk spooking the trout. I think that awareness in this way is one area in which trout and grayling angling has significantly developed in recent years. There are always those anglers, however, who walk right to the edge of a stocked still water and spend the session trying to cast to the far bank, ignorant of, or ignoring, the need for cover; but that is stocked fisheries, and even if catches are respectable, that does not make it good practice.

Anyway, you have fished enough on wild waters to know the profound difference a stealthy approach makes, particularly when the water is clear and calm, as here.

We have been here half an hour now, talking and setting up, watching the water for only those two rises, and you can barely contain yourself any longer. While I hang back in the grass, you crawl towards the bank, staying very low, and well back from the water so as not to spook any fish patrolling in close. Even if you cannot see them, they will probably be there, and one wrong move from you and they will be spooked. Even more significantly, they will then dash for cover and communicate the danger to every fish in the vicinity. It is always good to watch an experienced hunter-fisherman, and you have this just about right now, moving slowly and deliberately, with no sudden movements, keeping everything off the skyline.

As you settle in, 2 metres back from the water's edge, you peel off enough leader and line by holding the nymph firmly between finger and thumb of the 'line' hand. With the reel drag set light it is easy to draw off line and you just lay this out on the goose-cropped grass to your right. Always, as you know now, the problems occur on 'take-off or landing'; once the fly is in the air or out on the water, it is all under control, or should be. It is crucial, therefore, to have it in a state on the shore in which it is under similar control, ready for the casting process.

When you were a beginner, an instructor showed you the time-honoured and reliable way of extending line and developing into a cast, by using the surface tension of the water, a high rod tip and a roll cast to set off the process. This is wholly inappropriate for wild water fishing, however, and you have learned, as with so much, that there is a better way. Now you have a firm, safe grip on the fly with the leader and few metres of fly line lying gently coiled on the grass. As soon as you begin the casting process you will lift the rod tip enough to nudge the fly line into motion and throw it backwards into a dynamic D-loop, with easily enough momentum to develop the casting process. But now you wait again, frozen there, watching. You whisper that you saw a trout – a rainbow – skulk out of a weed channel and into the open, cruising through before becoming invisible again among the weed.

A few more seconds, which probably feel like minutes to you, and you lift rod and line into motion, slowly at first, and keeping the tip down as low as you dare to avoid the bank-side foliage. The nymph clips into the nearest open pool, a mere 3 metres out. It is a little short, but this is fine. It is always best to cast short at first, because there just might be a fish lying in closer and also you will then avoid spooking the 'prime' target water by lining it. The most important fish is the closest one.

You can see the tippet slowly drawing under the surface as the nymph sinks. Judging when it is deep enough is not easy, but you have it about right because as you ease into a slow figure-of-eight bunching, the nymph misses the fronds of milfoil. It must look like a damsel nymph approaching the bank. There are more adult damsels in the air now, so we know they are climbing up the reeds where they will go through ecdysis. You finish the retrieve by gradually lifting the rod tip, hanging the fly there a few moments, almost in the reeds, before lifting cleanly off and into the next cast. This time the nymph touches down almost 2 metres beyond the first cast, on the far side of the open pool among the milfoil. Again you watch the tippet slowly draw away, but then, well before you would start your retrieve, it abruptly stabs downwards.

Simultaneously, we both see a glint of trout's flank. You lift in reflex, tightening down on the line, and there is that thrilling surge of energy from the fish that transmits and translates itself to the core of us fishermen, especially you, in contact. It is a rainbow and after its initial submarine whirl it goes ballistic. You resist the urge to stand up, and just hold the rod tip vertical. The danger comes now as the fish runs. If it were a brown trout, especially the size of some of them in this alkaline tarn, it would undoubtedly bolt into the milfoil, but rainbows seldom do this, and prefer to dash for open water. To an extent you must allow this, because even a #4 weight, with the inertia of trailing fly line, can exert too much pressure and the hook-hold, or tippet, can suffer. If a hook-hold fails, well it fails, and no damage is done. If a tippet breaks then this is an actual problem with our sport. The sight of a trout with a hook in its mouth, trailing a length of tippet is just ugly. I think it is one of the great sins we fishermen commit – and we have all done it. Nowadays, more of us fish barbless, as you are doing, so this is less of an issue, but even so there is much too much virtually indestructible leader and tippet material littering the world's lake- and riverbeds, and that is our fault.

The fish surges out into the tarn and several strands of milfoil are caught on the leader. Just as quickly the trout rushes back towards you, as if seeking sanctuary in the pool from which it was hooked. You hand-line, keeping the rod tip up all the time, applying side-strain when necessary, and you do begin to gain control, with careful changes of angle. Sometimes we can significantly shorten the fight by choosing a moment to lift the fish to the surface and turn it in towards the bank. Arthur Cove nearly always beached his fish, and he would deal with them very quickly like this. When the fish is drawn into shallow water, or into the reeds as here, it will invariably turn on its side, and it then loses control of its speed and direction through the water. I suggest this to you and, as the fish powers along under our bank you abruptly apply strain, lifting the fish's head into the reeds. A sudden, explosive sweep of its tail and it pushes itself further into the reeds, right up against the bank at your feet.

From the moment of hooking it has taken ninety seconds to this stage. The fish is still coursing with energy, but on its side, it is still. Those anglers who 'play' with fish, thinking it better to tire them before bringing them to hand or net, nearly always over-exhaust the fish to the extent that if it is released it will often die, which is another sin in the sport, and a terrible waste. It is far better to risk applying pressure at the right moment when the fish is close to the bank and draw it into the shallows, where it is suddenly incapacitated. We can do this with soft rods and very fine tippets, much finer than the 0.14 mm copolymer that you are using today. It is mostly a matter of timing.

We are staring now at the consequence of this approach; a gorgeous, naturalized rainbow trout, well over 1.3 kilograms and pulsing with energy, lying in a bed of milfoil and reeds, with the Diawl Bach curled into the scissors of its jaw. As I snap off a few photos, you quickly twist the hook out and gently turn the fish and face it out into the tarn. As soon as it is upright, it kicks its tail and in a moment it has dissolved back into the waters and the weeds. I tell you that I have watched fly-fishing excellence and I can see that you feel the same way, because you are grinning and speechless, and trembling a little. I mention also that the fish you have just caught will probably be feeding again this evening; but it will be more difficult to catch next time!

You will need some time to calm down, and so will the disturbance. You are wondering if the capture of the rainbow will have spooked the other fish in this area of the tarn. Surprisingly, however, this is rarely the case. I remind you of those times on the river, when you find a tightly packed shoal of grayling in a pool: you can catch and release several of them without even moving your feet, but as soon as one is pricked, or is lost early in the fight, this seems to communicate danger to the others in the shoal. I think this has to do with the fish being lost in the immediate vicinity of others, and this undoubtedly causes alarm. If a fish is drawn away from the shoal in a successful capture, and then returned away from that shoal, even by a few metres, the general level of alarm remains low. So it is with lake trout, particularly when they are cruising and actively feeding, as here.

As if to allay your fears we see a rise over by the island, and soon afterwards another halfway across the tarn, about 30 metres from where we are kneeling. There are a lot of damsels either hunting or in their mating flights and we have noticed a few caddis skittering across the surface. There have even been a few crane flies too, crawling about in the shore-side grass. If any of these fall onto the water the trout are sure to take them.

Another rise over by the far shore convinces you that it is time for dry fly. You are thinking about a caddis, but I immediately recommend a hopper variant. The latter are more generally representative of all manner of trout food-forms on these upland tarns, particularly of heather and crane flies, though they are passable for caddis on the surface as well as the larger chironomids. Besides, I remind you of Cove's dictum that when you come down to the shore of a lake and there are caddis in evidence, if you see a buzzer, then put a buzzer on; and if you don't see a buzzer, then still put one on! Perhaps this is extreme, but I completely subscribe to the point: trout seem to be selective of most other food-forms in preference to caddis, particularly on still waters during daylight hours. Of course there are exceptions; just think of the Irish midland loughs in the summer, or the grayling rivers of northern Scandinavia. Such waters, however, are quintessential

Feral rainbow from the tarn, on the nymph

Trichoptera habitats and the various species of caddis present represent the most important food-form at this time of year.

You recall a July day on Stocks Reservoir, in Lancashire, when we drifted in gentle winds under a very bright sun. We fished hoppers then, and the pink and amber variants were demonstrably the most effective. These are what I recommend now, and perhaps because the colour of the natural insects is mostly a pale brown or dull orange, the amber might be preferable. We both hesitate, however, because experience has shown us that the dull, tup pink version is remarkably effective in sunny conditions, for both brown and rainbow trout, as Brian Ledbetter told me all those years ago. In spite of the colours of the prevalent naturals today, therefore, you select a size 14 pink hopper to replace the DB nymph, on the same long tippet.

You are being so careful. During the summer months, when they are at their most selective, wild or naturalized fish demand that you make the right choices, and minimize the casting. Everything has to be kept efficient, because every cast you make is adding to the disturbance. It is far better to hold back, observe, make the best fly selection in terms of prevalent conditions and past experience, and then make your presentation. There is elegance in the efficiency of this, and I think it portrays the best of our sport. It is invariant of the type of water, river or lake, or the discipline; it is simply good practice.

Being on our knees is uncomfortable now and I suggest we pull back a little way from the bank. You make a couple of exploratory casts close in, and then we ease back and feel the relief of standing. Here the grass comes to waist height and we are hidden well enough. With the breeze gentle from behind and slightly from left to right you can cast easily and achieve a very light touchdown. Your next cast puts the hopper about 8 metres out, very close to a clump of milfoil on the surface. The ripple disguises the floating tippet and you slowly figure-of-eight to bring the hopper into clearer water. The fly rocks slightly and again we catch a flash of trout flank. That is a refusal, but nothing to be alarmed about. Wild fish will often do this in calm conditions when the feeding is good; unless everything is perfect, they will reject. Their awareness might, at worst, be marginally increased.

The first cast, however, always offers the best chance of success. This is more pronounced on the river, of course, when that first drift over a target fish is always the most important. Subsequent drifts lead to diminishing returns, but on the lake, where fish patrol, often on well-defined hunting routes, you might have dozens of casts in the same area before a cruising fish finds your fly.

You cast again to the same general area, inching the hopper through the open pool water. Nothing happens and the following three casts to the same area also produce no reaction from a fish. We do not think you have spooked the trout, and neither do we believe that the pink hopper is the wrong fly, but they are obviously reluctant to rise. We noticed that the rise-forms we have seen have not actually broken the surface, as if the fish have taken a nymph or pupa, sub-surface. I suggest you degrease the hopper by rubbing it gently in the damp grass at the water's edge, and then cast to exactly the same place as before. We know there is at least one trout cruising through there.

As soon as the fly touches down, you draw it half a metre, gently, so that it breaks through the surface film and slowly sinks. As earlier with the nymph we watch the tippet sink away, and again you adopt the very slow figure-of-eight. You have almost run out of clear water space as the fly approaches some near-surface milfoil, when there is a sudden stab on the line and the water bulges. You had the sense to keep the rod tip well up, and this absorbs the shock of the take.

Now you are on your own; you and the fish, because this is a big, wild brown trout and there are lots of problems out there for you to solve. Anything I say or do will just confuse you in the ferociously exciting event that is unfolding and you have to deal with it your-self. In this moment, I doubt if the fish realizes it is hooked, but it soon will and then it will instinctively dive for cover, and there is plenty of this, almost surrounding the pool. Between you and the fish is a channel, but in places this is no more than a metre wide. A single pulse of the fish's tail will drive it deep into the sanctuary of the weed and I doubt that you will be able to extract it from there.

The trout whirls, obviously now aware of great danger, but it remains in the open, skirting along the edge of the weed. Its power is immense and you feel completely humbled by it, but I notice that the rod is well up and you are not keeping too much tension on the line. If you were to tighten down too much now, the fish would be even more alarmed and would certainly bolt into the nearest obstruction. Even with more powerful tackle you would not be able to prevent this. Indeed, it is a common miscon-ception that big fish require powerful tackle. In reality, it is nearly always better to deal with a big, energetic fish with a softer rod (and light fly line or leader-only) because they then seem not to be so alarmed and may often become quickly subdued. If one leans heavily against a fish, the reaction is usually extreme and this is often when a fish is lost, with a hook-hold giving way or, worse, the tippet breaking.

Apart from the power of the fish, your biggest problem is the milfoil. There are a lot of long strands coming up off the main beds and, as the trout scythes through them, a lot will pull away and gather on the leader. The weight of it being trailed along could be too much for the hook-hold. This is always a problem when there is too much fly line lying in and on the water between rod and big fish: the weight of this dragged through the water often tests the weakest point in a tackle rig detrimentally. You are keeping the rod tip high and almost all of the fly line is suspended in the air, so only the leader is cutting through the water. As the fish dashes, so the line hisses, like no other sound in our world. For the moment, the trout remains in the open pool and this is where you want it. To attempt to draw it through the channel towards you at this stage would be doomed, because as soon as it approached us on the bank it would surely spook and dive into the weeds. Timing will be crucial here.

After about three minutes, the trout begins to probe at the far fringe of milfoil, and that way certainly lies its sanctuary. You sense this all too well and gradually apply more side-strain to ease it towards the channel. You have measured it about right because the fish cuts out of the pool on a tangent in this direction. We have a glimpse of the thick, spotted shoulder and back of the fish and its dorsal fin slashes out of the surface. You keep

Long, lean spring trout from the tarn

up the momentum of the strain, by hand-lining rather than on the reel. This is fine, so long as that retrieved line doesn't catch in any of the plethora of bankside foliage. Another moment and the fish is there, pirouetting, just 3 metres away. This is make or break now. Either you or the trout will give an extra surge of power; you in order to lift its head like you did with the rainbow, or the fish in its bid to rid itself of the strange pressure at its head. I think that if the fish charges back out along the channel it will be lost; but it has to be your call, and it must be made now.

I stand well back as you sweep the rod sideways to lift the trout. Its head breaks the surface and it is pointed in towards the bank. Another kick of its tail propels it in the same direction and suddenly it is thrashing among the reeds, unable to turn. Keeping the strain with your right hand, line clasped between fingers and cork handle, you reach your left hand beneath the fish and lift it up onto the bank. You have done this a lot now with lesser fish and have learned that it is far more reliable than using a landing net, particularly among foliage.

This is the moment that sets itself forever in your mind's eye. There on the cropped meadow grass, with a pink hopper in its jaws, lies one of the ultimate prizes in the single-handed sport; a wild brown trout well in excess of 1.8 kilograms. In the English uplands this is exceptional, and throughout modern Europe it is increasingly rare. The wild places are being stolen from us by agriculture and the greed of the few who must seek profit no matter what the expense to the wild. This is what it comes down to: the beautiful fish we look at now, caught by a sportsman who has toiled for a long time in order to make such a moment possible. Very gently, as I fire away with the camera, you lift the fish with wet hands and ease it into the reeds by the channel through which you steered it. You hold it

upright for almost a minute as its gills work furiously as it gulps at the cool water, flushing its system with oxygen. You tell me you can feel the muscles quiver and tauten as the fish holds itself upright. A quiet sweep of its tail and it slips away along the channel, demate-rializing into the mysterious indigo folds of this high tarn.

What is possible when agriculture is kept away: feral rainbow from the tarn in the Howgill Fells

You are not trembling this time. Instead you seem very calm, but almost overwhelmed by the experience. Even as I ask the question about what you would like to do next, I know the answer. To fish on, moving around the tarn a little to new water, might well be produc-tive, because there are still good areas that have not been disturbed. But we should always know when to walk away, when any further pursuit will be anti-climactic. I always think that we should never end a session on a bad cast, or presentation, or something that has not gone well. But when that perfect moment comes, and passes, like the capture of your wonderful brown trout, then we really should leave.

So few casts; merely excellent presentation following careful observation, as well as considerable past experience to guide you, and yet you have caught two superb fish – a feral rainbow trout, on the nymph, and a big, wild brown trout on the drowned hopper. At the top of the hill by the farm gate, we look back towards the tarn, again at peace. We notice the flight of mallard in the distance, returning to this home which we have briefly perturbed. I know that you are just thinking about the magnificent trout, but I am wondering about how you have just fished with such elegance, and precision, while I, at your age, fishing on the lochs of northern Scotland, was so much more 'hit and run', or crude, really, in my approach. Of course, I caught a lot of fish, because there were a lot of fish in those days before the worst ravages of European agriculture set upon its destruc-tive path; but what I have just witnessed was better fishing.

CHAPTER SIX

Tailwater

Jusqu'à la frontière Européenne ...

It is early July and we stare out over fly-fishing paradise. This is the legendary Sava tailwater, in Slovenia; one of the world's great trout and grayling waters. I have fished this several times before, including during the 2006 European Championships, but this is the first time you have seen this incredible place. We are both so excited. I know what is to unfold, at least in part, while you have only an inkling, based on what I have told you, and from what you have learned about the historic significance of the Sava in the fly-fishing world. We are about a kilometre downstream of the confluence pool of the Sava Bohinkja and Sava Dolinka, the latter of which is dammed, several kilometres

Waters destined for the Sava tailwater

Grayling in the Sava

upstream, which makes the upper Sava into a tailwater. Right now, there is a blue-white pulse of flow, ripping along audibly as well as visually, so the dam sluices must be fully open, letting go the contained waters of the Triglav National Park in the Julian Alps. It is so incredibly motivating, this sight, and the expectation.

For about 10 metres from the bank on which we stand is very clear water, from Bohinkja's influence; but this abruptly disappears among Dolinka's white water, a line a metre wide, beyond which there is only that cold blue-whiteness, distinctive of tailwaters at full flow. I know what you are thinking. Here, fresh from all our trips to the Eden, where do we possibly start? How do we cope with this? The trick, in starting, is not to look at the entire immensity of it, the ultimate scale; but to reduce it, to limit the variables, to focus on a strip of river. We cannot hope to master the entire river, no matter how it tempts us. You must be realistic, keep all those variables to a minimum, and use your former knowledge of lesser places than this. You do not quite have the confidence to go straight to leader-only, so you mount a #3 weight line, tipped with a horsehair furl, and a double nymph rig, all on the Streamflex XF2+, which you keep in the 9½-foot format, unextended. Your single fly (a national rule in Slovenia) is a heavy Czech-style Rhyac,

with a 3.3 mm gold tungsten bead. You are drawn towards the seam, where the water begins to colour, reasoning that the fish will hold there. I mention that the water beyond that, which is very fast, will also hold fish (though mostly rainbows), at varying depths; but that the seam is indeed a good place to start.

Sava grayling going back

I think that you need to explore this area by yourself for some time, while the flow is so strong, wading along the comparatively sedate shoreline while pitching your nymphs at the seam. The fish should guide you beyond this, once you begin to engage with it all. With a last caution about the danger of venturing out too far in such hostile wading conditions, I walk off downstream about 100 metres, to an area which is extensive gravels, strewn with boulders, many of which are cushioned by their thick coats of water moss, again typical of tailwaters because this is one of the few plants which can tolerate such violent flow rates and being episodically covered and uncovered.

I have elected for leader-only on the Streamflex XF2 10-foot #2 and I, too, am going for a nymph, though lighter than yours; a 12 Czech-style PTN, with copper tungsten bead. I will alternate this with a smaller yellow quill nymph with gold bead. I glance upstream as you call out, to see you with rod bent, and a good grayling coming to hand. I can see that you are within comfortable 8-metre range of the seam, so know that you hooked the fish there and this is good because it will give you confidence in persisting with this for a while. Unless the flow begins to drop, fish will remain packed there.

I begin casting into the shallows, without even entering the water at first, pitching the flies into the pockets with most character. On the third cast a 30-centimetre grayling materializes from nowhere to take the nymph. The horsehair furl stops on the surface and I set the hook. This is followed by similarly sized fish coming every few casts. I cannot see a single one of these fish until it is actually hooked: I marvel at their invisibility. As my eyes become focused *in* the water, however, I begin to see the nymph, glinting (after changing twice, I notice that the quill nymph, with its gold bead, is slightly more visible in these conditions) and occasionally I see it disappear, which is the moment I lift into the fish. But I still cannot see the fish themselves. I find myself instinctively inching out into the shallows, never casting so far as the seam, and trying to gauge my pace – which is the real trick here – so that I am neither passing through too quickly nor wasting time on fished-out water. The most important fish is the closest one … I wonder at the fish you must be wading over, because you have not yet learned how both trout and grayling can be so completely invisible in very shallow water indeed in waters such as the Sava. Then again, almost every time I can bring myself to glance upstream, you are into another fish, so you are engaged, and this is surely good enough. 'The most important fish is the next one …'

With our subtly different approaches we are already into a routine with the grayling, while neither of us has yet had a trout, which must mostly be out in the open flow, not sheltering or feeding in the shallows as the grayling are. Nor have we yet had any really big grayling; these too must be lying out in the main flow, or on the riverbed in deeper water, there cushioned from the flow. It is not that they are not feeding out there; tail-waters are always rich in caddis and midges (in larval and pupal form), and usually in gammarus shrimps as well, and these are accessible to the fish even in very strong flows. It is often incorrectly assumed that fish will simply not feed while the dam sluices or turbines are releasing so much water, but even at such times, if the food-source is present, it is unlikely that it will be ignored. Because we have difficulty in seeing it does not mean that the fish have any trouble at all. Nonetheless, at least for now, it makes sense to concentrate on the most easily accessible fish in the calm, clear shallows, gradually extending our scope if the catch rate diminishes.

You call out and I can see your rod bent well over as a fish plunges deep, out towards the white water. You turn it quite easily but then it bolts, encircling you in the shallows. I am surprised when you shout out that it is a grayling. The speed with which it moved suggested it was a rainbow, but soon it shows its flank and you are able to skim it through the surface, to hand. Even at this range I can see that it is a big fish, around 45 centimetres, the best of the morning so far. With the numbers of grayling coming to the nymph, culminating with such a good fish, it also means that you will now be locked in position. As I am watching you I notice two rises, both on the clear water side of the stream, and I suspect these are to midges. They are very subtle, suggesting tiny flies, possibly pupae in the film, or emergers. It is enough for me, however, to take off the nymph and put up a single 21 heron herl plume tip. I also extend the tippet (of 0.12 mm copolymer) to over 3 metres because this will absorb shock much better than a short, fine tippet. Now I can hunt with what I love best.

A few steps back in towards the bank and upstream puts me in a position from which I can make a nice angled approach on the first rise that I had seen. I make a few specu- lative casts, fairly short, anticipating fish at closer range, but nothing comes to the plume tip. Finally, the very first pass over where I had seen that rise, up it comes again and sips the fly away. I set the hook and am immediately thankful that I had lengthened the tippet, because I hit it a bit hard and find that it is a good fish, immediately whirling off towards the deeper river. It moves very

The typical translucency of a Sava tailwater grayling

quickly and I am right, this time, in assuming it to be a trout. I see a silver/pink flash just before the fish rips into the fast water. Line is racing off the reel, and again I am thankful that it is leader, which has so much less drag than fly line and thus puts less strain on the hook-hold. So long as the fish remains upstream I allow it to expend some energy on the flow. If it drops too far below me, I will have to wade downstream, because fish on too long a line, downstream in flow of any significance, are frequently lost. The fish remains fighting with its head against the current and, abruptly, yields to a bit of extra pressure and kites back into the shallows towards me. A glimpse of extra flank and I know that the battle is won so that I can steer the fish, a beautiful rainbow of over 45 centimetres, to hand. Being a trout (rather than a grayling), I can slowly ease my line hand around and under the fish – held now on a very short line, with the furl in the rod guides – so that I can cradle and lift it out of the water on its back. As always, it is then completely motion- less and I can easily turn out the plume tip and flip the fish back, upright, into the stream. I reckon the whole process since the rise has taken perhaps two minutes, with 'air time' of less than ten seconds, and absolutely no squeezing of the fish (which is a killer). The trout flashes and dematerializes, like the released grayling, safely returned to its tailwater hunting grounds. I have done no more than disturb it: it will be feeding again by this evening.

It is now late morning and we are both well into double figures, and I think you have caught around twenty, mostly the average-sized grayling with just a scattering of larger fish. Your catch rate continues rather higher than mine, though the dry fly is picking out the better quality fish, including my trout. You have pushed right to the

Into a big rainbow on the Sava: Keith Wallington

edge of the clear water and can pitch your nymphs beyond the seam, so that when you have each drift nicely under control, with the Rhyac on point, fishing somewhere close to the riverbed, you are dead-drifting right on the seam itself. This is good, speculative fishing. I am concentrating on the shallows, watching closely for the few, but distinctive, risers.

My peripheral vision and hearing pick up a few more splashy, energetic rises out in the fast water. I see a dipper, the first of the day, flitting out from the far bank to perch momentarily on one of the big boulders in mid stream. It is eyeing its own feeding grounds, and I am suddenly alert because it signals a change. Another splash out over the main river and then I hear it: a diminution of the rush of flow. The tailwater is falling away. The turbines and sluices are closed and the waters are being held back. You have not noticed it yet – you have never experienced this – and I can see that you are pushing further out into the river, chasing the seam, which is becoming less distinct and structured. I begin to wade quickly up towards you, casting speculatively. I am suddenly impatient. I know that we can continue here, for as long as we like, even until the flow returns, but I know also that there is something exceptional awaiting us if we are bold enough to venture upstream, to the confluence pool. It has happened before.

We walk along the shoreline and then through the pines on the river bend until we come to the broad tail of the confluence pool. All the time you are talking about the

incredible number of grayling. There was a period of about fifteen minutes when you had a take on every single drift, hooking about one in three. I calmly try to prepare you for what is possible now. From past experience I expect the water to drop a little more and then remain low and stable for up to four hours. The fish will completely change their feeding behaviour, moving throughout the river, concentrating on the hatch which is bound to occur at this time of year, in low water conditions. You can see that the clarity is increasing almost as we watch. Here on the tail, fish are already rising regularly. They are mostly grayling, but we cannot see any insects, so again suspect that for now they are midges. I suggest that we will soon see pale wateries, or possibly medium olives, and if this occurs the fish will go into a feeding frenzy. Nothing incites preoccupied feeding behaviour in a river like these Ephemeroptera.

You cannot hold yourself out of the water any longer and decide to continue with nymph, though you have put on a smaller PTN. I climb in well downstream, on the rapid, because I am going to cross to the far side and wade up towards the top of the pool. This is an area that is accessible only during low water. As I begin to cross, you are already into a grayling. You say that you will change to dry fly later, when you see the pale wateries, but I wonder if you will get that far, because the nymph will continue to work very well on the pool's tail, and this will keep you locked in for several hours. You are already into a 'numbers' day, and we all need those from time to time.

Neil Berry into a huge rainbow on the Sava tailwater

I find myself on the cusp of what I recognize as a boundary state in our sport. I am by myself now. You are drifting off into my peripheral senses and, as I wade up close to the shoreline, I am watchful of the calm surface up and across the stream, focusing on the foam lane easing down from the mouth of the Dolinka, snaking and spreading as the flow rate diminishes. I can see quite a few midges, and even an occasional pale watery, all concentrated, as always, among the foam. Fish are cruising here, and occasionally rising. They appear to be in small shoals, like packs, almost as if they are taking it in turns to slide along under the foam and pick off the invertebrate flotsam which is so vulnerable above them. About two-thirds of the way up the pool to the river mouth is an enormous gravel bar, at the bottom of which I can wade out into the pool itself, leaving the shore and the overhanging tree-line behind me and opening up 360-degree access to the surrounding river space. Already, as I have waded up, I have put several casts to fish rising close to the shore, and have been rewarded by two lovely 35-centimetre rainbows. The plume tip is simply perfect here; close enough GISS to both midges and pale waveries, while the leader in combination with the gentle #2 Streamflex is giving almost disturbance-free presentation.

As I very slowly wade out over the gravels I pick out an increasing number of fish, almost all rainbows. Some are lying on the gravel, in ranks, as if poised or resting, though most are on the fin, cruising in tight shoals, obviously feeding. They waft in and out of view, but I redouble my estimate of the trout population here almost by the minute. In this area bounded by a comparatively deep channel each side, the river mouth and the deeper water of the body of the pool – a total area of perhaps 900 square metres – I now think there are several hundred trout, perhaps even thousands. There may even be a similar number of grayling, possibly even more, though these are completely invisible. In the 10-metre circle around me, therefore, in an area approaching 80 square metres, there might be in the region of a hundred fish. I try to narrow down the options, focusing on the foam lane, which itself varies in width from barely a metre to 10 metres as it wafts down the pool. The fish show me what to do, because the ones on the riverbed are not good targets; they are not feeding, at least on dry fly. I watch a pack coming up the foam, about 25 metres down from me. There is a very slight downstream breeze, coming from the river mouth, so I elect an-across-and-down cast, settling the plume tip in the centre of the foam lane with a lot of slack leader on the surface, rod tip held high so that I can track the dead-drifting fly downstream, maintaining contact. I wonder how many unseen fish I am lining, but with the leader, rather than fly line, it does not matter. I am intercepting the rainbow trout as they travel upstream, harvesting the increasing numbers of invertebrates hatching off the gravel.

There is a rise to a natural within a metre of my fly, and a few seconds later the plume tip itself is engulfed by a porpoising rise. Before I set the hook the trout is moving on upstream looking for its next prey, but then, feeling the stab, it instantly bolts, careering off towards the main body of the pool and jumping 30 metres away within just two or three seconds. Only rainbows, in tailwaters, can move so fast with such dashing energy. Twice more it jumps, out in the body of the pool, away from the feeding shoal. With the

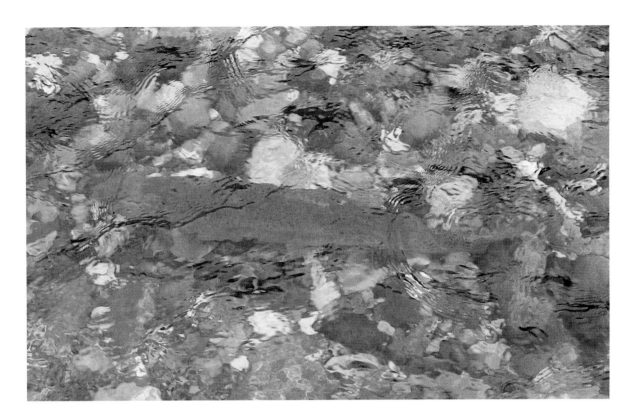

Ultralite set on minimum drag and the rod tip high, there is little tension on the line so that when the trout goes ballistic and crashes back into the water, even at that range, the hook-hold survives. As the trout dashes back towards me I can barely reel in fast enough and have to sweep the rod tip behind me, then hand-line to maintain control. Having expended so much energy the fish soon turns its flank and I can guide it to hand. It is not quite as big as the trout I caught downstream, before the waters fell, but its fight has been the better and the more spectacular. It is a magnificent, blade-finned wild trout and even as I turn the plume tip loose it thrashes its tail and showers me with spray. It seems to have been an enormous commotion, but as I dry the fly I can see several fish rising, mostly moving up the foam lane, apparently completely undisturbed by the hooked fish.

I am so completely absorbed in the moment. Guided entirely by the moods and movements of the patrolling trout, I am able to ease into a routine. I target a fish and try to focus on just this, while peripheral vision takes in the rest. I keep the plume tip very dry, because, as always, only when it is completely so do the trout accept it. While there are very few midges visible now, there are a lot of pale wateries, all apparently hatching off the gravels in the Dolinka's mouth, 40 metres up from where I am wading. I am constantly adjusting the casting angle, and my position, while doing a lot of false casting so that I can keep the fly dry, finally setting it down where I anticipate the next rise. Plume tips are never rejected, but there are so many naturals on the surface that it is sometimes missed,

A Sava tailwater rainbow cruising by

Tailwater grayling on a double nymph rig, leader-to-hand

only to be taken on the next delivery. After the first hour and a half in the pool I am losing track of numbers (I do still count, even after all these years). In truth, I have hooked and lost as many as I have brought to hand, and though this can be fatal to the catch rate with grayling, because of the alarm communicated throughout the shoal, with such tightly packed, preoccupied, feeding rainbows it usually makes no difference at all. Today, the feeding behaviour is so competitive that almost none of the pale watery duns drifts clear of the gravel bar or escapes into the air. The fish seem oblivious to the minute disturbance of the leader in the air or touching down, or to my wading, and even to the careering and crashing of hooked, released or lost rainbows.

I am now so engaged with the feeding fish that I can pick them off at will, being more selective than at the beginning. It is no longer enough to place the plume tip in the path of just any of the fish. I am looking for the larger specimens, though with the rise-forms to such small Ephemeridae being typically subtle, this is not always obvious. I am also surrounded by risers. The foam is now indistinct and spreading, because Dolinka's flow is feeble, a tiny fraction of what it had been just two and a half hours previously.

I notice that there are what appear to be a pod of large rainbows nudging right up into the river mouth itself, intercepting the pale wateries as they hatch. The breeze, though very gentle, is still from this upstream direction and I find myself with the wrong angle to allow good turn-over. Even though there are so many trout continuing to feed across and down from my position on the bar, I am drawn to the fish up in the mouth, so I wade farther out, right to the edge of the bar and up towards the confluence point between Bohinkja and Dolinka, a wooded area which is completely inaccessible from the bank, and only approachable during very low water conditions from the river itself, as now. I am vaguely aware that I am being seduced by the conditions, because if the waters rise again I will be cut off, with my only escape being via this closest bank and a very long walk over difficult terrain. I tell myself that I will know when the flow returns and will quickly be able to wade back the way I came before the rip and depth increase too much. Even so, the water is close to the top of my waders before I manage to gain a reasonable foothold on the edge of the gravel bar, from which I can begin my approach on my target trout. I now have the breeze coming from right to left, down the flow such as it is.

I wait for any disturbance that my approach might have made to settle and for the trout to rise confidently, which they do almost immediately. The closest fish, about 10 metres directly upstream and poised on the crease between feeble flow and a bankside eddy, is the most obvious target, both because of its proximity and because it is essentially away from the other trout. I have to be very accurate, because fish feeding on such a narrow feed lane will invariably not move off station to take flies drifting even a few centimetres off course. I miss or cast too short half a dozen times before the plume tip touches down right on the lane and falls among the natural pale wateries. The trout rises, but I do not strike, because I can see that it rose to a natural that was almost touching my plume tip. If I had tightened or struck I would have put the fish down for sure. 'Never take your eyes off your fly …'

Again the fly dead-drifts on the lane and this time I tighten into the minuscule rise. The waters detonate as a huge rainbow goes ballistic. I am stunned and can only hold the rod tip up and quickly check that the gathered line is free of any obstruction. Before I have time to do anything else the loop of line is already gone, with more being stripped off the reel. The trout whirls off across the river mouth, already rushing along the far bank and beginning to turn back towards the confluence pool. Again I am so thankful that it is dragging only leader behind it. I am astonished by its speed. I glance at the reel and see that there is not much backing to go. Sixty metres downstream, in the direction of the pool tail – where I strangely note that you are still fishing – the trout leaps again and it looks big even at that range. I marvel at its energy and size, of course, but more so at the recent memory of the tiny rise-form with which it had taken all those pale wateries, and the plume tip. It swims out into the body of the confluence pool, now heading upstream towards the Bohinkja. A huge arc of leader hangs in the air between the rod tip and where it enters the water, and I can hear it hiss as it is ripped along. I feel a sudden sense of control, however, because I am now able to reel in some line while keeping the rod tip well up and relying on the soft action to absorb any shock. Then the fish rushes directly towards me and I have to hand-strip in the line to keep up. Within a few metres of me it jumps again and it is like a depth charge. I cannot prevent myself taking a step backwards. This time, as it re-enters the water, I tighten into nothing. I retrieve the line and see that the hook has opened a little. I am angry, which is unusual because I do not really mind when a hook-hold gives way (though I always hate breaking on a fish); but this trout was immense and I would dearly love to have brought it to hand and taken its measure.

I break off the fly and tie on another identical pattern, turning back towards the Dolinka river mouth where I can still see other big rainbows continuing to feed. They are in line astern, both up- and downstream of my position. I select the closest, directly across the stream, and set the hook on the first drift. It seems to take ages to draw the fish in close enough to see the fly deep in its mouth, which means that I have to flip it on its back and reach down with the forceps in order to slip the hook and release it. It feels heavy in my hand and I estimate it at upwards of 50 centimetres, but it seems small compared with the giant just lost.

Again I am back in a routine, with obvious and selectable targets lined up on the stream as the pale wateries continue to hatch. There are some larger Ephemeridae also on the surface now, probably medium olives, and some are being taken, though I am convinced that even the very large trout (and I can see three of a size comparable to the fish I had hooked earlier) are focused on the smaller flies: which in itself I find a wonder of the natural world.

As I am drying the plume tip by rubbing on what is now a very damp cotton shirt, I am abruptly tense and aware, even though I cannot for a moment understand why. There is a change in sound. The birdsong has gone and there is an increasing throb of flowing water. I cannot see the fish out there and simultaneously realize that the flow has increased. It must have been mere seconds, but I now find myself in danger of being knocked off my feet. The water is already up to my waist. Without reeling in I push forwards, directly into the river mouth, knowing at least that it is still sufficiently deep and that there is only reasonably level gravel out there, rather than boulders which would produce massively different depths and make the river impassable. I am going with the pace of the river, rather than fighting it, relying largely on past experience of fast water, and probably also on instinct. I reach the far bank and continue as quickly as I can down towards the rapid at the tail. I notice that you are still fishing down there, so you have not noticed that the water is rising, or that the pulse of released water has not yet reached you.

I shout to you to get out of the river, but then all I can do is concentrate on reaching the rapid, knowing that I have probably less than three minutes to cross it before the full ferocity of flow would make it impossible. I feel that I am bouncing from footfall to foot-fall; but at last I am at the tail and, though the river is fast here, it is shallow. Glancing upstream, I can see that the translucent waters have metamorphosed into a ferocious, blue-white torrent, but I can still see the boulders and gravels of the rapid, so push on without hesitation. With enormous relief I make it to where you are now standing, on the home bank, with your hand outstretched to help me from the tumultuous river. We are both laughing like idiots!

It has been an incredible day, with each of us catching upwards of fifty fish; you mostly grayling on the nymph, with mine mostly rainbows on the plume tip (exclusively so up on the confluence pool). You tell me that it is the best day's fishing you have ever experienced, and that you have caught two grayling in excess of 45 centimetres. You estimate that you have actually hooked well over a hundred fish; and all of this has been in six hours of fishing, including the two hours we spent downstream. 'And I saw that huge trout you hooked – it jumped very close to me. I reckon it wasn't far off 4.5 kilos!' I do not disagree, and tell you that the hook opened.

We walk slowly away from the miraculous Sava tailwaters, now roaring behind us on the rapid, transformed. We too have been changed, especially you, because one cannot experience such remarkable events with a fly rod and not be affected, almost beyond a power to describe it all. We have been at our respective boundary states – the frontier as I recognize it – and perhaps extended ourselves a little beyond, to find new territory out there; new possibilities. Only tailwaters can do this, and probably only remarkably few of those.

* * * * *

Finally, at the end of the season, we are here on the San, far into the extreme south-east of Poland, below massive Lake Solina, and the turbines at Myczkowce, where the tailwater races off through ancient beech forest – surviving the wars and dreadful ethnic crimes of much of the last century, and for now comparatively safe from the ravages of the Common Agricultural Policy (which has done more to ruin European landscape and wildlife than wars ever did). The river gradually deepens and loses its vigour as it makes its way through the basin low country, falling away from the Carpathian range, which is its source. We journey along its upper regions, down through scatters of islands, and glides that begin with a boulder-strewn rip and then run on over gravels and thick plant growth for half a

*The San River, below
the islands at Zaluz*

San grayling during the BWO hatch

kilometre with trout and grayling habitat that is perfection; the lime-rich waters and the variety of substrate an invertebrate paradise. Here we pause, because in these places is the potential for memories with a fly rod that are unbeatable, perhaps especially so in the autumn as the pale wateries and caddis species give way to the natural wonder that is the San blue-winged olive hatch.

It is the last week of September and the leaves are beginning to turn, occasionally being brushed from the branches to litter the forest floor and the river's surface. The prolific weed growth is mostly dark green now, having lost its brilliant summer vigour, and the shallow flow wafts over gleaming, clean gravels, though where the current is slowest there is also silt. In the margins we can see millions of orange gammarus, all migrating upstream, against the flow. Daytime temperatures can reach into the high 20s at this time of year, while in the early morning we can have frost. Next month it will snow for sure, and the blue-winged olives will be immune from all the seasonal changes, or perhaps encouraged by them in their urgency to hatch, mate and lay the foundations of next autumn's miracle hatches.

At this moment of the season, on this river, *this* tailwater, we are humbled. Fly-fishing for trout and grayling does not exceed the potential of the San in autumn. It might be hugely challenging, or it might be a blitz of hatch and fish-hunting mayhem. We arrive in the late morning. The sun gleams through thinning cloud and a variable breeze ripples the long glide upstream and trembles the willow leaves along the shores, underneath the beech expanse that reaches up the slopes beyond. Very few fish ring the surface and, as yet, there is no evidence of a fly hatch.

You elect immediately for duo, nymph under dry, choosing the inevitable Oppo for the dry fly, set on a short dropper a metre up from an olive quill nymph on point. The river is low and clear, typical of autumn San, so the Oppo and the nymph are both small, with the nymph being very slim. You know the value of this, particularly late in the season. Fish will commonly reject an over-large nymph, or even one that is too bulky; though with good presentation, a small,

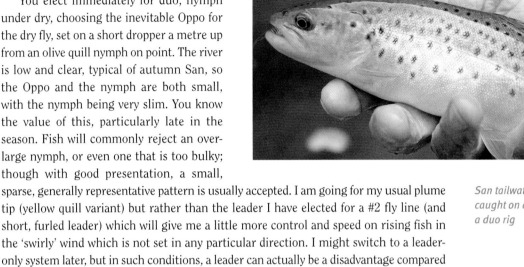

San tailwater trout, caught on an Oppo on a duo rig

sparse, generally representative pattern is usually accepted. I am going for my usual plume tip (yellow quill variant) but rather than the leader I have elected for a #2 fly line (and short, furled leader) which will give me a little more control and speed on rising fish in the 'swirly' wind which is not set in any particular direction. I might switch to a leader-only system later, but in such conditions, a leader can actually be a disadvantage compared to fly line, because when we manage to wade into position in terms of range and angle on a fish, we can often find that the wind has changed and ruined our presentation window, necessitating that we move again. Continuous wading like this disturbs the water and is bad practice in that it can over-damage the invertebrates in the substrate and weed-beds, and when fish are not showing regularly the whole situation is exacerbated because we are constantly finding and losing these prospective targets, moving way too much and increasing the disturbance factor. It is ugly fishing, and thus far better to slow down and be careful about selecting targets, moving at them according to the wind; easing our way in and waiting for the correct conditions so that the final cast will afford the best possible presentation. In this context, a fly line is advantageous, being a little less susceptible to the variable wind and allowing greater accuracy and speed, at reasonable range and a greater angle of attack, than is possible with a leader.

Surrounding us is a mixture of pocket water, short glides and rapids, with the huge glide upstream. You move right in among the pockets, casting as you wade into every likely looking drift and I notice that you are supremely confident with your wading now: you barely need to look down into the water to check out the riverbed, so you can concentrate on the set of the Oppo and seldom cover the same drift twice. You prowl across the river, like all good river anglers, using your whole body in the approach, not just your casting arm. This is very efficient searching technique, so suitable for water and conditions like this with few fish showing. Immediately you are into trout – good 'bread and butter' 20- to 30-centimetre fish – each one a picture of wildness and beauty. They come to both dry and nymph, with perhaps an emphasis on the latter, but this will change through the day, and depending on the type of water you are covering.

John Bailey nymphing towards the top of the 'no kill' sector

'The Break' below the islands on the San 'no kill' sector

I head off 50 metres upstream where the pockets are longer, like mini-glides, with well-defined foam lanes and probably greater potential for grayling. Waiting a while in the shallows by the shore I watch the water. I want a target: the first fish of the day is still important to me.

Thirty metres out, on the first of a swathe of foam lanes on this complicated section of river, is a tiny dimple. Watching more intently I can see an occasional pale watery dun among the flecks of foam, and by the time I see the second dimple – probably the same fish – my eyes have adjusted and I can see that there is actually a reasonable hatch. I also have a feel of the wind and therefore the ideal compromise for the angle I need to approach the foam lanes here. Before wading out to within range of this prime, observed target, however, I 'fish my way in', subconsciously aware that the most important fish is the closest one, whether or not it has been seen. I flop the plume tip out just 5 metres from my position, even as I take the first step, and a little trout whisks it away in a flash. Before I reach the ideal position with which to cover the first fish I had noticed, on the foam lane, I have two more trout, both close to 30 centimetres, and both unseen fish from water less than knee-deep.

It has taken less than five minutes to reach the intended position in order to have the ideal presentation on my prime target fish, and already I have picked out other risers, beyond. The plume tip touches down a metre up-drift of the riser and falls, dead, among the flow. Ignored or unnoticed for three drifts, I repeat the cast because it is extremely rare for plume tips, particularly a 19 or smaller, to be rejected by feeding fish. Sure enough, the fly is snatched away; not by a grayling as I had hoped, but another lively trout.

Out in mid river, 40 metres from either shore, is the essence of a glide, perhaps 30 metres long and consisting of two merging foam lanes, spreading at the tail where the water bulges over boulders and gravel. I

Beautiful cock brown trout off the San tailwater

wade towards it, from downstream, and see the occasional rise among the foam and the scatter of pale wateries. The approach to such water is always tricky. Ideally, one needs to cast from below, targeting any fish that are lying on the tail, which they inevitably do. The angler is less visible from downstream, with the fish facing up and away, and is also hidden to an extent by the shallow, broken water of the tail. Casting across fast water like this, into slower flow upstream, however, will very quickly mean drag – poor presentation and control. This is another area where the leader wins over heavy-mass fly line, because it can be kept off the faster water, particularly with the help of a long rod. With the #2 weight line, however, I have to be especially careful as I approach close to the tail, giving myself as open an angle as I can and using a raised arm and high rod to keep as much fly line in the air as possible. Indeed, at first, I am casting only a few metres of fly line, reaching over the tail so that little more than the furled leader and long tippet are on the water; again, using the whole body in the approach.

Moving very slowly into the mid-river glide, I take trout after trout, all good fish upwards of 25 centimetres, with two of them around 35 centimetres. By noon, having fished since 10 a.m., I have caught eighteen trout, twelve of them from the glide, in which I have barely moved and merely altered my angle and range on the numerous rising fish. It is astonishing that such an area can hold so many trout, and I know that I have not caught them all. They continue to rise at the sparse hatch, although there is, abruptly, a noticeable, qualitative change in the rises. They are slower, gentler, though still substantial. They also seem more localized, varying very little in their position. Even though I have not caught a single grayling, I suspect that most of the rises I now observe are indeed this species.

Almost directly upstream of my position, at around 10 metres, towards the top of one

Brown trout typical of the San tailwater

of the foam lanes, is a regular riser that I must already have covered a dozen times. Again I place the plume tip up-drift of this target only to watch it fall down towards me, rejected. My suspicions strengthen as this happens for several casts while the fish continues to rise at the Ephemeridae on the feed lane. I notice, however, that quite a few of the naturals also slip past, untroubled by the target fish. Unless they are spooked, trout will never leave such easy prey on the surface to drift by for waiting competitors downstream!

Realizing that there must be something wrong with the presentation – because it is never, I think, the plume tip at fault – I change my position slightly, opening the angle so that I can have a cleaner drift over the fish without it possibly being alarmed by tippet or furl falling overhead. One more barren drift and then, sip, and the plume tip is gone. Instantly I confirm that this is a grayling, different, now hooked, from any of the trout. It is powerful, though covering less distance in each run, questing for the riverbed, which in places here is 1.5 metres deep, even in the very low water. Soon it is at hand, a magnificent 42-centimetre cock fish with the plume tip lodged in its upper lip, easy to twist out without even handling the fish. I am relieved about this, because while trout are very easy to subdue simply by flipping them on their backs, grayling are not. With the latter it is always best when the fly is easily gripped while the fish is still in the water. If the fish must be held, then it should be cradled, preferably while still mostly in the water, while forceps find and grip the hook. No fish should ever be squeezed, *at all*, because the

damage thus done is usually, finally, fatal, even if the poor fish swims away. Imagine being gripped, even gently, by something fifty times your size. One can always tell, even if living in denial. I have seen it too often and it is, I now believe, the worst aspect, and enemy, of catch-and-release.

San grayling on the plume tip

There follows an extraordinary hour when the fish continue to rise to pale wateries, and a small scattering of blue-winged olives, though with those different rise-forms. Every fish caught is a sighted riser; seven grayling come to the fly, with not a single trout. I have experienced this strange phenomenon many times, and probably mostly on the San. It is as if one needs to fish through the obviously prolific trout before one can access the grayling. Then again, it is the evolution of the moment, because earlier the grayling simply were not feeding, while the trout were voracious. Now, even if the trout are still out there, the grayling are so focused on the hatch that the trout seem pushed off the prime feeding lanes. It is a fascinating balance: the dynamics of a mixed hatch along with two prime predator species, and I think that it is barely recognized by river fly-fishers, possibly because it is at its most noticeable only on outstanding tailwaters such as the San.

My great friend Wojtek, our group host, has built a fire on the shore where we climb out of the river at lunchtime and we all talk excitedly about the pale wateries and the large catches of trout. Very few grayling have been caught. Almost everyone has been

Why the San is one of the best trout and grayling rivers in Europe: run-off from pristine, protected forest

fishing nymph, or duo, and I suggest that this might be the reason for so few grayling. There are a few puzzled faces. I explain that the trout are much more aggressive and inefficient feeders, moving a great deal and not fixed in a feeding pattern in terms of both position and rhythm, as are grayling. Nymph and duo approaches are excellent for these catholic trout, but the larger grayling require much more precision, with very accurate casting and good imitations of their food forms. An Oppo or a Klinkhammer, which most of the group have been using, are fine for trout on the broken water, but everyone has noticed how the grayling have mostly ignored these. Really, only a small plume tip will do, matching the size of the ephemeral food forms, as well as their position in the surface film, evidenced by my catch of good grayling in the last hour of the morning session. Someone remarks about that, concerned about the lack of grayling in his catch.

'You don't catch too many grayling because you don't fish for them', I suggest.

'But I am; I'm fishing for the trout and the grayling together.'

'No, you are fishing for anything that will take your fly, and the duo gives you the fastest means of catching the most aggressive feeders in the river: the trout. That is why you catch few grayling. They feed differently and it is usually much more subtle than duo can allow, at least during a hatch. On a tailwater, if you want to catch big grayling, you have to fish for them, specifically.'

It took me years to work this out. You understand it now, but are happy to stay with the compromise method, mostly because you are happy catching trout, and you have had almost thirty this morning. You tell us all that you are going to continue with duo through the afternoon unless the blue-winged olives make a strong appearance, in which case you will switch to dry fly. The others are of like mind, though I am certainly going to continue with the plume tip. Even as we talk during lunch the olives are coming off the water, silvered in the sunlight, like snowflakes.

After lunch you and I walk up to the long glide upstream, leaving the others to continue exploring the pocket water. Wojtek is more adventurous still and makes the long hike up to the complicated and character-laden pools beyond the river bend above the glide. As we approach the tail, from the fast water, it is as this morning on the mini-glide, with fish showing, clipping off the olives before they escape into the broken water.

While we lunched: Pat Stevens into a big grayling on the San tailwater

Moving upstream on the tail ...

To the enormous,
shallow glide ...

They are obviously trout. You suggest that I go for them while you watch, because your duo rig will give no control at all on this accelerating water. As earlier, I can reach over this and achieve a reasonable distance of drag-free drift.

Three trout snatch the plume tip away before we have climbed over the sill into the glide. They are large fish for such shallow water, all over 30 centimetres, though this is often the case. Their rises had merely marked the surface and they had been patrolling water which could barely cover their backs. This is, however, typical of trout; so often in very shallow water, unless spooked, they will be mopping up the flies which would otherwise escape, even in the last few centimetres of a great hatch area. Many anglers pass by very shallow water thinking that the fish must be small there, but this is usually a mistake. I urge you to fish this afternoon over the next 100 metres or so of the glide, while I wade on upstream towards the top, where the water is slower below the enormous, shallow run-in, which is good hatch water.

Approaching an expansive section of river is always daunting. It helps to have at least one rising fish as a target, but even so it is all too easy to move too quickly and spook fish that are lying there, perhaps not feeding actively. Such fish are actually more susceptible to the nymph than the dry fly. They will often accept a nymph drifting close by whereas they are less likely to come up to the dry. It will all change during a rise, but it is bad practice to move fish off their chosen lies, and can severely raise the alarm level over a very broad area of river. I know this region of the glide very well, however, so I am able to move into prime areas, keeping the disturbance value low. I am also helped by two regular risers on well-defined foam lanes upstream. Glancing downstream I can see that you are

continuing your heyday with the trout. I prepare the plume tip, checking the knot and tippet, as I quietly ease into position, well short of the first foam lane and, as earlier, fish my way in, searching for closer-lying fish. A trout materializes from nowhere, in almost still water, and eats the plume tip. I am in perfect range for the rising fish now, so while I subconsciously prepare the fly again, by buffing it up on my cotton shirt (the best way of managing CDC), I fine-tune my stance and assess the rhythm of the fish's rise.

I know it is a grayling, just from the rise-form, and perhaps by its perfect, unvarying position on the feed lane. Using a #2 weight line will help me be accurate, though it will not touch down so gently as a leader, and this matters with big grayling unless they are feeding very confidently. Nonetheless, the furled leader will help, and the wind has dropped, so I have a good approach angle, downstream of the fish. Another trout rises nearby, but I ignore it. A trout that is not spooked will not go anywhere and I can catch this later on; right now I am entirely focused on the grayling. There is a mix of pale wateries and blue-winged olives on the river; not huge numbers, but even so my target fish is rising only to perhaps one in six. Long experience has taught me that though the temptation is always there to cast immediately at big grayling, it is nearly always a mistake to do so. Unless these fish are ready to rise, they will not, and a cast during the pause period has only the potential for alarming them. The more casts made, the greater the disturbance: it is a case of diminishing returns. Ideally, you want the first drift to count. The most important fish is the closest; the most important cast is the first one.

The fly is ready, perfect, the grayling rising confidently, and I am standing off downstream at almost 10 metres with a lovely 50-degree angle, in calm air. A short cast (which

San grayling on the plume tip

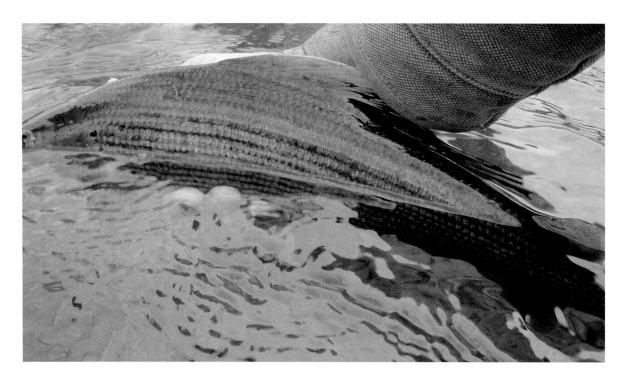

*Magnificent grayling
going back ...*

disturbs nothing) is followed by the plume tip 2 metres up from the fish, giving it plenty of lead, but not so much that there is the possibility of drag as it approaches the target rise area. Dead-drifted plume tips are very rarely refused by fish feeding on the surface, and this grayling is no exception, kissing it away on the first drift. Three minutes later it is on its side, in the current in front of me, measuring 45 centimetres with a splayed dorsal bigger than my hand. Again I can twist the plume tip free and watch the great fish whirl away towards the riverbed, dematerializing in the clear water as only grayling can. I am aware of more fish rising now, and more flies on the surface. I am buffing the plume tip and adjusting my position for the next target, just dropping downstream by two steps, and slightly further out towards the foam.

In a remarkably short time it has become routine; sighting the targets, adjusting position – which is slight because of the density of fish rising – and casting with a little lead on each fish. Almost all of them are grayling now, averaging in the mid-30 centimetre region, though I am able to pick out the occasional trout which are feeding on the periphery of the grayling shoals, dashing after every available fly, in abandon. In three hours, over a length of less than 50 metres, a lot of fish are caught, and I am both overwhelmed by their numbers and intoxicated with the mechanics of their capture. Towards the end of the hatch a very large trout appears from nowhere, unsuspected, and takes the plume tip. Once hooked it careers off to the far bank – its lair. I am too surprised by this exceptional fish, even though I have encountered them many times on this fabulous tailwater, and the tippet gives.

Along with the hatch, the afternoon is just beginning to fade away now, so I decide to leave the glide and head off upstream, towards where Wojtek is fishing, and search in the pockets, pools and mini-glides up there. I glance downstream and see you with rod bent, obviously happy with the sublime fishing at the tail of the glide. I soon come to a boulder-strewn section of river with varying currents and a sprawl of weed-beds. Being complex, with its turbulence and criss-cross of flows, it is more typically suited to trout rather than grayling, but it suits exactly what I want of the evening, because it is sure to hold fish that are not sated by the hatch on the slower water downstream – perhaps even some large trout. I am still rankled at being broken by the big brown on the glide. While the light is good, this section is also utterly perfect for prospecting with duo or nymph, but I am determined to stay with the plume tip, because in the evening, for sure, fish will be utterly preoccupied with surface flies, probably spinners.

The river is a little narrower here, around 80 metres, and looking across its features there are few rising fish, and those I can see are along the far bank. I decide to fish my way out very slowly, concentrating on covering every one of its multitude of holding areas in turn. Plotting a rough path (which will be altered by the fishing dynamics as they develop) I begin 'flopping' the plume tip out at about 6 metres in the very shallow water where I will be wading. There is no more than 2 metres of fly line extended from the tip. Two tiny fish mob the fly, but are not hooked, before I can place it on a feeble foam lane, beneath which I can clearly see the stones of the riverbed. My concentration is on the river beyond, and this too is a mistake because an inconsequential rise takes the fly away. I sense it

Late afternoon and prime time for the BWOs: working upstream on the San tailwater

Time for the hatch: above the islands at Zwierzin

rather than see it, and just tap upwards with the rod. A magnificent trout explodes from the shallows and careers off into the river. With the high rod tip, and nothing to snag the line, the fish is immediately on the reel and, in spite of its speed, I have the situation under control. In mid-river the trout spins and pauses. I am keeping on very little tension, only enough really to keep the fly line in the air – though this is considerably more than a leader-only rig would require. It is a crucial moment when a big fish is hooked and often one which places too much pressure on the hook-hold or tippet. It is not the mass of the fish that is the issue; it is its speed, or the product of the two – momentum. The soft #2 weight helps enormously, in two ways. First, the fish feels a lot less impact than against the pressure of a stiffer rod such as a #5 weight, and this has a definite calming effect. Second, of course, there is much more yielding against the elasticity of the soft rod, ultimately protecting the hook-hold.

Very slowly, the fish turns and dives down towards the riverbed. I feel the tippet drag against weed and try to lift the rod tip higher, cutting through the fronds of plant growth and hoping that the trout will push into open water. It does not take too much tension to open a 19 103BL, or to break 0.10 mm tippet. Again the fish bolts, this time downstream, towards faster water and this too presents the danger of too much strain. In practice, one has only a fifty-fifty chance of bringing a big fish that runs downstream to hand, particularly in heavy water. I am standing in very shallow water and by instinct (and from past experience) I back down the flow and am beneath the trout in a few seconds. Another

explosive lunge, upstream, towards where it was initially hooked, and I can ease up on its tail, while lifting so that it shows its flank. This is the moment when the fight is over and, provided one is in the right position, it is just a matter of keeping the lift constant, while slipping the line hand around and under the fish. As long as the movement is slow and gradual, avoiding surprise or panic, trout big and small respond invariably by lying subdued in the palm as they are eased slowly onto their backs. Grayling are the opposite and will writhe like eels, and if deeply hooked (which necessitates some manipulation to free them) are better netted.

The trout is brilliantly marked, with the characteristic bright orange pectorals of a wild San marvel; almost 50 centimetres in length and somewhere approaching 2 kilograms in weight. As the plume tip is twisted free I am in a state of wonder, as always, that this fish had been lying invisible, in such shallow, clear water, where I thought I could see everything. It had been hidden by no more than flecks of foam and its incredible camouflage. I had not even seen its shadow. It holds upright a moment in the current, with my hand under its belly. Still full of energy, it tests its tail on the flow and in an instant is kiting away into the stream, and again is merged into the magical waters. I find that I am trembling, not because of the capture of the big trout, so much as being almost overwhelmed by the nature of the situation; this special contact with an elusive hunter of the river. Finally, I am so happy that such fish can exist, in waters not yet wrecked by modern agriculture. We are on the cusp of things, and can still wonder.

Trout on the plume tip during the massed evening rise to pale wateries

As the sun sets and the intensity of light falls away, I work my way across the river, inexorably drawn to the fish I can see rising there. Twenty metres off I can make out far more than I had noticed from the far bank. There are also spinners on the water; a few blue-winged olives (sherry spinners), but mostly the pale wateries, which also have rusty brown abdominal segments at this egg-laying and spent stage in their life-cycle. While the light is still strong enough, I change the plume tip for a dark orange quill version, with a long, split tail of Coq de Leon, on a 21 103BL. The fish are rising with the delicacy of grayling, only the nebs of their upper jaws snipping the surface, though I know that they are trout because this is boulder-strewn, shallow and turbulent water which is not really the habitat of grayling. As I move into range and adopt a nice angle, almost square across the stream, slightly down, I can pick out four trout that I can cover in the 90-degree quadrant of river up and across from my position. There are also fish rising both up and downstream of these, as well as on the river's inside line, though I know that I have to focus on the target trout I have selected. I go for the most important, the closest …

Again, I marvel at the efficiency of the feeding, and the building numbers of fish on the surface. Like grayling, the trout are adopting very precise positions on the micro-feed lanes, where the concentration of spinners is highest. As the light diminishes, the flies are strangely more visible, while the trout make barely a mark as they rise to the spinners.

Each rise is accompanied by a barely audible sip; it is a subtle, sensory delight. The fish come quickly to hand at first; all good, fat trout between 25 and 35 centimetres, but as I find it increasingly difficult to pick out my fly among the spents, I become less accurate and the catch rate drops. I know it is not the fly – plume tips are never rejected if they are the right size and presented properly – but because of the sheer numbers of naturals; the trout are being selective of only those on their exact feeding point. Even the rhythm of the rise has to be right and I am surprised at this, because such is a quality of the feeding of big grayling and I do not usually associate this with the more aggressive feeding behaviour of trout.

Lovely 50-centimetre San grayling

For a period of perhaps thirty minutes I am overwhelmed by numbers, and by the buzz of life around me and consuming me. Long-eared bats and pipistrelles are in the air, also feeding on the spinners and the few, hapless caddis close to the river's shores, but the astonishment is in the numbers of feeding trout, and their accuracy. For these precious minutes I have so many targets to go for, on a tiny segment of tailwater; upwards of twenty. Not for the first time, I think that perhaps I should not be there, armed with my fly rod, and in truth I have been graced by more trout and grayling today than is probably my fair share in the scheme of things. Of course, I am a committed, lifelong fly-fisher, and catching these beautiful fish is as exciting now as it was when I was a young boy, except possibly more so in that the capture now is more satisfyingly purposeful.

At last, though, I can turn away, tear my focus from the targets, to see that Wojtek has come down-river and that you have wandered upstream to find us. Together we make our way to the meeting point as the river sings around us, and we talk about all the fish we have caught. You tell us that you caught more than thirty on the duo through the after-noon, almost all of them trout, but that when the evening rise started it took you by surprise and you changed to dry fly a bit too late, so you could not acquire a comfort with it. You feel that you probably wasted this opportunity, and I agree with you. An angler should always adapt immediately to changing circumstances, because, for sure, any situation will not last long. Duo is a comfortable, percentage method for daytime fishing on most rivers, including tailwaters, but it is hopeless for those immensely precise trout, and grayling, feeding on surface-bound Ephemeridae.

It does not matter at all. We have all been humbled by our day on the San River, and agree, as do the rest of the group, that this tailwater is the ultimate trout and grayling river in Europe, which really means the whole world, because they do not have European grayling on tailwaters elsewhere. We have experienced the boundary condition of what is possible in the single-handed fly rod sport. This is our frontier.

CHAPTER SEVEN

SUM OF THE PARTS

We have come full circle ...

I am always alluding to a myriad of tiny little parts of our occupation which make such a difference to our results out on the water. I catch myself doing this when guiding or helping others, and in writing articles about a particular technique or approach, in fact in almost every aspect of the sport as I practise it. Even when alone on the river I sometimes become acutely aware of a nuance of tackle or casting angle, say, which makes the difference between a successful presentation or failure. Many of these components are indescribable, or at least very difficult to convey in words, because they are born of long experience, stemming from countless failures before the light is glimpsed; but there are many others which can be conveyed and passed on, and such is the purpose of this chapter. I have already hinted at many of these acquired and learned aspects in other chapters, but I want to collect them here in a sort of holistic guide.

Approach, tackle and technique addressed to perfection: Tom Speak with three-weight and Rio triple zero into a good trout

The aim always is towards simplicity and minimalism, removing the superfluous and actually reducing the scope for faults which adversely affect presentation and control. This is what leads to our success and our satisfaction, and I suppose this is one of the most important components of the whole, and yet one of the most difficult to learn. Keeping things simple has become a subconscious tenet in my own approach and I am nowadays always suspicious of anything which introduces a complication, just as I am about new miracle flies, or materials and triggers in flies, which are claimed to be indispensable.

Concerning flies, you will have read repeatedly in Chapter 4 about minimalism, and also about keeping everything slim and sparse. I use comparatively few materials, and tie comparatively few patterns, and even few sizes within patterns. This approach has developed, however, from a long exploration of many thousands of types of fly, and variants, and a search for new materials and tying skills that might offer some developmental improvement. This is entirely healthy and continues with most of us all our fly-fishing lives; exploring, even though we tend to narrow-down the range and rely evermore on flies which have worked for us in numerous circumstances.

Arthur Cove's blunt statement, 'Any old bit of carpet wrapped around a hook will catch a trout', actually *promotes* the idea that what is so important is how that fly behaves in the water. That is to say its dynamics: how it sits on the water, or its sink rate, even the attitude with which it sinks. So, I urge those who spend time with me on the water, not to adhere to prescriptive fly dressings, nor to be concerned about having the exact materials for a particular pattern, nor even to be overly swayed by reports of some killer fly out there. These come and go. What is important is knowing exactly how the fly behaves, on and in the water. This is tantamount to having control over the fly.

I remember being given a Diawl Bach variant by a competitor in an England qualifier on Draycote Water. This was at a time when this particular pattern was enjoying one of its many fashionable periods and was, therefore, subject to enormous variation. The basic DB is delightfully simple, having half a dozen red game hackle fibres as a tail, a wound peacock herl body and a throat hackle the same as the tail. Frankly it ranks up there with the Cove PTN. As I've said, variations are rife: even the colour of the thread actually has an effect. It was not long before many of us began to favour green, orange or red thread instead of the standard dark brown, exposed at the head. Ribbing, producing a segmentation effect, was also incorporated, and then simple wire ribs (the original pattern had no rib) were replaced with fine gold or silver mylar, and latterly holographic mylar, or fine fluorescent thread. Then, of course, there were adornments of variously coloured 'wing cases', as well as a plethora of materials replacing the hackles in both throat and tail. Each of these additions or substitutions might be seen as a trigger feature; but in any case they were intended to improve an already successful fly. The pattern given me by my well-meaning friend actually bore no resemblance to a DB – I think the only common feature was a body of wound peacock herl. Because of all the crammed-in materials, also, the essential slim profile of the DB was lost, and it is the latter, just as in a properly tied PTN, that is its greatest merit. Trigger features certainly have a place in fly-tying, but the most important of these is the essential shape and structure of the invertebrate we are attempting to imitate. If we lose sight of this aim, then we completely miss the point (as will the trout).

As always, I am really writing about trout and grayling flies: moreover with an emphasis on wild or completely naturalized fish. Stocked trout exhibit rather different behaviour, and reaction to a fly, than do wild fish, and a consequence of this is that the lessons learned with stocked fish have limited value in the completely natural situation, and sometimes very little value whatsoever (though not invariably so). Those trigger features, or special patterns that have been developed on the reservoir, or small, still-water trout fishery, usually have rather limited application in the wild, if any at all.

The point I am making is that one should be focused not on combinations of trigger features, but on using these judiciously, knowing that it is nearly always best to have no embellishment whatsoever on a fly; that to show the fish 'less' is almost always 'more' in terms of a positive result, particularly with large trout and grayling. There are exceptions, but I seldom come across them. I have frequently been on the river fishing quietly away with small dries, or nymphs, for a streamer angler to wonder at the comparative difference in the size of our flies and the disbelief that anything so small as a 21 CDC plume tip, say, can often catch the largest fish in the river. The trick, of course, is to choose appropriate water for whatever is your choice of approach. I would no more attempt to present a plume tip to big rainbows sitting in 3 metres of tailwater, than the streamer angler would take on those same fish when rising to pale wateries on a glide. We should always marry our fly, tackle, and whole approach, to the most suitable water. I once fished the San with a group of anglers which included my friend Paul Procter. We all fanned out to various areas of the tailwater section and met up in the early afternoon to compare notes. I had fared rather better than others, fishing my inevitable 21 plume tips. Rather dismissively, I suggested that this had been possible because I had chosen the easiest water. 'No, J,' said Paul, 'you chose the most *appropriate* water.'

On this theme I might usefully add that there is a mindset, among both river and lake anglers, towards fly sizes that are generally too big and too bulky. The single most important trigger in a fly, in my experience, is its comparable size, and perhaps structure, to the naturals. If your fly is larger, or significantly more bulky, than the naturals, then there will certainly be a large number of refusals. I now never ignore this fundamental of our sport. If a fly is rejected more than once or twice, I downsize, and this almost always results in positive takes. Other than the caddis style of plume tip, the largest I ever use is a 17, even when very large Ephemeridae such as olive uprights or even *danica* mayfly are hatching. It always surprises me how the trout will pick out my diminutive offering among the naturals that might be three times larger. Importantly though, it does not work the other way around: put on a fly much larger than the prevalent naturals and you are inviting refusals. Anglers often remark about the ability of bulky flies such as Klinkhammers to bring up fish; but I always point to the nature of the water on which such flies are most effective, which is lively, broken water. Come down on the smooth glides and feed lanes and it is a completely different story. Besides which, one should never be afraid of fishing a tiny plume tip on broken water. Fish do not miss the natural midges or small Ephemeridae on such fast water: neither do they miss a 21 plume tip.

Structure should be a focal point. Just think of the delicacy of an upwing dun such as a pale watery. This is one of nature's most beautifully elegant creatures and, to the river fly-fisher, one of the most important. Large specimen trout and grayling frequently become preoccupied with this food-form, among many other ephemeral invertebrates, and anything other than the most delicately constructed offering will be rejected, no matter how good the other aspects of the presentation. CDC became popular in Britain only in the 1990s and at that time we had very little idea how best to use this material. We were intrigued by the buoyancy of this preen gland feather of the duck or goose, and recognized its potential, but usually simply used too much in a dressing, resulting in the age-old culprit of over-dressing, ruining the effect. At its best, the filigree structure of CDC is simply unbeatable, among natural or synthetic materials, for representing invertebrate wings. At its worst, we might just as well use a bit of old carpet! There is that much of a difference, and it all comes back to how much of this delightful material we use, and from what part of the feather. It is no accident that my standard CDC pattern has come to be known as the plume tip, because this is what is used in the dressing: only the tips of the duck CDC feather; two in a 19 or 17, and just a single one in a size 21 or smaller. It is no more complicated than that; but it took years of experimentation with patterns containing too much CDC, often stripped from the lower part of the flue, before I realized just how comparatively poor such flies were. Rather, it is the consistent, overwhelming success of correctly tied and deployed CDC that today still leaves me breathless at its effectiveness. CDC plume tips are far and away the most important trigger feature, or imitative feature, that a dry olive or midge, or in some cases caddis, possesses. I am not suggesting that a lovely body of stripped peacock quill, or split Coq de Leon tails, are superfluous, but they are, in reality, less significant in both dynamic and imitative terms to the effective river dry fly.

As in dry flies, over-dressing and over-sizing are similarly faults in nymphs and spiders, and indeed probably in traditional wet flies. I wonder now at how many times in my life I have failed to catch largely because I had chosen a fly that was too big or over-dressed, or both. I know it is many thousands. It is curious, too, just how long it takes most of us to learn this particular lesson. Much of my most formative fly-fishing, in the 1970s, was on the large English reservoirs and the sea-trout lochs of northern Scotland. I was very much indoctrinated by the fashion of those times, and I even remember Arthur Cove telling me that I should fish with the largest hook that I could 'get away with'; his claim being that it was more reliable to hook a fish with a big hook than a small one (something I completely disagree with nowadays). On Lochs Maree and Hope, also, as on all the sea-trout waters, the trend was for enormous hackled wet flies, or even larger dapping flies, all of which today seem ridiculous. We caught a lot of fish, of course, but this was because of the very large numbers present in these great fisheries in those days, and it was *in spite of* the comparatively poor flies (and other tackle) we used.

A requirement we have of nymphs is that they sink quickly to the required depth. In the swift-flowing stream this might be a metre or so, but in deep pools this can be much more. This is always a problem for the river fly-fisher. On a clear water river with significant flow and depth, such as we find running off the Alps, Pyrenees or Tatras – a great swathe of European rivers – we are often both captivated and daunted by the sight of huge trout suspended in the depths. We have a choice: either we place a nymph at the depth of those mesmerizing targets, or we abandon them and go in search of water which might hold such fish, but which is also accessible to flies presented on or near the surface. It is utterly pointless to present an unsuitably ballasted nymph or dry fly to these fish – though how many of us have spent countless hours in the attempt?

So, too, on darker waters, which might also have significant depth, though the fish are invisible. We are attracted to areas which our watercraft tells us are 'fishy', but then let ourselves down by putting out an unsuitable fly which drifts way over the trouts' heads. And few of us, really, can walk away, so the challenge is on to drop a nymph deep enough. We can perhaps go along the route of a fast-sinking line, but this is seldom consistently successful, and in truth is hugely demanding. The loss of control is considerable and, for most of us, unacceptable.

A preferred route is to use a very heavy nymph, perhaps sacrificially on the point, dragging smaller, more-imitative patterns on droppers down into the depths. I have in mind, however, tailwaters where anglers can fish only single or double fly combinations, so the idea of a sacrificial nymph – there for ballast alone – is a non-starter. There is no reason at all why a dense nymph, designed to sink to extreme depths on a long leader and floating line, cannot also take fish. The trick is to keep the bulk to a minimum, as always, and to maintain contact with the fly. The 'hold time' on such flies is very short indeed, and if one is not in contact there will be many missed takes, most of them not even registering. Trout and grayling will pick up very heavy nymphs and eject them within a second. The brilliantly conceived Polish woven nymphs and Czech nymphs, for example, are dense, but not bulky, and these provide an excellent compromise. It is perfectly feasible to fish these, as singletons or in teams, down to about 2 metres, so long as the flow rate is not too fast – and if it is, then one is probably either in the wrong place or not fishing appropriately for the flow conditions. Modern tungsten-beaded nymphs, jig-style or conventional, also give us the potential for fishing successfully at much greater depths than hitherto. In this context, see my point in Chapter 4 about fishing a sacrificial nymph in conjunction with a completely un-ballasted, small pattern (even a spider) on very fine tippet.

One's focus should be on each individual fly (easy with a singleton, much more complex with pairs or teams). A bushy, hackled fly will sink much more slowly than a smooth, streamlined fly of the same weight. If you want depth, quickly, then keep everything slim, and dense; and keep in contact. The bulkier and denser the fly, the shorter will be the hold time; but bulk is the real killer here. Just think of the modern approach of fishing teams of varnished (un-weighted) buzzers on still waters. From a slowly drifting boat the nymph on point can easily achieve depths of 6 metres, particularly with leaders constructed from (dense) fluorocarbon. The hold time of these flies is very long, certainly several seconds. And remember that Arthur Cove never used lead in any of his nymphs –

I remember him claiming depths for his pheasant tails in excess of 5 metres on a slow retrieve. In all cases, buzzers or un-weighted PTNs, most takes are registered by feel rather than visually. The fish simply pick them up and swim off while searching for the next fly.

As a consequence of this concentration on attempting to achieve great depth, it is my experience that most anglers fall foul of the converse problem of fishing *below* the feeding depth of the fish. To an extent, fishing a team of flies (be they nymph, spider or wet-fly combinations) alleviates this, though not entirely, and when fishing singletons the issue becomes central to correct presentation. Placing a fly at or close to the feeding (or holding) depth of the fish, for as long as possible in a drift, is the crucial aspect of this. It is easiest with dry fly to rising fish and becomes increasingly difficult, almost proportionally, with depth. The near surface, however, is a special case and even very experienced fly-fishers can be caught out by this. There are numerous circumstances, particularly on the river, when fish are feeding just sub-surface and most of us observing this will assume dry fly. If we fish a nymph with any ballasting whatsoever, we will be beneath the taking fish, while a dry fly is also often rejected. Frequently, small shuttlecock-style plume tips can work on such fish, or even a semi-drowned pattern such as a black gnat or midge emerger (and never discount the hopper on still waters for this role); but this really is the domain of the spider, again as a singleton or in teams. This approach is significantly more demanding than either dry fly or weighted nymph with indicator, while at times it is utterly superior to either, and thus worth mastering. The beautiful reversed hackle style of spiders (*sakasa kebari*) used in the Japanese and Italian (*pesca alla Valsesiana*) fixed line approaches lends itself to sub-surface presentations. With these techniques, and with this mode of dressing, it is comparatively easy to hold the fly, with control, close to the surface.

Hook structure, in terms of wire strength and overall shape, is a hugely overlooked area of fly-tying. Many good dressings are utterly ruined by the inappropriate choice of hook. Dry flies need fine wire hooks, but these need to be as strong as possible. On the one hand it is pointless to dress a fine, sparse CDC pattern on a heavy wire hook, which will drown it, but on the other it is very poor practice to present a wire of questionable strength to large fish. The wonderful Japanese Tiemco 103 BL is the ideal compromise. For nymphs my own choice is the Fulling Mill grab gape and for spiders the 2499 SPBL (spear point, barbless), also from Tiemco. These are the best hookers, and holders, that I have ever found. Apart from the excellent wire strength:diameter ratio of these hooks, they also have the shape I want for the patterns I tie. The shape of a fly is largely determined by the hook on which it is dressed, and it is very difficult to manipulate the desired shape into a fly with an incorrectly shaped hook, so it seems sensible to start with the correct hook. There are, of course, other hook patterns than those just mentioned and readers might like to refer to Chapter 4 where this topic is discussed in detail particularly for flies in the sub-size 20 range.

In summary, so far as the fly is concerned, we need to think about general impression of size and shape, GISS, and add colour to the analysis. We must determine where that fly should be in the water column for any particular situation or, if it is dry, then its attitude on or in the surface. Its structure in terms of density, shape and materials used, and the

hook itself, are all considerations that effect its dynamics, and hence its presentation. We reason that the best trigger features are minimal and probably result in elements of exaggeration of features of the natural food-form, such as a pronounced segmentation, or a brightly coloured wing case. Singletons are always easier to deal with than teams, but when we are nymphing with two or three flies then these need to be chosen so that each enhances the behaviour of the others, so that the water column can be suitably explored and that we have control over all the flies. We should recognize that fishing a team of flies with skill is considerably more demanding than fishing a single dry fly and should recognize any old-school doctrine to the converse as being exactly what it is.

Tippets and leaders, and their connectivity to fly and fly line, are an endless source of both fascination and frustration. In one sense, keeping everything as simple as possible in this area, like every other, is eminently sensible, though some development, or sophistication, has such a profound effect on presentation and control that attention to certain details is recommended. Throughout this book I have referred to leader constructions and urged the fly-angler to explore possibilities beyond standard doctrine. While the leader is a component of the tackle, we make a mistake if we see it as such, rather than an

When simplicity and minimalism really matter: dry fly in a summer storm

With all the connectivity as it should be within a perfectly balanced and simple outfit: wild trout from the Welsh Dee on Streamflex with Greys Platinum three-weight

integral part of the whole connectivity between the hands and the fly. The fixed line approach completely bypasses the use of fly line and requires only a leader (in various forms) for the delivery and control of the fly. Increasingly, Western-style fly-fishers, at the very least on the river, are abandoning conventional fly lines and utilizing developing ideas with leaders – influenced by tenkara – so as to improve presentation.

The connectivity throughout the system is itself largely overlooked. We have all been guilty of simply relying on the knot strength in leader or tippet joints, or connecting fly to tippet, with scant regard for other properties, such as their bulk or smoothness through the rod guides. A bulky knot in a leader forms a fish-scaring wake when on the surface and, when retrieved through the tip guide while playing a fish, can be so jarring as to catastrophically stress tippet or hook-hold. Having long suffered the failings of such crude knots and junctions, I spent a considerable time paying attention to all aspects of connectivity.

I had a lucky early start in that Arthur Cove showed me the Turle knot back in the 1970s, and this single feature has made a vast difference to my catches ever since. The most popular knot for attaching fly to tippet is probably the tucked half-blood and, indeed, this is the knot I use for straight-eyed hooks. The trouble with the half-blood, however, in common with every knot other than the Turle, is that it is fixed around the eye of the hook and therefore can and does allow hinging as the metal eye slips through the knot. This sets the whole fly off-centre – off the axis of the tippet. You might think this has negligible effect, but it is always something that irritates me and I am convinced it is certainly detrimental to presentation. The Turle, however, has the tippet threaded through the eye, while the knot itself beds down on the head dressing, around the neck of the fly.

For connecting two sections of tippet or leader, of same or similar diameter, a three-turn water knot is always reliable, significantly more so than the double-blood (and this for fluorocarbon, nylon monofilament or copolymer). I have noticed over the years that many anglers, actually most, tend to leave a tiny amount of the tags on the knot. I think this is to allow for any slippage but, in so doing, they are unleashing a nest of problems. In the first place, if a knot is subject to slippage, it is useless, failing in its function. The three-turn water knot, like any other, must be drawn down smoothly and tightly. Fully bedded down it cannot slip and the tags can be snipped completely flush to the knot. I have *never* had one slip. With no tags the overall effect is a smooth barrel of a knot which does not suffer the significant air resistance during casting which causes early collapse rather than clean turn-over. Neither does it give that tell-tale 'V' on the surface during retrieve. It might seem a tiny nuance of tackle preparation, but its effect is enormous.

Similarly, the connection of leader to fly line has often been problematical. The most popular connection has been a braided nylon loop, sleeved onto the fly line, with the leader attached to this either by a loop-to-loop or with a tucked half-blood to the loop. Many modern fly lines are now made with an integral loop. These are rather bulky and create a significant disturbance on the surface. They also do not marry well with fine leader material, which cuts through the polymer coating. The neatest connection I have discovered is made with a mini-loop of 18 lb braided monofilament, which is sleeved onto the fly line tip and fastened into place with Ghost thread or other fine fly-tying thread. I usually attach the leader directly to this via a tucked half-blood, though loop-to-loop is perfectly acceptable, even if a little more cumbersome. The mini-loop is smaller than those commercially available, and there is no plastic sleeve. The whipping of fly-tying thread is far smoother and creates no disturbance whatsoever. I do not use white braid, preferring an off-white or grey, with my favourite being Ghost thread, which is invisible to the naked eye.

Knots in any part of the tippet or leader are important, and not only the weakest one (which should be that joining tippet to fly). With leader-only systems there are knots or connections which will have to pass through the rod guides. In my presentation leader, there is a crucial knot between the running leader and the short section of steep taper, which is approximately 0.5 mm copolymer. This is formed with a very well drawn down two-turn water knot. The tags *must be cut absolutely flush to the knot* or they will catch on the guides, with ruinous consequences. A water knot will not slip if it is formed properly, so that we can trust it completely, neither does it need any form of knot glue. Cut the tags flush, or the whole leader system will be a hazard rather than the elegant presentation device that is its design. Everything between the fly and the reel must be kept as smooth as possible, which means free of any snag, kink or twist.

It is about minimizing the disturbance. Like any hunter, the fly-fisher is at his most

When the demands on tackle and technique are greatest; during a heavy summer storm on an alpine mountain stream

deadly when all movements are slow, and there is nothing to produce an untoward or unnatural reaction. The modern trend towards brightly coloured indicators, and even entire fly lines and leaders, is often counterproductive. Double World Champion Brian Leadbetter and I once shared a boat on Bewl Water. We were both catching a lot of trout, using teams of nymphs on Wet Cel intermediate lines. These were manufactured in a bright green colour which could be seen when they had sunk several metres below the surface, which was why I had dyed mine a dark olive. Brian asked me what line I was using. I replied that it was the same as his except that I had dyed it. 'Why have you done that?' he asked. I suggested that bright colours might spook fish to which he replied: 'No, it pulls 'em!' In fact, on that day we did catch roughly the same number, and so it had probably made no difference; but the fish on Bewl are stocked trout and, with wild fish, it most certainly does have a profound effect and I have witnessed it many times.

The fluorescent-coloured indicator is currently very much part of the river nymphing game, and many anglers tend to leave these in place even when changing to dry fly. On turbulent flow, or in coloured, stained water, the effect is usually negligible; but on smoother, clearer water it most certainly is not. So too with rod, reel and line flash, and

even bright colours on these items of tackle, which after all are sometimes moving quickly through the air, rendering them most noticeable. There is a trend towards bright thread and lacquering on modern fly rods – even very broad bands of bright colour on some tenkara rods – and anglers really should recognize the significant disadvantage that using such will result. I have seen too many big trout and grayling spooked by rod flash, or the proximity of an indicator not to know that we really should take extreme care with this often overlooked aspect of tackle.

Nymph fishers like to have some form of visual indication of a take, and this has precipitated all the various types of indicator that proliferate nowadays. A common feature is high visibility, but in most cases this aspect is overdone. My presentation leader incorporates a greased section of braided nylon monofilament or furled horsehair for the main purpose of adding casting mass in the right position of the leader, as well as buoyancy, but it also serves as an indicator when nymph fishing. The default colour is a dull grey and this, along with the long tags of tippet on the loops, is perfectly visible enough in most lights, even out beyond the 10-metre range. In coloured water I do occasionally replace this section with a dull orange braid, or even black, which is often the most visible of all.

All part of the quiet, stealthy approach: properly dealing with a fish without touching or netting it – calmly resting it on a bed of water moss for unhooking

An utterly crucial part of presentation is keeping the line tip afloat. Floating lines nowadays are far better than hitherto in floating uniformly, including at the tip, although with the amount of buoyant polymer at the tip being at its thinnest, this section of the line is liable to sinking. Also, if there is any breach in the polymer coating, even a minute crack, water will soak into the core by capillary action. The problems associated with this are huge and should never be underestimated. I have had more drifts ruined by a sinking line tip than I care to recall – it has been one of the tough lessons to learn on the river and it matters almost as much for spider/nymph fishing as it does with dry fly.

Drag is the ultimate enemy of the river fly-fisher and it is the interaction of fly line, leader and tippet with the current that produces it, exacerbated by wind drift and having poor control over the line. A sinking line tip compounds the problems and puts the angler completely out of control. While nymph fishing, also, the line tip juts down towards the fly and I am utterly convinced that it can spook fish. A lot of angers disagree with me on this point, but I have observed this too many times to be anything other than convinced by it. Actually, most of those who disagree are still-water orientated and point to the way that the floating line often sinks at the tip when fishing a string of varnished buzzers in calm water, to no apparent detrimental effect. Indeed, I believe this is one of the few exceptions to the general concept, because on the river, and in many instances on still water, the line tip absolutely must be afloat. We notice the effect of a sunken tip most obviously with a dry fly. Bear in mind that the fly will always follow the line. This is an inevitable consequence of physics. As we lift the line for a new cast, the dry fly will follow the curved path, beneath the surface, of the line tip, resulting in increased disturbance and also drowning of the fly. The latter might not matter so much with bulky caddis patterns, or comparatively bushy Klinkhamers or Oppos, say, but CDC is completely ruined and will require extra-vigorous false casting, at the very least, in order to blow the spray clear.

Fortunately, it is very easy to remedy the situation, and it is therefore a surprise that many anglers seem to endure the detrimental consequences of a sunken tip. A coating of Mucilin is all that is required, and a single application can last all day. The braided mini-loops, which are constructed from the same material as the braid sections in presentation leaders, are particularly good at absorbing Mucilin, to the extent that hardly any of the grease needs be applied to the line itself (or leader). One important point: use the red-tin Mucilin. The green label is silicone-based and interacts with the polymer coating of fly lines, speeding up their decomposition. Mucilin is the single most important item of peripheral tackle that I use.

The underwater drag of nymphs cannot be observed visually, though it can be felt to an extent. Again it is caused by interaction of line with the water, and also by the angler being in too tight a contact with the flies. The net effect is to move the nymphs at a speed faster than the current, or faster than the naturals could possibly achieve, even the agile darter olive nymphs, caddis pupae, gammarus shrimps or corixae, all of which are towards the speedy end of the invertebrate spectrum. River fishers everywhere often hold the line or leader very tight, particularly in what is known as 'leading' the nymphs. It is clearly a successful tactic and I suspect that this is largely to do with the excellent contact with the flies this produces, such that any taking fish is immediately registered, and hooked. It is claimed that leading the flies will induce fish to take. Undoubtedly this happens, but I believe this is usually the case with fish feeding actively (on nymphs), perhaps competing with one another for a sparse food source, rather than fish lying passively in wait for nymphs or hatch. In any case, I almost always adopt the opposite approach, doing everything I can to prolong a dead drift. It is a little more demanding, perhaps, because it is still important to stay in contact with the flies (and it is difficult to do this without moving them), but I have caught many thousand trout and grayling on dead-drifted nymphs, so I know that it is worth the effort. Oddly enough, I learned the value of a dead drift when nymph fishing mostly from fishing duo-style (nymph under dry), which is not a method that I particularly admire (and neither do many of the top Continental internationals in the contemporary sport). Using this method, however, one cannot help but notice that the best drifts are when the dry fly is drifting at the pace of the current, which means that the nymph also is drifting dead in the flow. The takes to the nymph, registered by the dry fly plunging away, are then always most positive.

Micro-drag is an extreme example of drag, but it is very common and actually suffered by most of us much more than the more obvious 'waking' of an out-of-control fly on the surface. Most anglers do not even notice it, but its effects are as ruinous to presentation as full-blown drag itself. The best dry-fly exponents never take their eyes off the fly from the moment it touches down until lift-off for the next cast. Such focus leads to an understanding of the line and tippet interaction with the surface, and ultimately to an enhanced degree of control over it. We watch the fly so intently that we observe its motion with respect to features nearby, particularly foam. Peripheral vision and other senses pick up enough of what is going on in the wider sphere, but all that really matters is the presentation of that fly through the drift. Any untoward movement relative to the natural flow of the neighbouring bubbles, or other flotsam, is micro-drag and we can be sure that if we can see this, so will the fish, and it will alarm them to the point of refusing the fly, or worse, a longer-term alertness. See this in the perspective of big grayling in slow water, which probably represent the greatest challenge we have: usually we have just a single chance at such fish – one drift – and it is so easy to spoil it with micro-drag.

The advice, then, is to become aware of micro-drag and learn ways to overcome it. Positioning of the cast, with slack or mends where necessary, will help. Keeping the range down as close as possible will help even more. Also, the more across the stream one casts, rather than upstream, the greater the surface-to-line interaction – because of the varied surface flow rates between angler and fly – which will inevitably and very quickly result in micro-drag. Do not be overly influenced by those who suggest you can overcome drag with appropriate line mends. Of course, these have an application, but they can also exacerbate the problem, by laying too much line across the varied currents, and also putting the angler significantly out of control. There can easily be far too much line, leader and tippet lying on the surface, with the rod tip high so that if a fish does take there is no hope of setting the hook.

All of this advice is geared towards learning how to fish the 360-degree river; being able to place the cast at any angle, up, down or across the stream, so that the ideal presentation of a dead-drifted fly can be achieved, with control. Line mends have their purpose, and so too does the angler's stance in the river, as well as the positioning of the rod tip on delivery and then throughout the subsequent drift as the tip tracks the leader and fly, absorbing slack line and maintaining contact without imparting micro-drag. Fishing the downstream dry fly is a hugely important tactic, which requires considerable practice to perfect. Do not listen to all the nonsense (stemming from some of the English chalk stream circles) about this approach being in some way unsporting. It requires significantly more skill to accomplish than does fishing upstream, largely because it is much more difficult to approach fish from this direction, and then to keep control of the fly falling way downstream.

I think this is a delightful approach to presenting a dry fly (and even more difficult to achieve with nymph). If practised with a leader-only rig, it can be combined with an upstream cast and continued with a few line corrections for up to 20 metres downstream, yielding total drift lengths of up to 30 metres, all dead-drift and under control, which is nothing short of astonishing. This, to me, is the perfect drift. Even with a strong downstreamer, necessitating delivery in a generally downstream direction, the rod can be 'stunned' with a very high stop point, with the leader and tippet even being dragged back towards the angler, and then dumped on the surface. The rod tip is maintained very high, slowly dropping while the coils of line are tracked as they straighten on the flow, thus maintaining contact with the fly. It is traditionally thought that a trout or grayling rising at a fly delivered in such a way will often be missed, because the fish is facing the angler and the tendency might be, therefore, for the fly to be pulled out of the mouth during the strike. In practice I have noticed no difference in hook-up ratio between fish risen up- or downstream; *provided the drift is dead*.

'Hold time' is that brief period for which a fish will hold onto a fly before ejecting, unless it is actually hooked. With a led or retrieved fly, the hold time is very short indeed. There is little time for visual registering of the take and usually such fish are hooked or lost in the moment that they are felt. Loch-stylers, often moving the fly quite quickly, however, experience those takes, both on and below the surface, when a fish turns on the fly and holds it for long enough for the angler to set the hook. This is comparatively rare on the river, where the norm is that a led fly will result in tactile registering of the take and the fish effectively hooking itself against the tension of the line, and commonly a higher frequency of failed takes, the so-called low hook-up ratio.

Once the fly-fisher has a period of practice with the downstream presentation of dry fly, the attempt should be made to deliver and control a single nymph in this direction, ideally with only a greased line/leader tip as indicator. I would suggest that this is probably the most exacting skill within the river repertoire, and to scorn it (as some bigots will) is utterly absurd.

A dead-drifted nymph will yield a longer hold time than one that is being led. Nymphs that are held on a tight line, such as Czech-nymph (under the rod tip) style, or with modern Euro-nymphing (akin to the Polish rolled nymph of the 1990s), will not yield a long hold time and again the hook-up ratio can be very poor with such methods, rather like the old 'down and across' with traditional wet flies. Even a fly line tip can impart enough resistance for a fish to eject the fly immediately. This was one of the great discoveries of fishing leader-only. We all noticed that the hold time could be extended to several seconds. Dan Svrcek, a former Czech team member, once told me that he thought that fish often picked up his nymph presented on a French leader (or an adapted Czech equivalent) and simply carried on feeding. I have experienced this effect many times with both nymph and dry fly. It happens because of lack of resistance felt by the fish, so there is nothing to alarm it, and the hold time is surprisingly long.

With regard to presentation on the 360-degree river, avoiding disturbance at close range is probably the most significant aspect of a successful approach. If you watch a cat hunting, or a hare in the open, you often see nothing at all until the animal moves, and it all becomes that much more noticeable as the speed increases. You will have noticed how trout and grayling, especially the latter, can be invisible, even in very clear water, until they move (and often it is the shadow against the riverbed that is noticed first). It is the same the other way around. If the angler steals into the water, taking supreme care with each footfall, stooping a little to keep any of the body off the skyline, keeping arm and head movements to a minimum, as slow as possible, it is surprising just how closely fish can be approached without spooking them. It is more difficult approaching from upstream, but still possible down to remarkably short range, certainly within 6 metres in most circumstances, particularly when fish are preoccupied with feeding. Use the cover of foliage or rocks behind you, or fast, broken water between you and your target fish.

One thing I notice a great deal when guiding anglers on the river is the tentative nature of their approach. Even when this is slow and methodical, it is not good for control. The angler is often tempted to make an over-range cast rather than using his feet to close

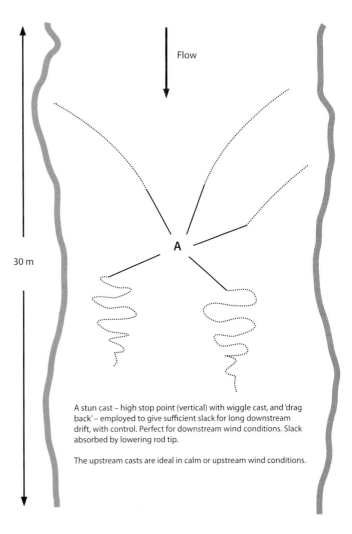

THE 360° RIVER

Flow

30 m

A

A stun cast – high stop point (vertical) with wiggle cast, and 'drag back' – employed to give sufficient slack for long downstream drift, with control. Perfect for downstream wind conditions. Slack absorbed by lowering rod tip.

The upstream casts are ideal in calm or upstream wind conditions.

The 360-degree river

Daniel Svrcek, the Czech team river master, demonstrating perfect nymph technique on the Dee

down the range and idealize the angle. The best approach to a target fish or area is one that is positive, with smooth movements rather than necessarily slow. In this context the feet become as important as the casting hand. In fact the whole body is used; something which leads to the best international competitors mostly having extreme fitness. Wading in the river often requires that the angler will be twisted away from having the perfect delivery angle, perhaps with his feet at different levels and requiring a whole host of casting nuances in order to deliver the best compromise cast, and drift, for the prevalent circumstances. The formal casting doctrine about arm positioning becomes far too limiting and is simply not good practice. The angler will often need to lift the rod arm to full extension, sometimes gripping around the handle's base (or even the reel) in order to keep line off the water or to minimize drag and maintain control. I discussed wading technique a great deal in *Tactical Fly Fishing*. Partly by being shown, but mostly by experience, the river fly-fisher develops an understanding of the use of his whole body in order to achieve the ideal approach to the whole gamut of possibilities on the 360-degree river.

Anglers have a lot of trouble dealing with broken water, or any faster current between the rod and the target. This is a problem particularly associated with fly lines and short rods. The significant mass of a fly line, even a #2 weight, results in it dropping almost vertically from the rod tip to the surface, and with a short rod it is impossible to keep very much in the air, avoiding the current which will set in drag. The lighter the line, or preferably leader-only, and the longer the rod, the better, in that progressively more line can be kept off the water, keeping the fly under control. This is one of the tremendous advantages of the fixed line techniques, tenkara and *alla Valsesiana*, in that the very long rod and lightweight leader often result in only the fly and a little tippet being on the water. This is wonderful for control, and presentation, and it is one Western-style fly-fishers can emulate using leader-to-hand and a long rod, though here, 'long' is somewhere between 10 and 12 feet.

In broken water, or otherwise, one should never underestimate the fish-holding capacity, which is nearly always much larger than we realize, even when the water is so clear that we think we can see the detail of every stone on the riverbed. How trout and grayling 'hide' even in the apparent absence of cover, is remarkable at the very least. The camouflage and poise of these fish is an elegant wonder of evolutionary survival strategy. Never assume you can see all the worthwhile fish in a stream.

A short while before writing this, on the Sava Bohinjka in Slovenia, I fished a stretch of the upper river during sunny, clear water conditions. My friends Lawrence Greasley and Neil Berry were downstream of me. On the far bank was a tangle of fallen trees and branches, offering shade and cover. On the edge lay trout and grayling, and I noticed one rainbow that must have been in the region of 1.8 kilograms in weight. From my position down and across from these fish, I estimated that there were up to half a dozen good fish here, with a scattering of small trout among them. I could not see any small grayling, though they, too, must have been present. Fishing a plume tip along the edge of the tangle, as far into the shade as I could cast it, I took three fish, all rainbows, with a best of about 40 centimetres. As rises dried up, it was clear that the fish were aware of danger, and slowly I made my way upstream in search of fresh targets. A few days later the group visited the same area of river and I had for company Gavin Walsh and David Uprichard. That morning I hurt my back badly and it was immediately obvious that I was not going to be able to fish very much. Gavin travelled off upstream, alone, hunting and exploring in the way he loves. I stayed with David, mostly watching him from the bank. In the early afternoon we came to the same tangle of timber that I had fished those days before. I remained on the bank while David fished his way down with nymph. My being unable to move with any speed actually produced the disguised blessing of being able to observe fish behaviour, and population, in the area. Among the tangle I was astonished by what I saw. As David worked his way downstream, the fish settled (it was as bright, as it had been days earlier) and I counted them, meandering among the cover of timber. I kept very still – a situation imposed mostly by the agony of my back – and counted at least a dozen very large trout and grayling in the lie. Those days earlier I had estimated no more than half that number. As I stood there motionless, more and more big fish materialized: a branch became a trout, a shadow revealed the presence of a huge grayling. I waited there a long while. David was out of sight and I became aware that I was observing a river at rest, free of disturbance, as the fish settled to their natural state. Some of them nudged out into the main river, onto the edge of the shadow, and I could see them nymphing. Others continued to hover, motionless among the fold of branches, while still more cruised and changed positions, even jousting a little for prime lies. In perhaps an hour I counted those dozen individual fish over the 40-centimetre mark, while the smaller fish – always more active or less settled than the big fish – were impossible to count. Days earlier, out there fishing, I had not begun to suspect the numbers of fish possible in this small area of river. My imposed, long watchful state on the shore allowed me a fascinating window into the world of the natural river.

Approaching fish is always a challenge for the fly-fisher, rarely more so than on the river where, ideally, it is preferable to close the range to sub-10 metres so as to have the best control and the best potential for presentation. As mentioned earlier, when the target has been selected, there may well be fish lying unseen between this target and your approach. It is always best to 'fish your way in' towards the prime target and enjoy the happy surprise of rising fish that have been previously unseen. Remember that a spooked fish, whether you have seen it or not, will swim away from you, which will be towards your target area, and this flight response will communicate alarm to other fish in the area. Moving straight towards the prime target, ignoring the rest of the river, usually collapses the catch potential dramatically. It is always so tempting to cast directly and immediately at a riser, especially if it is obviously a good fish, but why hurry? The fish is not going anywhere (unless you spook it by a sudden movement or over-range cast) and if you slowly fish your way in, casting all around the vicinity, but short, the fish will simply gain confidence and, being preoccupied with its feeding, will finally be easier to catch once you have adopted the right range and angle. The approach, therefore, is crucial, and this includes the movement of rod and line in the air, and even the spray that is cast off fly lines and braided nylon connectors (furled leaders are a little better in this regard). In calm, smooth water, such spray is noticeable and will frequently put fish down. It is a mistake to false cast in the direction of a target fish in such conditions, because the spray will shower down in its vicinity. It is far better to false cast 'off-line' before changing direction on the final delivery. The loss of casting efficiency because of this change of direction is minimal, and inconsequential at normal river ranges. It is also better to keep the rod tip low, side-casting (which is ideal for a leader-to-hand), so as not to encroach into the sphere of vision of the fish.

With river anglers tending to use finer fly lines, or leader-only, the issue of line twisting has developed. All fly lines are subject to twist: it is not a technical or manufacturing fault, and neither is it a casting fault, other than that it is the cast – and subsequent retrieve – which puts in the twist. Only if one keeps the line moving in the same plane as the rod, during casting, will there be no twisting; but this is impractical, because many practical casts (actually almost all other than the classic overhead), require considerable out-of-plane movement. With #4 weights and heavier, the twisting is barely noticeable, but probably the biggest problem of using leader-only, or a very fine fly line such as the Rio LT triple zero, is the twisting and coiling that occurs in the retrieved loop of line between the reel and the first rod guide or finger. Within a dozen casts this can be a serious problem in that it restricts line shooting and, worse, can jam the line up against the rod guide when a trout is running, resulting in the inevitable break. The remedy is simple, and it really is the only way of dealing with this issue. You will notice that long-distance, still-water or salt-water casts do not suffer this problem, and neither does the fixed line in tenkara. You need to cast the whole length of line or leader that is stripped off the reel. Just a few false casts will completely untwist the line. The long-distance caster does this by default, and with practice it becomes subliminal to the short-range river fisher. As soon as the first bit of twisting is noticed then, rather than attempting to pull it out under tension (which though tempting is useless and can easily damage the line by setting in a permanent kink), just extend the entire length of stripped-off line with a few slow false casts, ending with a long cast on a chosen target, or otherwise on a 'dead' bit of water, previously fished out.

There are so many technical and tactical aspects of our sport that make such a difference. All of the above have application for the competitive angler every bit as much as the non-competitive – although there are extra little nuances that can yield a significant performance advantage for the former. I am often asked about these when I coach and I find myself somewhat at a loss, because each should be seen in the context of particular situations – although there are some generalizations.

I remember back to my international competitive days and rediscover those moments which had such a profound effect on me. It seems that most of them stemmed from doing something that was not what others were doing. In all my international career I had seven different managers, and I recall that the best of them used me as something of a wild card. I must have been a headache for all of them, even those who allowed me my freedom out there on the water, but for most the final result was usually pretty good. I have never been one for following fad or, necessarily, the consensus. I have always preferred to analyse (though often with the help of my closest team-mates) and then follow wherever that leads me. In loch-style events, I was seldom one for staying with the pack on the 'percentage' water, where practice had suggested it would all be won because, on match day, it is *never* as it was in practice. One just has to adapt to the never-ending flux of the river or lake, and fish behaviour. There will be mistakes, and you will burn, then, in the scorn of your team-mates, and this is one of the worst feelings in the competitive fly-fishing world. And the more you rely on your own resources, rather than playing the percentage, team game, the greater the risk of catastrophe. Paul Page, one of the very best managers that England has thus-far had, once said to me that in loch-style, one can hide among the numbers (loch-style teams in Britain have twelve members), be lost among all those anglers and do the percentage thing. This is true, but frankly it gets you nowhere, and I never played this game. Crash and burn, or stunning victory: I had my share of both and, given the same situations and chances again, I would go for the same options in almost every case. If you don't take the risks, then you are an also-ran, almost by definition.

Outside competition it struck me some years ago what the key is that defines a certain level in the sport. For most anglers there is a degree of surprise when a fish takes the fly, while for the experienced, confident angler the surprise is when the fish *does not* take. This is a very simple, and perhaps obvious, statement which disguises the lengthy 'water time' that one has to put into fly-fishing to reach this magical level; but it is also, I believe, a very useful way-point in our venture. When there comes the time that our expectation is such that, on presenting the fly, a fish will almost certainly take, we know that we have passed through to a special place in fly-fishing. More to the point, perhaps, is that if the fish does not take we know that there is something intrinsically wrong with the presentation, or we have spooked the fish with our approach. We can, then, adjust very quickly, whereas the inexperienced will not have this realization and will persist in making the same mistakes. The experience leads us, by repetition and by trial and error, to this place where we have supreme confidence in the fly, the tackle, and our ability to use them with the presentation skills required. Thus, the process becomes vastly simplified, because if we are not worrying about whether or not the fly is the right one to use, say, then this is eliminated from the problem and we look elsewhere. Through time we address all the little aspects, as well as the more obvious, major issues such as casting mechanics and wading technique, so that we remove these, too, from the fish-catching equation. Finally, fly-fishing becomes this delightfully simple and minimalistic occupation in which we really can achieve homogeneity between the technical and tactical aspects of the sport and the freshwater habitat.

There is no short cut to acquiring this status. We all have to make the mistakes and learn by them, no matter who helps us or teaches us along the way, and we also have to put in the time on the water, which is probably the most important component of all. Years ago, I managed to reach this level, and stay there for quite some time, in loch-style, and perhaps with nymph fishing from the bank of large waters, but I eventually lost this simply because of lack of time on still waters. So today, the dry fly on rivers is very much my preferred approach and I will use this even in situations which are apparently much more conducive to nymph, or streamer. I have thus lost, to an extent, that supreme confidence which I once had with the nymph (though I never possessed this level with streamer). If I were to compete, I would have to attempt to re-acquire such skills, but this would mean stepping off the dry-fly plateau and making the long climb again with the nymph. Realistically, I do not think any of us can exist for very long at such high altitude in more than a single discipline, because there is simply not the time that we can spend on the water. In my loch-style days, I would be out on the lake perhaps three times a week. To achieve that expectation level with nymph on the bank I was fishing Grafham Water four evenings a week. I remember Arthur Cove telling me that he fished on average six times a week throughout the season, amassing over a ton of trout through the year: of course, with this history and expectation, he was surprised if the trout would not eat his pheasant tails! I catch in the region of a thousand trout and grayling every year, and in the last three years almost all of these have been on dry fly, and most of those on the CDC plume tip. In fact, during 2011, in a total catch of just under 1,200 fish, 1,040 were caught on dry fly, with more than 900 of these on plume tips. This is not meant as a boastful set of statistics, because large numbers of fish are no measure at all of the elegant skills in our

sport; but it does give some idea of the efforts necessary in order to achieve this extraordinary level of which I am writing. The numbers, even on some of the great rivers I fish, would not be possible without that utterly supreme confidence in my approach, including the leader and the fly, and, ultimately, the presentation.

The idea of presentation has come full circle. It is an expression of something that has always been there with us fly-fishers and we have developed it, in pace with our increasing sophistication. Although perhaps sophistication is not the right word here since this implies complexity: we find at the sporting frontier that it is all a long way from complex. It is, as I have stressed throughout this book, so delightfully simple and minimalistic. I have as little cluttering up my approach today as did the little boy in the Weald and the chalk downs of southern England, although things are rather more elegant and efficient, resulting from countless hours spent on the water. The core, running through it all, from the vastness of great still waters to mountain streams, from tailwaters to the Eden, has been the tenet of presentation, even before I had the word or the description for it. I suppose that this is where the complexity comes to the fore, because it would be impossible to achieve the final, simple approach without all those experiences, all the mistakes made, all the happy accidents and discoveries, all the triumphs; all those hours and all those tens of thousands of fish – we have come a long way.

A magnificent feral rainbow from the tarn on Streamflex XF2+ three-weight

CHAPTER EIGHT

Eden

Everything has changed ...

Though this is true, the Eden remains the most remarkable, surviving, mixed wild trout and grayling river system in England, on such a comparatively large scale. I live where I do *because* of the Eden and I have put more fishing hours into this river than any other in the world. It defines the fisherman into which I have evolved. It is thirty-five years now since I first put a fly on these waters. Back then I knew there was something special about the place, even though I was, at that time, more orientated towards large still waters, mostly in the form of Grafham, Bewl and Rutland, and the northern sea-trout and brown trout lochs. I did not realize the enormous effect on me, the changes, the development, that this incredible river would nurture.

Magnificent late summer cock grayling on the Eden

A wild Eden trout weighing over 5 lb

My little sport – esoteric and extraordinary – has been the driver of my whole life, *la raison d'être*, the essence of my soul, defining a freedom of expression and exploration that has consumed me. I have experienced things that most people cannot even imagine, and yet they have filled my life. The value of these is beyond measure to me. My own, personal, sport exists at a boundary state, essentially with trout and grayling on the river – the Eden – and I call this a frontier; really the only true frontier I have ever known.

Mere minutes' walk from my house is a weir, dispersing the waters from the long flat upstream onto a gravel and boulder glide, flecked with water crowfoot, down past a disused mill, surging over another, smaller weir and then over scoured gravels beneath sandstone cliffs, curving through a deeper, slower section and on into the ancient town of Appleby. The scale of the river here is utter perfection for a fly-fisher, packed with features and ideal hatch water, particularly for ephemerid species. It is surely one of the most important grayling recruitment areas of the entire river; in late April or May the clusters of fish can be watched from the high banks and the size of some of the cock fish, with their flame-like dorsals wrapped around the hens, is staggering. I once caught a trout here, immediately under the big weir, at over 60 centimetres and probably not far off 2.3 kilograms in weight, and every year I encounter exceptional fish here. They just keep on coming, throughout the year. In 2010 I caught over 200 sizeable trout and grayling from

Eden grayling on the plume tip

this area alone. I am sure that a lot of them were caught more than once, but even so the populations of fish – resident and nomadic – are very high.

Almost everywhere I travel, I fly-fish, and I am usually very happy doing so, even if the quarry are not wild trout or grayling (though they usually are); but it always strikes me that of all my fish each year, a third of them are from the Eden, and I am never so comfortable as I am here. It is my home. I realize, also, that this is where I have probably learned the most, with the possible exception of the San, in Poland. After all, with so many river hours spent over such an extreme range of conditions afforded by all the seasons of the year, within a lifetime of exploration, the effect must have been profound.

I cannot choose a single day, or even mesh together incidents or sessions, into a single chapter about this river. Again, I could fill a book with my times on the Eden alone, so much has been learned and discovered here on what I consider to be my home water. Perhaps that will be another book? Everything I do, how I fish, on rivers elsewhere, even on Europe's great tailwaters, is merely an extrapolation or adaptation of my approach to the Eden. Here have been the greatest discoveries: the vital importance of wading technique, closing down the range and choosing the optimum angle on a fish according to prevalent conditions; the subtle differences in behaviour and response to the fly between trout and grayling; the crucial aspect of a small, sparse fly and the incredible value of dry

Typical markings on an Eden valley trout going back

fly – specifically CDC plume tips – almost at all times through the year. The list goes on, diverging from these more obvious lessons learned. It was on the Eden, also, that I discovered my leader-to-hand approach, finding elevated levels of presentation and performance without dependence on crude fly line. Here I escaped from prescribed, English fly-fishing doctrine and explored a wild river from first principles, almost *ab initio*. All those hours when I was free to experiment here afforded this possibility. It could have happened on the San, or any number of European rivers, given the time on the water; but in the event it has been the Eden, with consolidation and honing of the approach on numerous other rivers and, to an extent, still waters.

Fish behaviour on the Eden is translatable to rivers anywhere, though there are exceptions. On waters as divergent as the big fish rivers of New Zealand or South America, or the mountain torrents of central Europe or western Scandinavia, we push out beyond anything we encounter on the Eden, though even in such places it is all a matter of scale and adaptation of the lessons learned on our more sedate, temperate waters. The principles of presentation are, after all, scale-invariant. Up in the Alps and Dolomites, or in the ferocious flows tumbling off the Jostedal Glacier in Norway, when one might think other rules apply, the discovery is both surprising and comforting. I am as happy on these waters with plume tips and pheasant tails, and leader-to-hand or horsehair tipped, lightweight fly

lines, and the cherished 10-foot #2 Streamflex, as anywhere. Of course there are limits, boundaries, and we will always continue to drift right up to these and beyond in our own development and in the sport more generally. That is from where the real progress, and discovery, are derived. The doubters, the bigots, the old school, might dismiss it all; but then they miss the whole point and cannot share the adventure. Not that there is anything wrong at all with remaining within our comfort zone, though we should not enforce this on others, any more than the pioneers should entirely dismiss the more traditional or classical backbone of the sport.

Because of its virtues and the values of what it can teach – in so many ways, in fact – the Cumbrian Eden should be at the very heart of fly-fishing in Britain, and way beyond. Its scale, by English standards, is huge, even if it is small compared with the mainland European giants. Some other English rivers, such as the Test and Itchen, are more famous perhaps, but only in historical context, because now, in this century, they have nothing like the environmental value or the impact on the sport's development that the Eden still possesses. In truth – and I am sure this will be realized in years to come – the Eden is England's last great river. As I write this chapter, I know that we are on the cusp of times. The Eden is dying: there is no doubting that, even though the powers that be are in denial. And beyond, throughout England, Britain, and deep into mainland Europe, even to the

Magnificent Eden valley trout

*Eden trout on the
plume tip*

legendary tailwaters of Sava and San, the fate of all trout rivers is almost inevitable.

An old friend of mine who has fished the Eden for many more years than I have, refers to my generation as the last of the wild trout hunters. He has seen the gradual degradation of these waters over seven decades and to listen to him describing how it used to be is both remarkable and depressing. Even twenty years ago, when I was just beginning to know the river, the flows were more stable, the banks hardly over-grazed, the ranunculus beds more prolific, while the trout population was enormous. Farming activity has been utterly destructive to the river. From its many sources up on the wild openness of the Howgills, Pennines and Lakeland fells, drainage for agricultural purposes, massive over-grazing with ever-increasing arable farming exploitation of the valleys, have all had detrimental, even catastrophic, effects on the river system. Only the fishermen really notice the damage, because we wade through the silt, experience the unstable flows and witness the loss of water crowfoot and invertebrate diversity; we observe the changing fish population dynamics.

The agricultural lobby and the political spin will tell us otherwise, but those who really know the river also see the truth. We should have absolutely no time for those with a personal agenda who deny the facts. Neither should we have further patience with those who suggest that research needs to be done. This is nonsense: the cause of habitat

The perfection of winter grayling from the Eden – tenkara and PTN

degradation is obvious. We see, also, that this extends beyond the Eden and Cumbria, throughout Europe, begun by the post-War political drive towards food security and the auspices of the Common Agricultural Policy. This is all an unworkable system that bene-

Eden trout going back

fits only the farmer, the landowner and the supermarket. All else loses, most particularly the wild environment and so too, finally, do we. The Eden bewitches me to this day. I often find myself wanting to drag our political masters to the waterside so that they too can see what the agriculturally orientated policies really mean to the environment they risk.

Perhaps my generation *are* the last of the wild trout hunters – though actually I think not. Neither do I think that the Atlantic salmon will disappear, nor even the sea-trout, though these will continue to be exterminated in certain, agriculturally

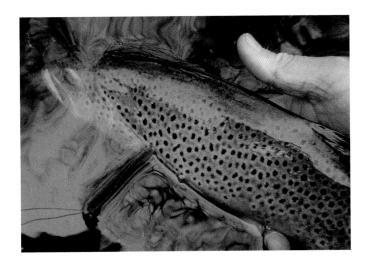

Eden, on the plume tip

vulnerable locations. In my lifetime fly-fishers everywhere have become more adventurous, more skilled and more sophisticated. We have travelled so broadly, experiencing geographical as well as technical frontiers within the sport, and have extended our scope towards the extremes. We have found fish in rivers and lakes where few if any were caught on fly not so many years ago, and we will continue so to do, even though it is difficult right now to forecast exactly how, as the last wild places become exploited or spoiled, and as our technical ability is currently so manifestly high. Thirty years ago, I could not have even glimpsed the possibilities with the fixed line or leader-only techniques that so many of us routinely deploy nowadays, usually for greater numbers and larger fish than we hitherto either expected or realized.

As grotesquely damaged as our rivers have become (and the Eden is no exception to this), they can repair, and they can also continue to exist as trout and grayling rivers, albeit in a degraded state. The biology changes in order to minimize the effect of the constraints – the siltation and bank erosion, the nitrate run-off – and life persists, while adapting; from plankton through to invertebrates and the fish that feed upon them. If there is sufficient clean, cold water, even the trout and the grayling survive, along with the anadromous, salmonid visitors from the ocean.

Because of its large scale, which effectively buffers the system, there remains a good diversity of invertebrates throughout the Eden. We still have March browns and iron blues, good hatches of large and medium dark olives, yellow May duns and olive uprights, and population explosions of the silt-loving *danica* mayfly and various chironomid species. Pale wateries, spurwings and medium olives are such that summer-long there is rarely a need to fish anything other than dry fly and these finally yield to outstanding hatches of blue-winged olives, the ultimate autumn upwing that is of such value to trout and grayling. Caddis species, starting with the grannoms in early spring through to the *Rhyacophila* and *Hydropsyche*, the cinnamons and great reds of high summer, are also prevalent, though many of us have noticed that, as the feeder becks become degraded by over-grazing and drainage damage, and loss of water crowfoot, the diversity and abundance are falling.

Encouragingly, however, there are several sections of these becks that in recent years have received some care and attention, or conservation measures, mostly in the form of tree planting along the banks, preclusion of grazing farm animals and the massively over-sized modern tractor, and the reintroduction of ranunculus. In all cases the habitat impact has been positive and species have returned, right up to the wild trout (absolutely without

Upper Eden feeder beck, early in the restoration phase

217

Water crowfoot coming back in the beck

stocking), and even otters. It is all too little, but it does at least demonstrate unequivocally that the farm damage can be reversed. I also think it goes way further than this. When one sees an undamaged or repaired English river – these utterly perfect stretches of upland beck, and the main river itself, bursting with life – the sense of well-being is beyond measure, as is the understanding of what we lose by allowing agriculture to ruin these immensely precious habitats.

For all our differences and preferences, our philosophies and approaches, we fly-fishers have but one enemy, and that is the destruction of wild waters and habitats, all over the planet. Human activity and population are putting colossal pressure on trout and grayling rivers, largely via modern, unsustainable farming practice, in the short term. The European Common Agricultural Policy, or rather the way it is used and abused by those comparative few who benefit enormously from it, is utterly destructive of the environment, and temperate zone rivers are particularly vulnerable. I think now that what a life in fly-fishing in such places has taught me more than anything else – much more important than expedient and elegant means of catching fish – is that these waters are valuable beyond measure. I have been blessed to fish throughout most trout regions of the world, especially perhaps on the San, Sava and Eden, and while I have discovered so much of

personal value in terms of fly-fishing technique on these rivers, what endures is the memory of all their miraculous habitats.

This being the case, I feel in a way that I have written this book just in time, while it has relevance, while there remains expansion in the sport and scope for us all, wherever the fly rod takes us. In time, also, in the sense that I still have the will to be out there on the wild waters, honing my personal approach, discovering and moving on, catching trout and grayling and moving on, and broadcasting what I find. There are still fresh peaks or plateaux to strive towards, and I perceive that probably the highest one of all is not within the technical or tactical aspects which have captivated me and led me to my appreciation of presentation. It is, rather, in the conservation of those river and lake habitats that have given me so much through fifty years. Without clean, cold waters, and undamaged landscapes through which they flow; without the habitats that support wild trout, not only is our sport meaningless, but the entire world is impoverished.

I want to be more positive than this; to think that our generation can still make amends and that the next will be able to explore these fabulous environments that have consumed me in my fly-fishing life. At the time of writing, my grandson is just weeks old. By the time he is of an age when he can flex a fly rod, I want to be able to take him down

My most precious trout of 2012; utterly wild Eden valley trout on the restored beck

Summer trout from the Eden

to the Eden and have him cast at rising wild trout. Finally, it is our choice; yours and mine. We can ignore it all and allow agriculture its way, or we can determine to confront this at every level open to us, right up to European legislation. At the very least, we can watch and care for those streams and lakes we visit regularly; to see that the conservation measures that are already in place – by law – are actually being observed and, if not, to inform the relevant authorities. This is certainly a minimum, because if we, the anglers, do not seek to protect our freshwater habitats, no one else will, because no one else, really, can see or care for the largely invisible wildlife of the underwater world.

The breeze is warm, and upstream, so I am going to head down to the river now. There are bound to be a few olives coming off, and probably midges in the calmer folds of the overhanging foliage. I will use the 10-foot #2 weight and a leader, with the inevitable plume tip. We have come a long way, travelled far out from the core of classical fly-fishing to some of the world's last, great trout and grayling rivers; but right now I'm home, on Eden.

Index